CONTENTS

INTRODUCTION

1 THE NEW EDITION

This new edition of *Success at First Certificate* has been developed in response to comments from teachers and students from all over the world. While the features that make it such a well-liked course have been retained, the following is a list of the new edition's components and the principal changes:

Student's Book

- updated illustrations, now in full colour throughout
- extra exercises on the directed writing section of Paper 3 (Use of English)
- additional problem-solving activities for Paper 5 (Interview)
- nine new Listening Tests.

Workbook

- a new component to extend the range of the course (see page 7).

Cassette

- the main cassette remains unchanged from the previous edition so that teachers can continue to use their original cassette with the new edition.

Listening Tests Cassette

- contains the recordings for the nine new Listening Tests.

Teacher's Book

- includes answer keys for the new Workbook
- provides a Revision Test for each unit for the teacher to copy.

Also available:

- *Success at First Certificate* Practice Tests 1 and 2
- *The Interview* video (for Paper 5)

2 TYPES OF TARGET LEARNER

Success at First Certificate is designed primarily for learners preparing for the First Certificate. However, as will be seen, the material is also relevant to several types of learners who have no intention of taking FCE. But let us look first at the FCE learner.

Who or what is a typical 'FCE' learner?

This kind of learner has completed some kind of intermediate course and should already be familiar with but not usually proficient at such 'intermediate'

English as: basic tense distinctions (present and past, present perfect and past, progressive forms in present and past); basic conditionals and modals; various future forms such as 'will' and 'going to'; basic distinctions between adjective and adverb; comparatives etc.

Furthermore, this kind of learner is almost always learning in a group or class with a teacher. The course may be of the 'intensive' or 'longer-term' type. Some of these learners are attending courses in England. The greater proportion of them are attending courses, usually not of the intensive type, in their own countries. These learners are usually in their teens or are young adults. But even if they are still in their teens, they usually want to be treated in an adult fashion. There is a particularly pressing need with learners at this level to present what can be called 'common-core' English in a new and interesting light. 'Common-core' English is the kind of lexis and structure found in a wide variety of texts and uses, from non-specialist 'general interest' type English to basic scientific and technical materials. Typical FCE learners have often had some exposure to this kind of English before, often suppose they already 'know' it, but almost always have all sorts of problems in using it accurately.

A second and related need at this level is to expose the learner to and give him or her practice in a range of lexis and structure called for specifically in the FCE examination. The learner is usually not familiar with a great deal of this lexis and structure or with some of the techniques for manipulating it, such as transformation and word-building, which s/he will need in the exam.

Who are the other 'non-FCE' learners this book can be used with?

The FCE exam is sometimes – and we think quite mistakenly – seen as a 'rather academic type of examination'. The inference is that only a certain type of learner will be interested in materials designed with this exam in mind. However, experience has shown that there are many other kinds of learner who can and do benefit from an 'FCE-type' approach. Such 'other types of learner' include:
- those preparing for, or already attending post-secondary courses at university or other types of institution where English is used as the medium of instruction in various subjects (Medicine, Psychology, Engineering and Computer Sciences, Business Administration and Management courses etc.)
- upper-secondary school learners

SUCCESS
at
FIRST
CERTIFICATE
■■■ *new edition* ■■■

TEACHER'S BOOK
with Revision Tests

R. O'Neill, M. Duckworth & K. Gude

Oxford University Press
Walton Street, Oxford OX2 6DP

Oxford New York Toronto Madrid Delhi Bombay
Calcutta Madras Karachi Kuala Lumpur
Singapore Hong Kong Tokyo Nairobi Dar es Salaam
Cape Town Melbourne Auckland

and associated companies in
Berlin Ibadan

Oxford and *Oxford English* are trade marks of
Oxford University Press

ISBN 0 19 453266 6
© Oxford University Press 1991

First published 1987
Second edition 1991
Third impression 1992

Typeset by Promenade Graphics Ltd.
Cheltenham, Glos.
Printed in Great Britain by
St Edmundsbury Press Ltd,
Bury St Edmunds, Suffolk.

– participants in a wide range of so-called 'general courses' who want English not only for 'general communication' but also as a means of acquiring further information about the world around them; that is, the type of learner who may have no specific exam aim but who sees English as a kind of 'tool for further development'.

3 TIMING

How much time is necessary for – a typical Focus?

The first three Focuses in particular of each unit are designed as 'lessons'. A 'lesson' in this sense usually takes at least $1\frac{1}{2}$ hours (often broken into two 45-minute sessions) unless the teacher decides to set certain parts of each Focus (such as vocabulary work, transformation exercises in language study, and other practice components) for homework. If the teacher does this, a 'lesson' can often be covered in one hour. Each unit contains at least three such 'lessons' (Focuses 1–3) with clear options for two more lessons (Focuses 4 and 5). We say 'options' because only the teacher can decide if a class can be left to do Focuses 4 and 5 as homework or not. Certainly at the beginning, and probably until well into the course, the teacher needs to devote some class time to Focuses 4 and 5, in order to explain and monitor what is required. We predict that at the very least, most teachers will do a minimum of ten 'Focus 4' composition practices in class, or at least start the students off in class with the writing of the model compositions. Most teachers will also find it useful to spend some classroom time on the revision and extension exercises in Focus 4. This is particularly true at the beginning of the course and with very good classes becomes less necessary as the class grows used to doing some of these things on their own, without classroom supervision by the teacher.

How much time is necessary for – the whole book?

A great deal depends on class size, motivation and other factors. But it can be said with absolute certainty that at the very least, sixty double lessons and ideally an option of at least ten more such double lessons will be necessary to do justice to the book and the rich and varied material it contains.

4 OBJECTIVES

What are the objectives of the course?

1 To cover the different requirements of the five separate exam papers in a varied, interesting and thorough way.

2 To do this so that not only exam requirements are met but so that the learner's general communicative competence develops and grows.

It is sometimes argued that these two objectives are incompatible; that studying for an exam such as FCE automatically means that the learner only acquires 'exam techniques' and that these are of little or no real use otherwise. It is obvious that among other things, a course and the book on which it is based must prepare learners to do the exam by giving them practice with exercises and tasks similar to those of the exam. Learners have to be familiar with the format of the exam papers. They have to be free to use their English to the best possible effect when doing the exam, and not be worried by the format or puzzled about how to go about the mechanics of the exam. But it is equally obvious that the art of passing the new FCE exam goes far, far beyond this alone. *No learner without a broad base of communicative English can hope to pass the exam.* Therefore, the aim of this Teacher's Book and of any teacher with the learner's best interests at heart must be to find ways of using FCE-type exercises and tasks so as to extend and improve this communicative base. There are many things which the teacher can do; s/he can make, for instance, the most of possibilities for group and pair work so that activities become more communicative. The tasks and exercises in *Success at First Certificate* are also designed so that students are not just performing mechanical operations on surface structure, but thinking about how alterations in surface structure affect meaning. The tasks and exercises also try to involve the personality of the individual student so that s/he is communicating about his/her own ideas and opinions. See for example the questions about Alison and Platchett on page 34 of the Student's Book where students are asked to visualize these people for themselves.

5 THE EXAMINATION

The First Certificate exam consists of 5 papers:

Paper 1	Reading Comprehension	1 hour	40 marks
Paper 2	Composition	$1\frac{1}{2}$ hours	40 marks
Paper 3	Use of English	2 hours	40 marks
Paper 4	Listening	about 30 minutes	20 marks
Paper 5	Interview	about 15 minutes	40 marks

See 'About the exam', page 8, for more detailed information, which is also provided in the Student's Book. The Teacher's Book gives teachers suggestions about how to train their students for the demands of the different papers. The Teacher's Book also points to suitable opportunities for getting students used to working under the time pressure they will meet in the exam.

6 METHODOLOGY

The body of the Teacher's Book gives detailed suggestions for teaching each section of each unit. However, there are a number of general teaching points we would like to make:

Interaction

It is a good idea if the teacher varies as much as possible the ways in which the class work together, so that sometimes a pair of students work together, sometimes a small group, sometimes a large group, and sometimes the whole class. Tasks which are usually done alone by the student, such as reading, blank-filling, answering multiple choice questions, compositions and so on, can also be done together with another student or students. Students can learn from each other and there will be an increase in the amount of language being used and learnt.

Thinking grammar

Success at First Certificate asks students to apply an inductive approach to learning the grammar rules of the language, that is, working from examples to the rules underlying them. Rather than being given the rules, students are led into a process of discovering them, often by being asked to think about differences in meaning produced by different structures. They can check whether their ideas are correct by looking at the Grammar Summary at the end of the Student's Book. This discovery process is an important part of the methodology of the course and rules about the language learnt in this way are absorbed much more deeply and memorably.

Picture discussion

The Teacher's Book suggests different ways of making the pictures in the Student's Book a starting point for classroom discussion. The basic methodology is to encourage students to describe accurately what they can see in the picture, then extend the conversation to a wider topic, as happens in Paper 5 (the Interview). As more candidates are now opting to be examined in groups of two or three, suggestions for dealing with pictures as a group or in pairs are also included.

Ideas are given in the Teacher's Book for further discussion and extension activities. It also gives practice in functional language which students will need in Paper 5.

Reading

The Teacher's Book gives ideas for developing students' reading skills. Ideas are given for prediction and information gap activities. Passages can be split up and the parts given to different groups and used in a number of ways. Guidance is also given for training students to deal with the kind of multiple choice questions on reading passages they will meet in Paper 1. Students are encouraged to justify their choice of answer and explain why the other answers are wrong.

Use of English

These sections cover all the question types found in the FCE, i.e. gap-filling or cloze passages (note the gradual reduction in help given to students for this), dialogue completion, paragraph completion and writing letters from notes.

Problem solving

The activities under this heading provide practice for the third part of Paper 5 (Interview) in which students may be asked to take part in a problem-solving activity. The examiner presents a problem and a choice of possible solutions and expects the candidate to comment on the solutions saying whether each is acceptable or not and giving reasons.

Language Study

These sections ask students to think about changes in meaning caused by changes in surface structure, and to arrive at the rules themselves. Students are then given a reference to the appropriate section in the Grammar Summary at the end of the book against which they can check their insights. They are given practice in the structures through transformation exercises. Note that the transformation exercises in these sections are of the same format as the exam but some have a different purpose, that is, they may concentrate on one structure in order to teach it, whereas in the exam students will be asked to do transformations for a variety of structures. The transformation exercises in Focus 4, however, do practise a variety of structures.

Vocabulary

The sections on vocabulary cover word building, phrasal verbs, and words often confused because they are similar to each other, such as *travel*, *journey*, *voyage* and *trip*. Students can be asked to tackle these exercises in pairs or groups, discuss different meanings and approaches and arrive at their own conclusions, before comparing their results with those of other pairs or groups of students. Dictionaries are an often neglected resource in the EFL classroom and suggestions are made in the Teacher's Book for encouraging students to use them.

Listening

The listening passage tasks closely resemble those in the exam, and students are taught to look through the tasks and predict what they are going to hear and what they will be asked to do, e.g. fill in information, tick boxes, mark routes or answer multiple choice questions. Students will hear the passage twice in the exam and be expected to perform the required task during two plays with only a short pause between each play. There is no opportunity to stop the tape half way through a play. This method is also recommended in the classroom, although it is suggested that students and teachers can listen to the passages stopping whenever they wish *after* the required task has been performed, as long as it is made clear to the students that this will not be possible in the exam.

Composition

Writing a composition can be a lonely process and the teacher the only audience for the result. The Teacher's Book makes suggestions for writing compositions in class as well as for homework, and for doing them in pairs and groups, so that students can plan their writing together and learn from each other by sharing ideas. Teachers are also encouraged to devise a way of displaying students' work on the walls of the classroom so that other students can read and enjoy it.

It is suggested that teachers and students together devise a simple code which they all understand for marking work and indicating what kind of mistake the student has made, e.g.

sp = spelling
wo = word order
Nu (Number) = student has written a plural instead of a singular, or vice versa.

This is a good way of making sure that students understand why they made a mistake and of encouraging them to try and correct their own work.

Revision and extension

The revision and extension exercises come at the end of each unit. The exercises at the end of odd numbered units (1, 3, 5, 7 etc.) extend and build on the language covered in the units. The exercises at the end of even numbered units revise the structures and vocabulary which have gone before in the format of Paper 1, Section A of the exam, thus consolidating what students have covered so far *and* giving them exam practice at the same time. It is suggested that these revision and extension units should be used diagnostically so that students become aware of the areas they are weak in, and do further work on them, for instance looking at the Grammar Summary and redoing the appropriate input section in the Student's Book.

Listening Tests

This new listening material is separated from the main text of the book (appearing in the Revision and extension sections, Focus 5, of every second unit). The aim is that it should be treated as testing material, either in class or by students working on their own. The tapescripts and answer keys are to be found on the relevant pages of the Teacher's Book.

7 WORKBOOK

The Workbook contains twenty units that are thematically linked to the twenty units of the Student's Book. Each unit has a new authentic passage, vocabulary exercises and extensive grammar revision. There are four Progress Tests – one after every five units. The answer keys for all Workbook exercises are to be found after the teaching notes for the relevant unit.

The Workbook can be integrated with the Student's Book in a variety of ways. When preparing each unit of *Success at First Certificate* it would be useful to look at the Workbook in conjunction with the Student's Book and decide which exercises you want to use in class and which ones students could work through on their own.

8 REVISION TESTS

Some new revision tests can be found at the end of this Teacher's Book. Each set of ten questions is based on a unit in the Student's Book. Putting these Revision Tests in the Teacher's Book is a response to teachers who want testing material that will not have been seen by the students.

You may make photocopies of the tests for classroom use but please note that copyright law does not normally permit multiple copying of published material.

ABOUT THE FIRST CERTIFICATE EXAM

The Cambridge First Certificate in English exam is held twice a year in June and December. It consists of five different papers. The exam has a total of 180 marks, and the pass mark is about 100 out of 180. There are five grades. Pass grades are A, B, C and Fail grades are D and E. You are not allowed to use a dictionary during the exam.

PAPER 1   READING COMPREHENSION   1 HOUR
(40 MARKS)

Section A In the first section of this paper you have to answer 25 multiple choice questions. These test your knowledge of grammar, vocabulary, and other items like phrasal verbs and prepositions. (*See p. 16 for an example.*)

When you answer the questions, look carefully at each of the choices you are given. If you find one of the questions difficult, try to work out which of the answers are definitely wrong, and guess the answer from the choices that are left. Never leave a question unanswered.

You should aim to spend about 15 minutes on this section and you get one mark for each correct answer.

Section B In this section, you are given 15 multiple choice questions based on three reading passages. The questions test your comprehension of different varieties of written English. (*See p. 2 for an example.*)

It is very important to read the questions extremely carefully. Often you will find that more than one answer seems to be right. You must consider all of the answers, and try and decide which one is the best.

You should aim to spend about 15 minutes on each passage. Remember that you get TWO marks for each correct answer. The marks for Sections A and B are added up and then turned into a score out of 40.

PAPER 2   COMPOSITION   1½ HOURS   (40 MARKS)

In this paper you have to write two different compositions from a choice of topics. You may have to write a letter to a friend, a formal letter, a story, a speech, or give your opinions on a particular subject. If you have studied a set book, one of the questions will give you the chance to write about it.

Each composition should be between 120 and 180 words, unless you are told otherwise. Marks are given for organization and content, grammatical accuracy, using correct and suitable vocabulary, and using natural, fluent English. (*See FOCUS FOUR of each unit for this paper.*)

You should aim to spend at least 5 minutes planning each composition, about 30 minutes writing it, and at least 5 minutes checking it.

PAPER 3   USE OF ENGLISH   2 HOURS   (40 MARKS)

Section A The first exercise of this paper is a cloze test. This is a passage with blanks—you have to fill in each blank with one word only. The best way to do this question is to read the whole passage through once or twice, and then try to fill in the blanks. If you find any blank very difficult, do not waste too much time on it, leave it and come back to it later. (*See p. 3 for an example. Note that in earlier units you are given clues to help you approach this exercise.*)

The second exercise is usually a sentence transformation exercise. This is a set of ten sentences which you have to rewrite so that the meaning does not change. The questions test your knowledge of grammar, and often require you to change sentences from direct to reported speech, active to passive, etc. (*See p. 40 for an example.*)

The remainder of Section A varies. There are often exercises to test word building (*see p. 3, Exercise A*) or your knowledge of phrasal verbs (*see p. 38*). You may also be asked to write a letter from notes (*see p. 54*) or to complete a dialogue (*see p. 35*).

Section B This section is a mixture of reading comprehension and composition. You may be given an advertisement, a notice, or some other type of text or diagram. You are usually asked to use the information from the text or diagram to complete several paragraphs which show that you have understood it. (*See PARAGRAPH COMPLETION exercises, e.g. p. 5.*)

Marks for this paper are given mainly for getting the most important pieces of information correctly sorted out; however, grammatical accuracy is also important.

You should allow about 45 minutes for Section B. The total number of marks for the paper is 40, about 32 for Section A and 8 for Section B.

PAPER 4   LISTENING   ABOUT 30 MINUTES (20 MARKS)

In this paper, you will usually be given three different types of listening activity, but these can vary a great deal. The recordings you hear may be telephone conversations, announcements, parts of a radio programme, etc. English will be spoken at normal speed. Usually you will be given one form filling, one multiple choice, and one or more other type of exercise. You will hear each recording twice.

PAPER 5   INTERVIEW   ABOUT 15 MINUTES   (40 MARKS)

In the first part of the interview you will be given a picture (or possibly a cartoon, advert etc.) to look at. The examiner will first ask you to talk about the picture itself and then to discuss more general topics related to the theme of the picture (*see PICTURE DISCUSSION headings, e.g. p. 1*).

In the second part of the interview you will be given two or more short passages which will also be related to the theme of the picture. You will be asked to talk about one (or more) of these passages e.g. where it comes from, who wrote (or said) it, what you think of the content etc. (*see PASSAGES FOR COMMENT headings, e.g. p. 11*). You no longer have to read any passage aloud.

The third part varies. Usually you will be given some realistic material (in the form of an advertisement, leaflet etc.) and you will be asked to take part in an activity related to the material (typically the activity involves role play, problem solving or discussion). You can choose to talk about a set book or a project for this part of the interview (ask your school or your Examination Centre about these options).

Marks are given for fluency and grammatical accuracy, pronunciation and stress, communicative ability and range of vocabulary.

ABOUT THE BOOK

Success at First Certificate is an integrated course divided into 20 topic-based units. Every eight-page unit has five parts, each starting on a new page. Each of these five parts is called a 'Focus'.

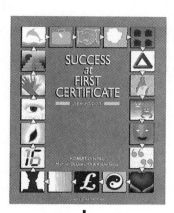

UNITS

| 1 | 2 | 3 | 4 | 5 | 6 | 7 | 8 | 9 | 10 | 11 | 12 | 13 | 14 | 15 | 16 | 17 | 18 | 19 | 20 |

FOCUS ONE **FOCUS TWO** **FOCUS THREE** **FOCUS FOUR** **FOCUS FIVE**

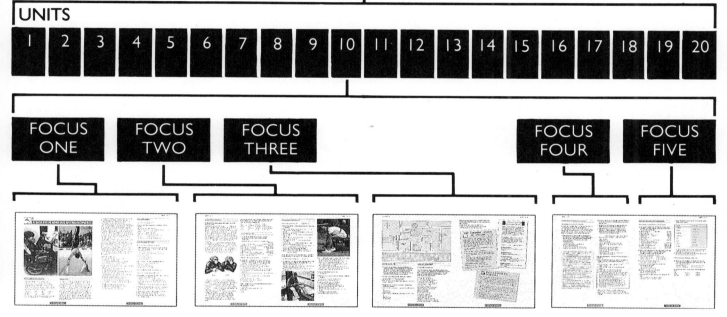

Each of *Focus 1–3* brings a fresh perspective to the unit topic together with integrated and varied language input and practice. The Focus input may be one or more of:

> PICTURE DISCUSSION
> USE OF ENGLISH
> READING
> LISTENING
> SPEAKING
> PASSAGES FOR COMMENT

Practice of vocabulary, structure and usage arises naturally from the input of the Focus. Practice activities and exercises may be one or more of:

> VOCABULARY
> LANGUAGE STUDY
> USE OF ENGLISH
> ROLE PLAY
> PROBLEM SOLVING

Focus 4 of each unit concentrates on the writing skill and the COMPOSITION paper of the exam. It provides models, and practice of all the types of composition (letter, narrative, speech, argument, description etc.) required in this part of the exam.

Focus 5 contains REVISION AND EXTENSION of key structures and vocabulary. Many of the exercises are in the form of the exam and there are cross-references where necessary to the Grammar Summary at the back of the book. This Summary provides clear grammatical explanations and examples.

There is an extra LISTENING TEST in every second unit. These tests are recorded on the LISTENING TESTS cassette.

The Syllabus pages show how each unit practises each of the five papers of the exam as well as listing the language study and vocabulary covered. ▷

SYLLABUS

1 A DOLPHIN AND AN ASTRONOMER

FOCUS	EXAM PRACTICE (P1A = Paper 1, Section A etc.)	LANGUAGE STUDY/VOCABULARY
ONE	Picture discussion (P5) Reading (P1B)	*say*, *tell*, *talk* or *speak*? How structure changes meaning Two types of questions with *who*
TWO	Use of English (P3A)	Which is the phrasal verb? *who*, *which* or *whose*? *stop doing* vs. *stop to do* When do you have to use *the*?
THREE	Listening (P4) Use of English (P3B)	Giving directions
FOUR	Composition (argument) (P2)	Advantages and disadvantages; link words
FIVE	Revision and extension	Word building (verb to noun)

2 TRAVEL WISELY, TRAVEL WELL

ONE	Picture discussion (P5) Reading (P1B)	*travel*, *journey*, *voyage* or *trip*? *little*, *a little*, *few* or *a few*?
TWO	Use of English (P3B)	*may*, *should*, *must* and *will*
THREE	Reading (P1B)	Phrasal verbs (position of *it* and *them* with phrasal verbs)
FOUR	Composition (speech) (P2)	Welcoming and introducing
FIVE	Revision and extension (P1A) Listening Test (P4)	Revision of Units 1 and 2

3 THE INTERVIEW

ONE	Picture discussion (P5) Reading (P1B)	Phrasal verbs *bored* or *boring*, *interested* or *interesting*?
TWO	Use of English 1 (P3A) Role Play (P5) Use of English 2 (P3B) Listening (P4)	Word building (noun to adjective/adverb)
THREE	Reading (P1B)	Word building (*advise*, *adviser*, *advice* etc.) Requests and intentions
FOUR	Composition (describing an object) (P2)	Adjective order
FIVE	Revision and extension	*do/does* or *am/is/are doing*? *will do* or *is/are doing*?

4 SECRET MESSAGES TO OURSELVES

Page 25

FOCUS	EXAM PRACTICE	LANGUAGE STUDY/VOCABULARY
ONE	Picture discussion (P5) Reading (P1B)	Small words with big meanings (*so, neither* etc.)
TWO	Listening (P4)	Direct and reported speech
THREE	Use of English (P3A)	Review of verb forms Phrasal verbs (*take* and *run*)
FOUR	Composition (narrative) (P2)	Punctuation and layout of direct speech
FIVE	Revision and extension (P1A) Listening Test (P4)	Revision of Units 3 and 4

5 NEIGHBOURS

Page 33

FOCUS	EXAM PRACTICE	LANGUAGE STUDY/VOCABULARY
ONE	Picture discussion (P5) Reading (P1B)	Ways of asking for permission (*Is . . . permitted? Do you mind . . .? etc.*)
TWO	Use of English (P3A) Listening (P4) Problem Solving (P5)	Asking people not to do things Asking politely Reporting direct speech
THREE	Use of English (P3A)	Word building (noun ⇄ verb) Phrasal verbs
FOUR	Composition (semi-formal letter) (P2)	Complaining
FIVE	Revision and extension	Review of verb forms (*do, did* or *have done?*)

6 DOES HONESTY ALWAYS PAY?

Page 41

FOCUS	EXAM PRACTICE	LANGUAGE STUDY/VOCABULARY
ONE	Picture discussion (P5) Reading (P1B)	*I wish* and *If only*
TWO	Reading (P3)	Describing films
THREE	Use of English (P3A) Listening (P4) Speaking (P5)	Regrets with *wish* (*I wish you had/hadn't . . .*) Word combinations (*cassette-player, dish-washer* etc.)
FOUR	Composition (formal speech) (P2)	Structure and language for a 'farewell' speech
FIVE	Revision and extension (P1A) Listening Test (P4)	Revision of Units 5 and 6

7 LETTERS TO AN ADVICE COLUMN

FOCUS	EXAM PRACTICE	LANGUAGE STUDY/VOCABULARY
ONE	Reading (P1B)	*money, pay, cash, salary, wages* Is it still going on?
TWO	Use of English (P3A)	*lend* or *borrow*? *fault, error* or *mistake*? Conditionals (1 and 2)
THREE	Listening (P4) Use of English (P3A)	*still, yet* or *already*? Another look at reported speech
FOUR	Composition (argument) (P2)	Expressing an opinion
FIVE	Revision and extension	Conditionals (1 and 2)

8 SPACE WARRIOR MADNESS

FOCUS	EXAM PRACTICE	LANGUAGE STUDY/VOCABULARY
ONE	Picture discussion (P5) Reading (P1B)	Three types of past action
TWO	Use of English (P3A)	*so* or *such*? *ache* or *pain*?
THREE	Speaking (P5) Listening (P4)	*used to do* or *be used to doing*? Phrasal verbs
FOUR	Composition (describing people) (P2)	Adjectives describing appearance and character
FIVE	Revision and extension (P1A) Listening Test (P4)	Revision of Units 7 and 8

9 THE FACE BEHIND THE MASK

FOCUS	EXAM PRACTICE	LANGUAGE STUDY/VOCABULARY
ONE	Picture discussion (P5) Reading (P1B)	*although* and *despite*
TWO	Reading (P1B) Speaking (P5) Use of English (P3A)	Word building
THREE	Listening (P4)	*avoid* or *prevent*? Phrasal verbs *mustn't* or *don't have to*?
FOUR	Composition (informal letter) (P2)	Phrases, beginnings and endings etc. for informal letters
FIVE	Revision and extension	Word building (noun ⇄ adjective)

10 WORDS AND FEELINGS

FOCUS	EXAM PRACTICE	LANGUAGE STUDY/VOCABULARY
ONE	Picture discussion (P5) Reading (P1B)	Comparisons
TWO	Use of English (P3A)	*give, cause, make* or *bring?*
THREE	Listening (P4) Role play (P5)	Phrasal verbs Preferences
FOUR	Composition (narrative) (P2)	Use of tenses to suggest sequence
FIVE	Revision and extension (P1A) Listening Test (P4)	Revision of Units 9 and 10

11 SCENES FROM A ROMANTIC NOVEL

ONE	Picture discussion (P5) Passage for comment (P5) Listening (P4) Use of English (P3B)	Descriptive adjectives *wedding* or *marriage?*
TWO	Reading (P1B)	Gerund (*going*) or infinitive (*to go*)?
THREE	Use of English (P3A) Listening (P4) Role play (P5)	*who, which* or *that?* More kinds of comparisons
FOUR	Composition (a talk) (P2)	Order and sequence of a descriptive talk
FIVE	Revision and extension	Infinitive with or without *to?* Gerund (*going*) or infinitive (*to go*)?

12 A STUDY IN CONTRASTS

ONE	Reading (P1B)	*Not only . . . as well*
TWO	Problem Solving (P5)	*lie* or *lay?* *bring, take, fetch, carry* or *wear?* *have something done*
THREE	Listening (P4)	Phrasal verbs The passive
FOUR	Composition (argument) (P2)	Arguing for and against
FIVE	Revision and extension (P1A) Listening Test (P4)	Revision of Units 11 and 12

13
A SHOPPER'S NIGHTMARE

FOCUS	EXAM PRACTICE	LANGUAGE STUDY/VOCABULARY
ONE	Reading (P1B) Role play (P5)	Relative clauses without *who*
TWO	Picture discussion (P5) Listening (P4)	*what* clauses
THREE	Use of English (P3A) Role play (P5)	Phrasal verbs
FOUR	Composition (describing places) (P2)	Using *with*, *who* and *which* to combine adjectives
FIVE	Revision and extension	The passive Forming opposites (with prefixes)

14
MYSTERIES OF MEMORY
Page 105

ONE	Picture discussion (P5) Reading (P1B)	Words connected with memory
TWO	Listening (P4) Use of English (P3A)	*should have*, *must have* or *might have*? *whose*, *which* or *that*?
THREE	Use of English (P3A)	Word combinations
FOUR	Composition (giving directions) (P2 and P5)	*Follow the signs to . . .* *When you get to . . .* etc.
FIVE	Revision and extension (P1A) Listening Test (P4)	Revision of Units 13 and 14

15
THE MAN IN THE PARK
Page 113

ONE	Picture Discussion Reading (P1B)	Talking about a long time ago
TWO	Use of English (P3A)	Reporting suggestions *cost*, *value*, *expense*, *price* or *worth*?
THREE	Use of English (P3A) Listening (P4)	*if* or *unless*? *until* or *by*? Word combinations
FOUR	Composition (sequence) (P2)	Use of link words and time expressions for a sequence of events
FIVE	Revision and extension	Further forms of the future Four types of infinitive Review of tenses

16
SERVANTS OF THE FUTURE
Page 121

FOCUS	EXAM PRACTICE	LANGUAGE STUDY/VOCABULARY
ONE	Picture discussion (P5) Reading (P1B)	*false* or *artificial*? *clean* or *wash*? *needs doing* *myself, yourself* etc.
TWO	Listening (P4) Use of English 1 (P3A) Use of English 2 (P3B)	*small enough . . .* or *too small . . .*?
THREE	Use of English (P3A)	Phrasal verbs *do* or *make*? *to* or *with*? *-ing* clauses as the subject of a sentence
FOUR	Composition (giving advice) (P2)	Positive and negative advice
FIVE	Revision and extension (P1A) Listening Test (P4)	Revision of Units 15 and 16

17
DEATH-TRAP
Page 129

ONE	Picture discussion (P5) Reading (P1B)	More about the passive
TWO	Listening (P4)	*could, managed to* and *couldn't* *must have been done* *must be done*
THREE	Use of English (P3A and P3B)	Giving advice
FOUR	Composition (argument) (P2)	Discussing different points of view
FIVE	Revision and extension	Modals

18
THE WOMAN WITHOUT A NAME
Page 137

ONE	Reading (P1B)	*in case* and *if*
TWO	Picture discussion (P5) Listening Test (P4)	Phrasal verbs with *make* *careful* or *careless*? *if* or *whether*? *a, an* or *some*?
THREE	Use of English (P3A)	*had better/had better not*
FOUR	Composition (describing a process) (P2)	Use of the passive to avoid repetition
FIVE	Revision and extension (P1A) Listening Test (P4)	Revision of Units 17 and 18

 19
LEAVING HOME

FOCUS	EXAM PRACTICE	LANGUAGE STUDY/VOCABULARY
ONE	Picture discussion (P5) Reading (P1B)	Phrasal verbs Cause and result in conditional sentences
TWO	Use of English (P3A)	*between* or *among*? *It's time . . .*
THREE	Use of English (P3B) Listening (P4)	Prefixes
FOUR	Composition (letter and narrative) (P2)	Formal and informal letter styles
FIVE	Revision and extension	*if, unless, when* or *in case*? Conditional 3 Conditionals 1, 2 and 3 Mixed tense forms

 20
THE LOST CIVILIZATION

ONE	Picture discussion (P5) Reading (P1B)	Revision transformations 1
TWO	Listening (P4) Use of English (P3A)	Review of phrasal verbs 1
THREE	Reading (P1B) Passages for commennt (P5)	Revision transformations 2 Review of phrasal verbs 2
FOUR	Composition (narrative) (P2)	An account of an event
FIVE	Revision and extension (P1A)	Revision of Units 19 and 20

GRAMMAR SUMMARY

Page 161

1 A DOLPHIN AND AN ASTRONOMER

FOCUS ONE *SB 1–2

- ■ PICTURE DISCUSSION
- ■ READING
- ■ VOCABULARY
- ☐ *say*, *tell*, *talk* or *speak*?
- ■ LANGUAGE STUDY
- ☐ How structure changes meaning
- ☐ Two types of question with *who*

PICTURE DISCUSSION

Divide class into 2 groups: A and B. Divide students in groups A and B into pairs. Tell pairs in group A to answer questions 1–3 about picture 1 **only** and group B pairs to do the same for picture 2. Allow 2–3 minutes, then invite pairs from each group to tell the rest of the class **one** of their answers.

Now ask pairs from each group to prepare two more questions about their own picture to ask students in the other group. Walk round helping with questions if necessary.

With the class in groups of 3–4, allow 3–4 minutes for students to answer questions 4 and 5. Choose students at random from each group to report back to the rest of the class on their conclusions for No.4, dealing with each animal in turn and making sentences like:
I think spiders are useful to humans because they do not harm us or our belongings and they kill flies.

For No.5 invite comments from each group, encouraging students to say why they reached their decision.

Topics for further discussion

(The examiner may move on to topics of this kind in Paper 5, after talking about the picture.)

1 Ask students to describe any pets they keep or would like to keep at home.
2 Should animals be kept in captivity? If so, where is the best place to keep them, e.g. zoos, safari parks?

Give students 2–3 minutes to think about these topics before asking them for their opinions. Encourage a natural discussion and be prepared for disagreement. Write the following expressions on the board for students to use:

* References throughout are to the relevant page numbers in the Student's Book.

Expressing disagreement
I'm afraid I don't agree at all.
I don't think that's the case.
I disagree.

Expressing agreement
I couldn't agree more.
That's exactly what I feel.
That's quite right/true.

READING

Allow 4–5 minutes for students to look through the multiple choice questions **before** they read the passage. This is a useful exam technique because it gives the students something to look for while they are reading the passage.

Tell students to 'skim' read the passage (glance through it quickly) for general meaning, then read it carefully a second time and in pairs or groups of 3 choose the best answer.

Ask students to read out parts of the text to justify their choice of answer. They can use the following expressions:

Justifying choices
It isn't A, B or C because . . .
It must be/is D because . . .
It can't be B because . . .
I don't think it's A because . . .

▶ Answers
    1C   2A   3C   4D

VOCABULARY

say, *tell*, *talk* or *speak*?

With students' books closed, introduce the verbs *say*, *tell*, *talk* and *speak* with your own examples, e.g.
*Now, listen to what I'm going to **say**.*
*I'm going to **tell** you what to do next.*
*I'm **talking** about four verbs which are often confused.*
*You're learning to **speak** better English.*

Write the following patterns on the board and ask students to copy them into their notebooks for future reference:

	say that
say	say something to somebody
	said, '. . . . . . .'

tell	tell somebody that tell somebody to do something tell the truth/lies/a story tell somebody how to do something
talk	talk to somebody talk about something
speak	speak to somebody speak well/badly speak French/Japanese

Ask students to make sentences of their own using the four verbs. Ask individual students to read out one of their examples and ask the other students to say whether it is correct or not. Invite students to correct any sentences they think are wrong.

Ask students to open their books and complete the exercise individually. When they have finished, they can compare their answers in pairs.

▶ Answers

1 speak	4 tell	7 speak
2 say	5 speak/talk	8 say
3 talk	6 tell	

LANGUAGE STUDY

How structure changes meaning

EXERCISE A

With students' books closed, write sentences a)–f) on the board. Ask students in pairs to discuss what the difference in meaning is between each pair of sentences and what causes it.

▶ Suggested answers

a) *Sound*	– sound in general
b) *The sound*	– definite article *the* suggests a specific sound
c) *Who loves . . . ?*	– We don't know the subject but we know the object of the sentence.
d) *Who does M. love?*	– We know the subject but we don't know the object of the sentence.
e) *Stop to think*	– The infinitive refers to what happened **after** *stop*.
f) *Stop thinking*	– The gerund or *-ing* form refers to what happened **before** *stop*.

Ask students to open their books, match sentences a)–f) with sentences 1–4 and rephrase the sentences they cannot match.

▶ Answers

1 e)   2 f)   3 d)   4 c)

a) Sound in general travels very fast through water in general.
b) A particular kind of sound (which has been mentioned) travels very fast through a particular area of water.

Two types of question with *who*

EXERCISE B

▶ Answers

1a) Tom		1b) Dick	
2a) Jack Ruby		2b) Kennedy	

EXERCISE C

▶ Answers

1 Who broke the window?
2 Who always leaves the door open?
3 Who did Cleopatra love?
4 Who does the teacher work for?
5 Who likes doing exercises like these?

FOCUS TWO   SB 3 – 4

- ■ USE OF ENGLISH
- ■ VOCABULARY
- □ Which is the phrasal verb? ▷ GS 9.1
- ■ LANGUAGE STUDY
- □ *who, which* or *whose*? (and *that*) ▷ GS 11.1.1
- □ *stop doing* vs. *stop to do* ▷ GS 5.3
- □ When do you have to use *the*? ▷ GS 3.2, 3.3

USE OF ENGLISH

Ask students to skim read the passage silently for general meaning. Tell them not to worry about the meaning of individual words. Allow 2–3 minutes. Encourage students to summarize the content of the passage by asking a few check comprehension questions, e.g. *What kinds of creatures are mentioned? What can these creatures do?*

Ask students to look at the words at the end of the passage which are to be inserted in the blank spaces. Explain the meanings (or ask students to explain the meanings) of the words, giving as many different examples as possible of how the words could be used, e.g. *besides* = 'in addition to', 'as well'.

Ask students to work in pairs or groups of 3 and fill each of the numbered blanks with one of the words given (or a suitable alternative of their own choice).

Allow 5–10 minutes for this. Encourage discussion as to why answers are right or wrong as this teaches students to think through the possibilities and make intelligent guesses in an exam situation. Remind them that they can use the language for justifying choices given in Focus One.

▶ Answers

1	besides	11	capable
2	which/that	12	make/use
3	go	13	such
4	distances	14	learned
5	contained	15	who
6	number/amount	16	got
7	other	17	meant
8	seems/appears	18	been
9	hear	19	mistakes
10	branches	20	correcting

VOCABULARY

EXERCISE A

With students' books closed, write the words in capitals on the board and ask students to explain their meanings by giving synonyms, explanations or opposites, e.g.
appear = seem, come into view: (opposite = disappear).

Ask students to think of as many different forms of the words in capitals as they can, e.g. *appear, appearance, apparently*. This 'brainstorming' session will make them feel more confident about forming other words from those given, and provide good practice for the questions they will encounter in the exam.

Tell students to open their books, complete the exercise with an appropriate word formed from the one in capitals, and say what part of speech they have formed.

▶ Answers

1 communication (noun)	5 development (noun)
2 apparently (adverb)	6 corrections (noun)
3 intelligence (noun)	7 refusal (noun)
4 astonishment (noun)	8 angrily (adverb)

Ask students to use the words they have formed in sentences of their own, paying particular attention to stress and pronunciation. Notice the stress and pronunciation of the words in Exercise A.

1 kəˌmjuːnɪˈkeɪʃn	4 əˈstɒnɪʃmənt	7 rɪˈfjuːzl
2 əˈpærəntlɪ	5 dɪˈveləpmənt	8 ˈæŋgrəlɪ
3 ɪnˈtelɪdʒəns	6 kəˈrekʃnz	

Which is the phrasal verb?

EXERCISE B

With students' books closed, write examples a) and b) on the board and ask students what the difference in meaning is. Point out that the meaning of a) is obvious while the meaning of b) cannot be guessed from the individual meanings of each part of the verb.

Keeping books closed, ask students if they can give two different meanings for *look into, look up, go on, go up, go down* and then use the verbs in sentences of their own.

With books open, ask students to identify the phrasal verbs from the definitions given in their books in Nos. 1–5.

▶ Answers

1 b)   2 d)   3 f)   4 h)   5 h)

LANGUAGE STUDY

who, which or *whose*?

EXERCISE A

▶ Answers

1 which/that	4 which/that	7 who
2 who/that	5 whose	8 which/that
3 who/that	6 whose	9 who/that

You can use *that* in sentences 1, 2, 3, 4, 8, and 9.
You can only use *who* and not *that* in sentence 7.

stop doing vs. *stop to do*

EXERCISE B

▶ Answers

Picture 1
He stopped working. He stopped to have a cup of tea/coffee.

Picture 2
She stopped playing tennis. She stopped to do up her shoelaces.

1 They stopped talking. They stopped to listen to it.
2 They stopped eating. They stopped to look at her.
3 They stopped climbing. They stopped to have a rest.
4 They stopped watching television. They stopped to look out of the window.

When do you have to use *the*?

EXERCISE C

In pairs, ask one student to form sentences from the notes in 1–4 and the other to do the same for 5–8.

Ask individual students to read out one of the sentences they have completed and invite the other students to correct the answers if necessary.

▶ Answers

1 The sound on your television set is very loud.
2 Do you enjoy listening to classical music?
3 Do you like the music of Beethoven and Mozart?
4 The love of money is often the strongest feeling of all.
5 I am very interested in science.
6 I am particularly interested in the science of marine biology.
7 I do not like the food in this restaurant.
8 Everybody needs food in order to live.

FOCUS THREE   SB 5 – 6

- ■ LISTENING
- ■ USE OF ENGLISH
- ☐ Paragraph completion

LISTENING 🖾

Before listening to the passage, ask students to suggest ways of asking for and giving directions. Write a list of useful expressions on the board:

Giving directions

Turn right/left at . . .
It's the first/second on the right/left . . .
Go straight on.
It's opposite/facing . . .
Could you tell me where . . . is?
Excuse me! How do I get to . . .?
You can't miss it.

Ask one student to choose a secret destination on the map in the book, then direct the other students to the place chosen without saying what it is. The other students follow the directions on the map and have to guess what the destination is.

EXERCISE A

Allow 1–2 minutes for students to read through the instructions and make certain they understand what is required of them, i.e. to mark the route with a line and put an X indicating where the stranger wants to get to.

Play the tape through once without pausing.

Tapescript

A: Excuse me . . . do you live here?
B: Yes.
A: Oh . . . well, do you know where the English Language Institute is?
B: The English Language Institute? Uh, let's see.
A: They sent me a map showing me how to get there but I've lost it. I haven't even got the address.
B: Hmm . . . Ah, yes. I think I know where it is. Have you got a car?
A: No, I'm on foot.
B: Well, uh, as you go out of the station, just continue along the road until you come to the second set of traffic lights . . . then turn left into Castle Street.
A: Yes. Uh huh.
B: Walk down the street just a bit and take the first turning on the right . . . and carry on walking until you come to the park.
A: A park. Yes.
B: Well . . . let's see now, uh . . . walk through the park . . . but as you get to the end of it the path branches to the left and to the right . . . uh . . . are you following me?
A: Yes. The path branches . . . to the left and the right . . . uh huh.
B: Yes. Well, take the path that branches to the right . . . and then you come to Seaview Road which runs towards the sea . . . O.K.?
A: Yes . . . I . . . I think so . . . uh . . . yes.
B: And then, walk down *that* road to the first . . . uh . . . no . . . the second turning, turn left again down Butterfield Road . . . and . . . carry on . . . just go up the road; you come to another road that runs towards the sea but don't turn . . . just go straight ahead and the Institute is almost at the end of the road on your left, just before you come to Broad Street. Did you get all that? Aren't you glad you asked me?

EXERCISE B

Before listening for a second time, ask students to read through the questions in the exercise. Encourage students to make notes on any points they remember from the first listening. Play the tape a second time without pausing. Students add to their notes.

If necessary, when checking the answers, play the tape a third time, stopping at any problem sections, but stress that students will only hear the material twice without pauses in the exam.

▶ Answers

1 The English Language Institute
2 on foot
3 Walk down Seaview Road and take the second turning left into Butterfield Road. The Institute is almost at the end of the road on your left.

Now ask students to do Exercise C in pairs.

Extension activity

Students are often asked to give or ask for directions during the interview (Paper 5). Give practice in this activity by taking into the lesson copies of maps of a town or city all the students are familiar with. Choose a number of destinations and get students in pairs to ask for and give directions to the places you mention. Students can then choose destinations of their own to direct each other to.

USE OF ENGLISH

Paragraph completion

Students may be asked to do this kind of activity in Paper 3.

Divide the class into 3 groups. Ask each group to read the notes about one student who wants to go on a language course.

Ask each group to skim read the adverts for the three different organizations running courses and to choose the most suitable course for **their** student. Tell each group to appoint a 'secretary' to write down a report in about 50 words to read out to the rest of the class, explaining why the group has chosen that particular course.

Point out that although the groups should not try to find new words for every point they make, they should also try not to repeat large sections of the advertisements in their report.

▶ Sample answer for Ahmed Fauzi, aged 38.

We/I think Ahmed Fauzi should apply to The International School's Hastings Centre, as he would like to be by the sea. The Centre offers two-week courses for businessmen throughout the year, accommodation with host families and a full programme of social activities, so he will be able to meet other students.

Students should now be sufficiently prepared to write the other two paragraphs on their own, either in class or for homework.

FOCUS FOUR   SB 7

■ COMPOSITION (argument)
□ Advantages and disadvantages

COMPOSITION

EXERCISE A

Introduce the first expression in the list of words and phrases and ask students to explain its meaning and usage, e.g. *first of all* is used to introduce the first item in a list, or the first point you are going to make. Other possibilities are: *firstly, the first thing is . . . .*
Repeat the procedure for the other items in the list.

In pairs ask students to fill in the numbered blanks with one of the words or expressions suggested, trying not to use the same one twice. Ask pairs to compare answers when they have finished.

▶ Suggested answers

1 However	6 Moreover/In addition
2 First of all/Firstly	7 As a result
3 In addition/Moreover	8 In conclusion
4 On the other hand/	9 On the whole
However	10 To sum up
5 Firstly/First of all	

EXERCISE B

▶ Answers

1 Introduction	3 Disadvantages
2 Advantages	4 Conclusion

Point out the importance of the introduction and conclusion, and the development of the composition in paragraphs 2 and 3. Tell students this formula is one which should be adopted for all compositions they write and will help them to produce a clear, logical composition.

EXERCISE C

In groups of 3 or 4, ask students to make two lists of points mentioned in the composition:
List 1 – *Advantages of living in the country*
List 2 – *Disadvantages*

Write (or ask a student to write) the two lists on the board, dealing with any differences of opinion between the groups.

▶ Answers

ADVANTAGES	DISADVANTAGES
– closer to nature	– fewer people, ∴ fewer friends
– peace and quiet	– less entertainment
– life slower	– fewer shops
– people more open, friendly	– fewer services
– less traffic	– fewer jobs available
– safer for young children	– longer, more expensive journeys to work
	– less excitement

EXERCISE D

With books closed, ask students to write down a) as many advantages and b) as many disadvantages of TV as they can think of. With books open, ask students to look at Exercise D and add any points 'for' and 'against' they have not already mentioned.

▶ Answers

ADVANTAGES	DISADVANTAGES
– good company	– bad for the eyes
– can be educational	– stops people from talking to each other
– cheap	– discourages people from taking exercise
– good for old people living alone	– makes reading seem less attractive
– good for children	– can create problems in the family
	– stops people going to theatre, cinema, etc

EXERCISE E

Ask students in pairs to follow the instructions which appear in the box.

Tell students to prepare a joint composition (which they both copy into their exercise books).

When they have finished, ask them to exchange compositions and read each other's work. This will encourage students to write clearly and legibly so that the examiner will have no problems reading their writing.

FOCUS FIVE   SB 8

■ REVISION AND EXTENSION
☐ How words change from verb to noun
☐ Pronunciation changes with *-ion*

REVISION AND EXTENSION

As this is the first unit the exercises here are mainly extension.

How words change from verb to noun

EXERCISE A

With students' books closed, give examples of how nouns are formed from verbs, e.g.
announce – announcement, survive – survival, wash – washing, protect – protection.
Point out the different endings and the vowel change in *survive – survival.*

Write the words in the exercise on the board and ask students to make them into nouns. Put the nouns on the board. After this rub everything off the board and ask students to do the exercise in their books. Tell them to fill in the blanks with the correct form of the word in capitals and say what part of speech they have formed.

► Answers

1	agree (verb)	7	arrive (verb)
2	agreement (noun)	8	arrival (noun)
3	mean (verb)	9	astonish (verb)
4	meaning (noun)	10	astonishment (noun)
5	live (verb)	11	collect (verb)
6	life (noun)	12	collection (noun)

EXERCISE B

Further examples of words in categories a)–e) are:

a) employ – employment, retire – retirement, content – contentment;

perform – performance, avoid – avoidance;
rehearse – rehearsal, propose – proposal;
permit – permission, reduce – reduction;
prefer – preference, correspond – correspondence;
depend – dependency, urge – urgency
b) tell – tale (vowel change), grieve – grief (consonant change), prove – proof (consonant change)
c) house/z/ – house/s/
d) re'ject – 'reject (stress shift and vowel change)
e) cut – cut

EXERCISE C

In pairs, ask students to complete the table of missing words. Check that students understand the meanings of the words by asking them to explain the meanings with synonyms or paraphrases.

Point out the changes in pronunciation, spelling and/or stress as indicated in the answers below.

► Answers

suggest /sə'dʒest/	*suggestion /sə'dʒestʃən/
*explain /ɪkspleɪn/	explanation /ˌeksplə'neɪʃn/
satisfy /'sætɪsfaɪ/	*satisfaction /ˌsætɪs'fækʃn/
*permit /pə'mɪt/	permission /pə'mɪʃn/
interfere /ˌɪntə'fɪə(r)/	*interference /ˌɪntə'fɪərəns/
*appear /ə'pɪə(r)/	appearance/ə'pɪərns/
encourage /ɪn'kʌrɪdʒ/	*encouragement /ɪn'kʌrɪdʒmənt/
*deliver /dɪ'lɪvə(r)/	delivery /dɪ'lɪvərɪ/
see /si:/	*sight /saɪt/
*breathe /bri:ð/	breath /breθ/
give /gɪv/	*gift /gɪft/
*export /ɪk'spɔ:t/	export /'ekspɔ:t/
prove /pru:v/	*proof /pru:f/
*practise /'præktɪs/	practice /'præktɪs/
advise /əd'vaɪz/	*advice /əd'vaɪs/

* words supplied by the students themselves

Pronunciation changes with *-ion*

EXERCISE D

Ask individual students to read out a verb and noun from the examples and point out the changes, e.g.

decide /dɪ'saɪd/	decision /dɪ'sɪʒn/
express /ɪk'spres/	expression /ɪk'spreʃn/
confuse /kən'fju:z/	confusion /ˌkən'fju:ʒn/
decide /dɪ'saɪd/	decision /dɪ'sɪʒn/

Ask students to pronounce (either individually or in chorus) the noun forms in the exercise.

▶ Answers

add – addition /əˈdɪʃn/
divide – division /dɪˈvɪʒn/
persuade – persuasion /pəˈsweɪʒn/
confess – confession /kənˈfeʃn/
impress – impression /ɪmˈpreʃn/
possess – possession /pəˈzeʃn/
inflate – inflation /ɪnˈfleɪʃn/
suspect – suspicion /səˈspɪʃn/
pollute – pollution /pəˈluːʃn/

WORKBOOK KEY *WB 1 — 4

UNIT 1

EXERCISE A

1 B   2 D   3 B   4 A

EXERCISE B

Mammals: chimpanzee, whale, leopard, etc.
Birds: eagle, robin, crow, etc.
Insects: cockroach, mosquito, ant, etc.
Fish: salmon, sardine, shark, etc.
Reptiles: cobra, tortoise, crocodile, etc.

EXERCISE C

1 whose	5 whose	9 whose
2 which	6 which	10 which
3 who	7 who	
4 which	8 which	

EXERCISE D

1 Who went with you/Who did you go with?
2 Who did you sit next to?
3 Who did you talk to?
4 What did you say to him?
5 What did you do then?
6 What was on?
7 Who took/drove you home?
8 Who could prove it?

EXERCISE E

1 told	6 told	11 talking
2 said	7 speak	12 talking
3 say	8 told	13 said
4 talk	9 said	
5 said	10 said	

EXERCISE F

suggesting: 7	repeating: 8
threatening: 2	denying: 5
claiming: 9	warning: 3
replying: 1	admitting: 4
promising: 6	advising: 10

EXERCISE G

1 He warned me not to go too near the dog.
2 He threatened to hit me if I didn't stop talking.
3 I asked how he was and he replied that he was fine.
4 He admitted stealing the money.
5 He denied having anything to do with the robbery.
6 She promised she would never forget me.
7 We suggested that he should go to the cinema.
8 He repeated that he thought I was making a mistake.
9 He claimed that he had seen a ghost.
10 He advised me to talk to her and say how I felt.

EXERCISE H

1 come down	6 looked into
2 looked up	7 went up
3 looking into	8 come down
4 look . . . up	9 go on
5 went on	10 gone up

EXERCISE I

1 T   2 F   3 F   4 F
5 T   6 T   7 T   8 T

EXERCISE J

1 ozone layer	6 nuclear power
2 polluted	7 waste
3 sewage	8 greenhouse
4 exhaust	9 global/world-wide
5 rainforest	

*References are to the relevant page numbers in the Workbook.

FOCUS ONE   SB 9 – 10

- ■ PICTURE DISCUSSION
- ■ READING
- ■ VOCABULARY
  - ☐ *travel, journey, voyage* or *trip*?
  - ☐ *flight, drive, ride* or *tour*?
- ■ LANGUAGE STUDY
  - ☐ *little, a little, few* or *a few*? ▷ GS 3.1

PICTURE DISCUSSION

In pairs ask students to prepare lists of everything they can see in both photographs. Ask pairs to compare lists.

Give students some useful language:

Position

Write the following expressions on the board in the position they refer to, e.g.

In the top left hand corner	At the top	In the top right hand corner
	🧍 In the background	
On the left	In the middle, centre	On the right
	🧍 In the foreground	
In the bottom left hand corner	At the bottom	In the bottom right hand corner

Tell students to take it in turns to ask each other where the items on their lists appear in the photo, e.g.
Where's the . . . ?
Can you tell me where the . . . is?
It's/They're . . .

Now ask students in groups of 2–3 to answer questions 1–3, then prepare a brief comparison of the types of transport shown in both photographs to answer No. 4, e.g.
Travelling by bicycle is much slower/healthier/more interesting than travelling by plane.
Travelling by plane is quicker/more expensive/less relaxing than travelling by bicycle.

Invite students to share their ideas with the rest of the class after they have discussed No. 5.

Topics for further discussion

1 Describe anything interesting which happened to you (or someone you know) at an airport.
2 What kind of security problems do airports face nowadays?

Extension activity

Give students 3–4 minutes to prepare a short talk on either of the above topics and ask two or three students to give their talks to the rest of the class. The rest of the talks could be spread over several lessons so that all students have the opportunity to give the talks they have prepared.

Encourage the other students to interrupt politely and ask for repetition or clarification of anything which they do not understand or would like to comment on. These expressions might help the students:

Interrupting politely

Excuse me! Would you mind repeating that, please?
Sorry, what did you say? I didn't quite catch it.
I'm sorry but I couldn't quite hear/didn't quite understand what you said.

READING

Divide the passage into three parts as follows:
1 *I have learned . . . an important meeting.*
2 *The second rule is . . . very embarrassing.*
3 *The third . . . air travel.*

Divide the class into 3 groups. Ask each group to skim read a different part of the passage, and to write two to three comprehension questions for the other groups to answer. Allow about 5 minutes for this. Ask each group to skim read the sections they have not yet read, then ask each group to take it in turns to ask the others their questions.

Now ask students to read and answer Nos. 1–7 in their books. Allow 5–10 minutes. Invite students to compare answers and comment on whether their colleagues' answers are correct or not. Encourage students to say why they agree or disagree with the answers given.

Students can now be asked to produce a written summary of the passage in note form.

VOCABULARY

travel, journey, voyage or *trip*?

EXERCISE A

▶ Answers

1 voyage	3 trip
2 journey	4 travel

EXERCISE B

▶ Answers

1 trip	3 journey
2 travel	4 voyage

flight, drive, ride or *tour*?

EXERCISE C

With students' books closed, elicit or explain the meaning of the four words:
flight = journey by plane (noun)
drive = journey by car (noun and verb)
ride = sit on a horse, bicycle, be carried along in a vehicle (noun and verb)
tour = go on a guided excursion, usually for pleasure but could be an official visit (noun and verb)

Ask students to make sentences of their own using these words.

With students' books still closed, read out the sentences in the exercise and ask students to suggest which of the words above could fill the blank. Read the whole sentence first then pause at the blank on the second reading.

Now ask students to open their books and write in the answers.

▶ Answers

1 ride	3 drive
2 tour	4 flight

LANGUAGE STUDY

little, a little, few or *a few*?

EXERCISE A

Read out the examples a)–d) and see if students can explain the difference in meaning from your intonation and attitude.

Some possible answers are:
a) *little* = not much (uncountable)
b) *a little* = some (uncountable)
c) *few* = not many (countable)
d) *a few* = some (countable).

Now ask students to match the explanations in Nos. 1–4 to the sentences in a)–d).

▶ Answers

1 c)   2 a)   3 d)   4 b)

EXERCISE B

▶ Answers

1 There were *a few* people in the queue in front of me.
2 *Few* foreigners visit Tulsa.
3 There are *a few* good restaurants in Tulsa.
4 There has been *little* rain lately.
5 There was *a little* rain yesterday.
6 Here's *a little* money for you.
7 I have *little* talent for music.
8 When I travel, I always take *a few* books with me.
9 There are *few* books I enjoy reading more than once.
10 There are *few* people I really trust.

FOCUS TWO   SB 11–12

■ **USE OF ENGLISH**
☐ Guided discussion and writing

■ **LANGUAGE STUDY**
☐ Different meanings of *may, should, must* and *will* ▷ GS 7

USE OF ENGLISH

Guided discussion and writing

Explain that students are going with three friends to spend five days in San Francisco. There is a description of the friend beside each photograph. Refer students to the photographs of the friends and elicit a brief physical description of each one.

Ask students to read the information silently, then in groups of 2–3, discuss the answers to Nos. 2–3. Explain any vocabulary students may not know and ask a few comprehension questions to check understanding of subject matter.

Allow 8–10 minutes for students to write 2 or 3 sentences in answer to each question. Walk round helping if necessary then ask students to compare sentences with a partner.

LANGUAGE STUDY

Different meanings of *may*, *should*, *must* and *will*

EXERCISE A

Ask students to match the explanations 1–8 with the correct sentence a)–h).

▶ Answers

1 d)	3 h)	5 g)	7 c)
2 f)	4 b)	6 a)	8 e)

EXERCISE B

In pairs ask Student A to read out the sentence and Student B to supply the correct answer *may*, *should*, *must* or *will*. Reverse roles in each alternate sentence. Walk round the class listening and helping where necessary. See if students can explain their choice of answer. If they can't, the explanations below will help.

▶ Answers
  1 must (a reasonable conclusion)
  2 should (advice)
  3 may (asking for permission)
  4 may (a possibility in the future, saying perhaps something will happen)
  5 will (future simple – conditional 1)
  6 must (obligation or necessity)
  7 should (something that will almost certainly happen, as long as nothing unexpected prevents it)
  8 will (polite request)

EXERCISE C

▶ Suggested answers
  1 *May* I leave the office early tomorrow?
  2 You *should* study harder.
  3 You *must* take all the medicine.
  4 It *must* be 10 o'clock.
  5 It *may* rain tomorrow.
  6 *Will* you answer the phone for me?
  7 What time *will* the plane arrive in Paris?
  8 It *should* arrive at 12.10.

FOCUS THREE   SB 13–14

- ■ READING
- ■ VOCABULARY
- ☐ Phrasal verbs (position of *it* and *them* with phrasal verbs) ▷ GS 9
- ■ LISTENING

READING

In small groups, ask students to study the information from the travel brochure. Allow 5–10 minutes for this. Ask students to make notes in their exercise books under the headings which appear in the brochure:

PASSPORT CONTROL
BAGGAGE RECLAIM AREA
CUSTOMS
TRANSFERS

When they have done this tell them to close their books but keep their notes in front of them. Using the notes they have made, ask students to reconstruct orally the information they have extracted from the brochure. Invite the other students to correct or amend any inaccurate information.

EXERCISE A

In pairs, tell students to ask each other questions 1–8 in turn and decide whether they are true or false and why. Encourage students to give logical reasons for their answers. They may refer back to the original text at this stage.

▶ Answers
  1 False, because under CUSTOMS it says if you are transferring to another flight outside the UK, you do not need to go through Customs and Passport Control.
  2 False, because it is only if you are neither British nor a citizen of the European Community that you have to fill out a special form.
  3 True
  4 False, because you have to go through the Baggage Reclaim Area, even if you don't have to stop.
  5 False, because you can go through the Green Channel if you don't have more than the duty free allowances.
  6 True
  7 True
  8 False, because your final destination is Great Britain and you must therefore go through Customs at the first point of landing in the country.

EXERCISE B

▶ Suggested answers

1 All passengers arriving at Heathrow from outside Britain and not transferring to a flight outside the UK must go through Passport Control and Customs there.
2 If you aren't British or a citizen of the European Community, you have to fill out a special form.
4 If you have only hand luggage, go directly through the Baggage Reclaim Area.
5 You shouldn't go through the Green Customs Channel if you have any goods over and above the usual duty free allowances.
8 If you are transferring to a flight to another place in Britain or Northern Ireland, you should go through Customs and Passport Control at Heathrow.

VOCABULARY

Phrasal verbs

EXERCISE A

▶ Suggested answers (2, 4, 6 and 8 are the phrasal verbs.)

2 The inspectors will *examine* your luggage carefully.
4 The fire is *stopping burning*.
6 You should *check* your work again and make sure there are no mistakes.
8 Only a few colours *are suitable with* green.

EXERCISE B

Before asking students to do the exercise, give examples of the phrasal verbs in sentences of your own, asking students to complete the verbs if they can, e.g.
If you can't hear the TV, you can turn the sound . . . . (up)
If the radio's too loud, you can turn it . . . . (down)
The dress might fit you. Why don't you try it . . . ? (on)
Make similar examples for:
try (something new) out, break down (car), break up (relationship), look for something (you have lost), look after (an elderly relative).

Now ask students to write the appropriate words in their books for Nos. 1–8.

▶ Answers

1 up	4 out	7 for
2 down	5 down	8 after
3 on	6 up	

EXERCISE C

Ask students to close their books and play the tape through once without pausing, for general understanding.

Ask a few check comprehension questions to make sure students have understood the content of the conversation, e.g.
What's wrong with the figures?
Why can't the speaker see very well?
What other two things does the first speaker want the second speaker to do?

Play the tape a second time and ask students to open their books and follow the conversation, paying particular attention to the position of words like *it* and *them*. See if students can say when these words come in the middle of the phrasal verb and when they come after the verb.

Remind students of the rules:
With verbs which **can** be separated, pronouns come in the middle, e.g. *turn **it** on*, and nouns come in the middle or after, e.g. *turn **the light** on, turn on **the light***.

With verbs which **cannot** be separated, pronouns and nouns must come after, e.g. *look into **the matter**, look into **it***.

EXERCISE D

▶ Answers

1 Please go over *it* again.
2 And for God's sake, turn *it* off!
3 . . . Look *it* up in your dictionary.
4 Go through *them* all.
5 Put *them* on.
6 Look for *it*.
7 Turn *them* all on. / Turn all of *them* on.
8 Fill *them* all in. / Fill all of *them* in.

FOCUS FOUR   SB 15

■ COMPOSITION (speech)

COMPOSITION

Explain the type of speech students may have to write in the exam, i.e. a 'formal' speech to an audience of some kind but often including their own ideas or opinions. The speech, like the previous composition on SB p. 7, will consist of an introduction, development and conclusion, or summing up.

Stress that speeches should be polite, friendly, interesting and informative.

EXERCISE A

With students' books closed, read out the expressions listed in the student's book and ask students to explain what they mean (using synonyms or paraphrases) and when they would be used, e.g. – at the beginning or the end of a speech? – to introduce a point? – to make a polite request? etc.

If you can, take in a map of Central London (maps are often available from travel agents, tourist offices or British Council offices abroad). Point out the places which appear in the passage, e.g. The Houses of Parliament, Westminster Abbey etc. Ask students to skim read the passage, ignoring the blanks, then explain briefly to each other what the passage is about.

In pairs, ask students to fill in each of the blanks with one of the listed phrases. Compare answers and ask students to justify their choice of phrase.

► Answers

1 ladies and gentlemen
2 it gives me great pleasure
3 let me introduce myself
4 I would like to take this opportunity
5 after that
6 as I am sure most of you know
7 finally
8 May I also ask
9 please feel free to ask me any questions
10 Thank you for your attention

EXERCISE B

In pairs, ask students to read the instructions in their books and then write the courier's speech. Both students should copy down the speech as they plan it together. Try to pair students who are familiar with the same town or city (or choose the town or city where they are studying).

Stress the importance of planning the speech together, i.e.

1 Introduction
2 Details
3 Summing up/Conclusion

Go round the class giving help and advice where necessary. When students have finished, ask them to exchange speeches with another pair of students and compare what they have written. Ask one or two students to read out their speeches to the rest of the class.

Extension activity

Ask the class to imagine that a group of foreign students is coming to their school, and will spend a few days studying there and staying with them as visitors. Ask students (in different pairs) to write a speech welcoming the students to the school, and/or a speech saying goodbye to the students when they leave.

FOCUS FIVE   SB 16

- ■ REVISION AND EXTENSION
- ■ LISTENING TEST 1

REVISION AND EXTENSION

In pairs ask students to work on the 20 multiple choice items. Stress the importance when doing multiple choice items of trying out all the options to see if they work a) grammatically and b) with the correct meaning. Tell students they should be able to say why something is wrong. This makes the choice of what is correct much easier, e.g. in 1 all the options are possible grammatically but

A is the wrong meaning; *look up to* = respect
B is the wrong meaning; *look in on* = visit (unexpectedly)
C is the correct meaning; *look into* = investigate
D is the wrong meaning; *look through* = check details (in a document)

Tell students not to forget to check D before deciding that C is the correct answer.

Ask students to repeat this procedure for Nos. 2–20.

► Answers

1 C	6 D	11 C	16 A
2 B	7 C	12 D	17 D
3 A	8 D	13 B	18 C
4 C	9 A	14 A	19 A
5 B	10 B	15 C	20 B

LISTENING TEST 1

Tapescript

A: Hello. Tragical Mystery Tours.
B: Hello.
A: Hello.
B: I'm ringing up about the coach trips that you do. Could you tell me a bit about them?
A: Yes, we have two different ones. The first is called the Bus Trip to Murder, and well, it's basically a trip to all the places where there've been famous murders in London. And the second one, the Ghost Bus, goes . . . well, goes looking for ghosts.
B: Right. Could you tell me, on this Bus Trip to Murder, what is involved?
A: What is involved? Well, you'd pick up the bus at the Temple underground station . . .
B: Aha.
A: . . . and then go on a sort of macabre journey through the sights of the murders of Jack the Ripper and into the East End.
B: Aha.
A: You also go to Greenwich where we can get food and drink at the pub, and there's a commentary throughout, all in English.
B: Ah.
A: Finally . . .
B: Right, and . . . and how long does that last for? . . .

A: We leave at seven fifteen and we get back at about quarter to eleven.

B: Ah right...

A: Eleven at the latest – it just depends how long people stay in the pub really.

B: I see. Right, and there's the other ghost one as well. Is that ghosts in London?

A: No. Well, we take a route out of London and there's a commentary about ghosts on the way out, but it goes down to Chiselhurst in Kent.

B: Chiselhurst.

A: It goes around the caves in Chiselhurst and we have a tour round there, and then come back via the East End again, stopping at a different pub.

B: Er, and what happened at the Chiselhurst caves then? I haven't heard of them before.

A: Well, they're just very sinister and spooky really. And everyone gets a lantern that they can hold so they can see where they're going, and you walk through the dark caves and tunnels.

B: Aha. Right, and you can tell me how much these things cost?

A: Yup. They're . . . for an adult it's ten pounds fifty on both tours, and it's seven pounds for a child under twelve. And the Trip to Murder runs every day except Saturday and the Ghost Bus runs on Sunday nights and (When do Thursdays start? . . . Next week?) . . . and Thursday nights also. Starting from next week for the winter season.

B: So, sorry, the Ghost Bus is only . . .

A: Only Thursdays and Sundays.

B: Only Thursdays and Sundays.

A: Yep.

B: Right, and the price, it's ten pounds, sorry what did you say? I can't remember.

A: Ten pounds fifty p for an adult and seven for under 12s.

▶ Answers

1 Murder
2 underground station
3 7.15 (p.m.)
4 English
5 Saturday
6 tunnels
7 Thursdays and Sundays
8 £10.50 adults, £7 children (under 12)

WORKBOOK KEY WB 5 — 8

UNIT 2

EXERCISE A

| 1 F | 2 T | 3 T | 4 T |
| 5 T | 6 T | 7 F | 8 F |

EXERCISE B

| 1 C | 2 D | 3 D | 4 A |

EXERCISE C

1 flight	7 ride
2 tour	8 travel
3 drive	9 expedition
4 trip	10 excursion
5 journey	11 visit
6 voyage	

EXERCISE D

1 went after	6 went on
2 went with	7 gone up
3 has gone off	8 go down
4 go over/through	9 go over/through
5 goes out	10 go with

EXERCISE E

1 I'm afraid my salary leaves me very little to spend on entertainment.
2 Fortunately I've made a few good friends since I came to live here.
3 I find very little time for reading.
4 There are very few jobs available in this area; Very few jobs are available in this area.
5 Very few people came to the meeting.
6 There were (quite) a few supporters at the tennis tournament.
7 You've been eating biscuits again. There are very few (biscuits) (left) in the tin.
8 Luckily I had a little time for sight-seeing on my last business trip.
9 Quite a few people were still at the party at 2.30 in the morning.
10 I've read (quite) a few of his books but I didn't enjoy many of them.

EXERCISE F

1 May	5 may/should	9 must
2 should	6 will	10 may
3 should	7 will	
4 will	8 should	

EXERCISE G

tube, liner, jet, taxi, motorbike, hovercraft.
suitcase, rucksack, luggage, handbag, holdall, briefcase.
harbour, quay, station, airport, docks, port.
outing, tour, trip, journey, excursion, drive.
track, line, way, route, path, lane.

EXERCISE H

Across:

1 FLIGHT NUMBER	12 RETURN
6 MAP	13 SEAT
8 SINGLE	15 ROME
9 DECLARE	16 VISIT
11 DELAY	17 LEFT LUGGAGE

Down:

2 LATE ARRIVAL	9 DUTY FREE
3 GATE	10 CUSTOMS
4 TO	13 SEA
5 BAGGAGE	14 TRAVEL
7 PLANE	

THE INTERVIEW

FOCUS ONE SB 17 – 18

- ■ PICTURE DISCUSSION
- ■ READING
- ■ SPEAKING
- ■ VOCABULARY
- □ Phrasal verbs (*come*)
- ■ LANGUAGE STUDY
- □ *bored* or *boring, interested* or *interesting*?
  ▷ GS 1.2

PICTURE DISCUSSION

Students should look at the picture for a couple of minutes. Divide the students into pairs. With books closed, ask the pairs to exchange as much information as they can remember about the setting and the people.

With books open, ask students who they think is conducting the interview and who is being interviewed. Tell them to give reasons for their answers.

Ask students to imagine the kind of questions and answers they might hear if they were at the interview.

Extension activity

Tell each student to prepare a personal CV (Curriculum Vitae or history of education and jobs). Write the following points on the board:
– where you went to school
– what exams you took
– what qualifications you have (if any)
– what job experience you have had (if any)

Now ask students to interview each other in pairs to find the answers to the questions above. They can invent details if they are still at school. They then write the CV for the person they interviewed.

READING

Tell students to read only the advertisement and make notes about it. Allow about 5 minutes for this.

With books closed, ask students to give as much information as possible about the advertisement using their notes to help them. Ask students to try and guess what the rest of the passage will be about. They can use the following expressions:

Giving opinions

I think it'll be . . .
I imagine it's probably . . .
I have an idea that it'll be . . .
In my opinion it'll be . . .

Tell students to skim read the whole passage silently. Allow about 5 minutes for this. Decide who predicted most accurately what the passage would be about.

Ask students to answer questions 1–6.

▶ Suggested answers
  1 She seemed surprised that the applicant was a man.
  2 Personal Assistant to the Sales Manager etc.
  3 – came across the advertisement in the local paper
    – wrote a short letter signed 'Chris Neale'
    – received a brief note asking him to come for an interview
    – they did not send a proper application form or ask for a photograph
  4 It says *had come across it, had written* etc., which tells us that it happened before the interview.
  5 He had done clerical work, he knew about computers and he spoke Spanish.
  6 Mr Lambert had thought he was a woman.

SPEAKING

Other suggestions for 'men's'/'women's' jobs:
– looking after children
– doing housework
– hairdressing
– dentist
– working on an oil-rig
– sailor

VOCABULARY

Phrasal verbs

EXERCISE A

Using examples of your own, ask students what the verb *come* + particle(s) means, e.g.
We wanted to move to the countryside but it didn't **come off**.
She **came up against** *a lot of opposition when she announced she wanted to work on a building site.*
You don't **come across** *many women bricklayers.*

In pairs, ask students to look at examples a)–c) in their books and match them with Nos. 1–3.

► Answers
   1 b)   2 a)   3 c)

EXERCISE B

► Answers
   1 off   3 up against   5 out
   2 across   4 round

LANGUAGE STUDY

bored or *boring*, *interested* or *interesting*?

Using examples of your own, see if students can explain what the difference between the −*ed* and the −*ing* forms is, e.g.
He was **bored** *so he left.*
He was **boring** *so I left!*

Suggested explanation: -*ed* ending for adjectives used to describe a person's feelings, e.g. *bored*. -*Ing* ending for adjectives used to describe the person or thing that produces those feelings, e.g. *boring*.

EXERCISE A

► Suggested answers
   b) and d) sound insulting
   a) might be used when two people are watching a film, or at a party, and the speaker cannot understand why the other person is not enjoying himself.
   c) might be used when the speaker is talking to someone who does not seem to have any interest in something, e.g. family photographs.

EXERCISE B

► Answers
   1 amusing   4 amused
   2 interested   5 interesting
   3 embarrassed   6 embarrassing

EXERCISE C

► Answers
   1 Did you find the story interesting?
   2 You will be shocked by this story.
   3 I'm not interested in computers.
   4 I find football boring.
   5 I am bored by this kind of exercise, too.
   6 You will be fascinated by the next unit.
   7 I hope you won't be disappointed by it / find it disappointing.
   8 I'm sure you won't be embarrassed by it / find it embarrassing.

See if students can make examples of their own about what *bores*, *fascinates* them and what they find *boring*, *fascinating* etc.

FOCUS TWO   SB 19 – 20

■ USE OF ENGLISH 1
■ VOCABULARY
■ ROLE PLAY
■ USE OF ENGLISH 2
☐ Paragraph completion
☐ Dialogue completion
■ LISTENING

USE OF ENGLISH 1

Before going into the lesson, write the fifteen missing words listed after the passage on flash cards. Write 1 or 2 sets, depending on the number of students in the class. Give each student (or pair of students) a card with one of the missing words written on it. Ask each student to make a sentence using the word on the flash card and read it out to the rest of the class.

Collect in all the cards and give students 3–4 minutes to skim read the passage, ignoring the blanks.

Spread out the flash cards on a table and ask students to pick out the word which they think would fill the first, then the second blank etc. Encourage students to explain why a word would not fit, if they think it is the wrong choice.

► Answers
   1 stores   7 bring/provide
   2 responsible   8 experience
   3 present/current*   9 applicant
   4 over   10 willing*
   5 requires/demands* 11 deal
   6 in   12 provide*

13	allowance	17	at
14	benefits	18	addition*
15	contributions	19	share
16	on	20	applications

*words supplied by students themselves

VOCABULARY

With students' books closed, write all the words in capitals on the board. In groups of 3–4, ask students to make lists of as many words as possible which can be formed from the words on the board. Give one example, e.g. *music, musical, musically, musician*. Allow about 5 minutes for this. See which groups can find the most correct words and check the spellings.

Ask students to say what parts of speech they have formed if they can, e.g. adjective, adverb etc.

Keeping the same groups, ask students to fill in Nos. 1–10 in their books, then use the words they have formed in sentences of their own without looking at the sentences in their books.

▶ Answers

1	secretarial	6	centrally
2	musical	7	friendly
3	additional	8	yearly
4	professional	9	monthly
5	personally	10	daily

Point out that *friendly, monthly, yearly* and *daily* are adjectives here, and *personally* and *centrally* are adverbs. Nos. 1, 2, 3 and 4 are adjectives.

ROLE PLAY

Give students a secret name, address and telephone number on a card. Write the following conversation on the board:

A: *Hello. 522 3658.*
B: *Oh, good morning. I believe you phoned earlier about the job advertised in the paper and left your number on our answering machine.*
A: *Yes, that's right.*
B: *Could you give me your full name and address, please?*
A: *Certainly! It's . . .*

Alternatively you could record the conversation and play it to the students in the class.

Divide students into pairs and ask them to practise a similar conversation using the 'secret' information on their cards. Ask them to reverse roles when they have finished. Encourage them to spell out any difficult words.

Now divide the students into small groups of 4 or 5. Split the small groups into two. Half the students read through the advert for the job in their books. The other half prepare to act out Role B. Allow about 5 minutes for students to prepare what they might say on the phone. Choose one student from each splinter group and ask pairs of students to act out the roles suggested in their books. Sit the students back-to-back so they cannot see each other. This gives the impression of a 'real' phone call, where there is no eye contact. Ask several pairs of students to do this so that most of the class have an opportunity to practise what they have prepared.

Extension activity

Take in a copy of the local 'Yellow Pages' telephone directory and ask students to choose an advertisement they would like to have more information about. In pairs, ask them to prepare a telephone conversation asking for and giving information about the product or service they have chosen. Again use the back-to-back technique. Write the following expressions on the board to help the students:

Asking for help

I wonder if you could help me, please?
I wonder if you could tell me . . . ?
Could you tell me . . . ?
Can you give me any information about . . . ?

USE OF ENGLISH 2

Paragraph completion

Divide the class into four groups and assign one candidate to each group. Ask all the students to read through the job advert again carefully and decide in their groups if their candidate should get the job or not. Ask each group to be prepared to give reasons for their decision. Allow 5–10 minutes for this.

▶ Sample answer

I/We don't think Thomas Woodward should get the job because, although he is the right age, single (so would have plenty of spare time) and is also interested in art and music, he has had no administrative experience and he hates all kinds of sports.

Ask each group to exchange information about their candidate. Now tell all the students to write a paragraph, using the language suggested at the end of the exercise, explaining why they think their candidate should/shouldn't get the job. Walk round the class helping where necessary. Students can then be asked to write similar paragraphs about the other 3 candidates either in class or for homework.

Dialogue completion

Write the sentence '*How did you hear about this job?*' on the board and show students how it can be reduced to note form, e.g. *How/you hear/this job?*

Point out which words are left out in the notes, i.e. *did*, *about*.

Explain that students have to reconstruct complete sentences from notes in the exam so they should look out for any important words which are missing. Write one or two of the sentences from the dialogue on the board in note form and see if students can reconstruct what was said orally. Point out the kinds of words left out; often they are auxiliary verbs, prepositions or articles.

With students' books open, ask students to write in the completed sentences and finish the dialogue themselves. Allow 5–10 minutes for this. Compare answers and point out that there may be more than one correct version.

▶ Answers

1 Have you ever done this kind of work before?
2 No. I'm afraid this kind of job is completely new to/for me.
3 Why are/were you interested in it?
4 It's difficult to say. It just sounds/sounded interesting.
5 What interests/interested you most about the job?
6 Oh, well. I enjoy meeting people and travelling/travel.
7 What did you do in your previous job?
8 I sold books in a bookshop.
9 Why did you leave?
10 I was having/had (some/a lot of) arguments with my boss.
11 What caused/was the cause of these arguments?
12 He was a very stupid man! He and I just did not get on with each other!

Ask students to act out their dialogue in pairs to see if it sounds natural and correct.

Extension activity

Students can practise this examination skill further by testing each other. Either individually or in pairs, they can write their own dialogue (or find one in a book in English), reduce it to note form and give it to another student to complete. This will help them to think their way into the mind of the person setting the exam and to discover why some words are more difficult to supply than others.

LISTENING

▶ Suggested answer

PREVIOUS EMPLOYMENT

Candidate 1 – selling books
Candidate 2 – working in travel agents

REASON FOR CHANGING JOB

Candidate 1 – had arguments with boss
Candidate 2 – had arguments with boss

PERSONALITY

Candidate 1 – hesitant, confused, impatient
Candidate 2 – confident, understanding, ready to learn

The following expressions may help the discussion:

Expressing certainty

There's no question about it . . .
I'm convinced that . . .
Without doubt . . .

Tapescript

(First interview)
A: Have you ever done this kind of work before?
B: No . . . uh . . . I'm afraid this kind of job is completely new for me.
A: Why are you interested in it?
B: Well . . . uh . . .
A: Yes?
B: It . . . it's difficult to say. It . . . it just sounds interesting.
A: Hmm . . . what is it that interests you most about the job?
B: Oh, uh . . . well . . .
A: Yes?
B: I . . . I'd enjoy meeting people and . . . and travelling.
A: What did you do in your previous job?
B: I sold books in a bookshop.
A: Why did you leave?
B: Uh . . . well . . . I had . . . arguments with my boss.
A: Arguments? What . . . what was the cause of these arguments?
B: He was a very stupid man! He and I just didn't get on with each other!

(Second interview)
A: Have you ever done this kind of work before?
C: No, I haven't, but it's the kind of job I've always wanted to do.
A: Really? Why are you interested in it?
C: Because I think it would give me a chance to use and develop some of the things I've learned in my previous job.
A: Which things?
C: Well, in my last job I met a wide range of people and developed an ability to deal with them. I think this job would develop that ability even more.
A: What was your last job?
C: I worked in a travel agency, arranging holidays and that sort of thing.
A: Why did you leave?
C: Well, it was an interesting job in many ways, and I felt I learned a great deal, but, to be honest with you, I had several arguments with the boss, and decided it would be better to find another job.
A: What were these arguments about?
C: He said he had told me to do things and that I hadn't done them. But the fact was he hadn't told me to do them. Perhaps he meant to, but he forgot. And when I told him he'd never told me, he became very angry and said I was lying. This simply wasn't true.
A: Oh. I see.
C: Please don't misunderstand me. I'm not criticizing my previous employer. In many ways I liked him very much. But he was overworked and accused not only me but other people of forgetting to do things. I think I learned even from that . . . from our arguments, I mean.
A: What do you think you learned from them?
C: I think I learned that it's important to ask not only your boss but the other people you're working with more questions about what you are supposed to do and exactly who is doing what.
A: I see. Very interesting.

FOCUS THREE SB 21–22

- ■ READING
- ■ VOCABULARY
- ■ LANGUAGE STUDY
- □ Requests and intentions (*Are you going to/ Will you go/Will you be going to?*)

READING

Type out or photocopy* the text. Cut the text up into parts and stick each part on a separate piece of card. Make further sets of cards like this so that you have one set for each group of 4–5 students in your class.

Shuffle the cards but keep them in complete sets.

Divide students into groups and give each group one set of cards. Tell students that they come from a government leaflet giving advice on interviews.

Ask each group of students to arrange the cards in what they consider to be the most appropriate order. Allow 10–15 minutes for this.

When students have finished and made their decisions, tell them to look at the reading passage in their books and see if their decisions were correct. They can now do the multiple choice questions.

► Answers to multiple choice questions
1 B   2 D   3 A   4 C

Extension activity

Ask students whether they think this is good advice and whether they can think of any advice of their own to add.

VOCABULARY

EXERCISE A

► Answers
1 applicants /ˈæplɪkənts/	=	people who apply
2 applications /ˌæplɪˈkeɪʃns/	=	forms to be filled in
3 assistants /əˈsɪstənts/	=	helpers
4 assistance /əˈsɪstəns/	=	help
5 employer /ɪmˈplɔɪə/	=	person who employs others
6 employee /ˌemplɔɪˈiː/	=	person who is employed

EXERCISE B

► Answers

VERB	PERSON (noun)	THING (noun)
apply	*applicant*	*application*
assist	assistant	*assistance*
interview	interviewer/ interviewee	*interview*
translate	*translator*	*translation*
criticize	critic	*criticism*
employ	*employer/ employee*	employment
think	*thinker*	*thought*
shop	*shopper*	shopping
speak	*speaker*	*speech*
love	*lover*	love
use	*user*	use
oppose	opponent	*opposition*
discover	*discoverer*	*discovery*
invent	*inventor*	invention

Employer/employee is like interviewer/interviewee.

Check learning: with students' books closed, read out the verb in each of the above examples and ask students to tell you what both types of nouns are.

EXERCISE C

► Answers
1 noun (thing)	6 noun (thing)
2 noun (person)	7 verb
3 verb	8 noun (person)
4 noun (thing)	9 noun (thing)
5 noun (person)	

VERB	PERSON (noun)	THING (noun)
rob	robber	*robbery*
compete	*competitor*	competition
observe	observer	observation
organize	organizer	*organization*
train	trainer/*trainee*	training
give	giver	*gift*
imitate	imitator	imitation
publish	*publisher*	publication
lose	loser	*loss*

LANGUAGE STUDY

Requests and intentions

EXERCISE A

► Answers
1 b) and d)   2 a) and c)

---

* You may make photocopies of page 21 of the Student's Book for classroom use (but please note that copyright law does not normally permit multiple copies of published material).

EXERCISE B

▶ Answers

1 Are you going to help me?
2 Will you help me?
3 Will you explain this word to me?
4 Are you going to explain these words?
5 Are you going to take this to the post office?
6 Will you take this to the post office for me, please?
7 Are you going to answer these questions?
8 Will you answer all these questions, please?

EXERCISE C

▶ Answers

1 b) Will you be going to the post office?
2 c) is an invitation
  d) is asking if you intend to come to the party (you have already had an invitation)

EXERCISE D

Introduce Nos. 1–8 orally and ask students to make appropriate sentences to find out if someone is planning to do these things using *Will you be . . . ? / Are you going to . . . ?*

▶ Answers

1 Will you be working / Are you going to work late this evening?
2 Will you be spending / Are you going to spend the holidays at home?
3 Will you be visiting / Are you going to visit London soon?
4 Will you be taking / Are you going to take the Cambridge Exam this year?
5 Will you be going / Are you going to go to the supermarket?
6 Will you be coming / Are you going to come to all the lessons next week?

Extension activity

Tell students in pairs to ask each other what they are planning to do
– tonight
– at the weekend
– at half-term
– at Christmas
– at Easter (or any other religious festival, e.g. Ramadan)
– in the summer

FOCUS FOUR   SB 23

■ COMPOSITION (describing an object)
□ Adjective order ▷ GS 1.1

COMPOSITION

Point out that in the exam students may need to describe an object in their composition – especially in questions which ask for statements or reports.

Take into the lesson some small, unusual, colourful objects such as pencil cases, jewellery, ornaments, bags, purses, wallets.

Conduct a 'brainstorming' session and write as many adjectives as the students can think of to describe the objects, all over the board in no particular order. Ask students to copy all the adjectives into their books.

Point out (giving a few examples, or asking students to make their own examples) that adjectives can describe: *colour, country of origin, shape, material, size, weight* and *age*.

Ask students to sort the adjectives on the board into these categories, according to the order in the table in their books.

EXERCISE A

Ask students in pairs or small groups to write at least 5 more examples of all the categories mentioned except *age*. Allow about 5 minutes for this.

When students have finished, ask them to use at least one of the adjectives they have written down in each category to describe an object of their own choice.

EXERCISE B

▶ Answers

1 a small blue German hair-dryer
2 a small flat black leather wallet
3 a beautiful red Japanese fountain-pen
4 an old Pakistani mahogany writing-desk
5 a round white china table-lamp

EXERCISE C

Describe an object to the students. They have to guess what it is, e.g.
It's large, brown, made of leather and you can carry things in it. (A suitcase)
It's small and round and made of china and you can drink out of it. (A cup)

Now ask students to do the exercise in their books in pairs. Write the following expressions on the board to help them:

Trying to guess

It could be . . .
It might be . . .
Is it . . . ?
I think it's . . .

EXERCISE D

Ask students individually to choose three or four adjectives to describe the objects mentioned in the exercise, then to compare their choice of adjectives with that of another student. Check that students give the adjectives in the correct order.

▶ Sample answers (there are other possibilities)

frying-pan	– battered / old / round
apple	– round / red / shiny
digital watch	– cheap / rectangular / plastic

EXERCISE E

▶ Answers

- new light brown leather
- long stainless steel
- small Egyptian copper
- square red French silk
- small plastic

FOCUS FIVE   SB 24

■ REVISION AND EXTENSION
□ *do/does* or *am/is/are doing*? ▷ GS 13.1
□ *will do* or *is/are doing*? ▷ GS 13.1, 13.3

REVISION AND EXTENSION

do/does or *am/is/are doing*?

EXERCISE A

Tell students to skim read the letter for general meaning then read it carefully a second time and choose the correct form of the verb.

▶ Answers

1 am writing	9 come
2 am staying	10 am looking
3 am doing	11 doesn't seem
4 am moving	12 deal
5 live	13 answer
6 am renting	14 suppose
7 is raining	15 starts
8 is getting	16 are beginning

EXERCISE B

▶ Answers

1 doesn't like, is thinking
2 want, hear
3 love, smell
4 prefers, does not taste
5 doubt, understand, are talking
6 appears, belongs
7 see, are meeting
8 is working, deserves
9 imagine, feels/is feeling
10 am measuring, need

will do or *is/are doing*?

EXERCISE C

In pairs, ask students to complete the conversation using *will do* or *is/are doing*, then practise reading out their completed conversations to each other. Point out the use of the abbreviated forms and encourage students to use them.

▶ Answers

1 Are you doing		8 'll give
2 am going		9 'll tell
3 won't be able		10 'll pick
4 'm meeting		11 'll be
5 're going		12 'm seeing
6 'll want		13 won't be
7 won't		

EXERCISE D

Divide the class into groups of 3 or 4 and ask them to discuss how certain they are that a) – h) will happen using the expressions suggested in Nos. 1–5. Allow 5–10 minutes for this.

Now ask students to write a couple of sentences individually about the statements using the expressions suggested beneath the grid. Encourage students to use as many different expressions as possible and explain any difficulties in meaning, e.g.

It's bound to happen	= It's inevitable / cannot be avoided
I'm convinced	= I'm absolutely certain / Someone has made me certain

WORKBOOK KEY WB 9 – 12

UNIT 3

EXERCISE A

1 C   2 B   3 D   4 C

EXERCISE B

Forestry: tree preservationists, tree surgeons
Fisheries: fishermen
Agriculture: agricultural engineers
Education and Librarianship: teachers, librarians, (technical teachers, building instructors)
Health: doctors, health educators
Business and Commerce: business entrepreneurs, accountants, (computer analysts and programmers)
Community and Social Development: social workers, community workers, town planners
Technical Trades, Crafts and Engineering: (technical teachers), boat builders, (building instructors, computer analysts and programmers), carpenters, petrol mechanics, (agricultural engineers)

EXERCISE D

1 came across
2 didn't come off
3 came up against
4 didn't come off
5 came round
6 came off
7 came up against
8 came out
9 came round
10 come across

EXERCISE E

1 annoying
2 surprised
3 embarrassed
4 bored
5 fascinated
6 amusing
7 annoying
8 boring
9 disappointed
10 disappointing

EXERCISE F

1 I have been appointed Operations Manager at London Zoo.
2 The Zoo is a major tourist attraction with (well) over a million visitors a year.
3 I will/shall be responsible for looking after visitors to the zoo/zoo itself.
4 They were looking for candidates aged between 28 and 45.
5 They also wanted someone with managerial ability and relevant experience.
6 Surprisingly, I got the job.
7 My starting salary will be around £22,000.
8 I am looking forward to starting work there.
9 I hope I shall be able to cope with the work that will be involved/what the work will involve.
10 Hope/I hope to see you sometime soon.
11 Give my love to all the family.

EXERCISE G

1 post/position
2 applicants/applications
3 salary
4 experience
5 qualifications
6 employees
7 management, staff
8 candidates
9 profits
10 appointment

EXERCISE H

Are you going to (do)? = intention
Is it going to (do)? = probability
Will you (do)? = a request
Will you be (doing)? = something that will be in progress in the future

1 Will you open the window (please)?
2 Are you going to wash your hair tonight?
3 Will you be attending the next committee meeting?
4 Is it going to rain this afternoon?
5 Are you going to tell the truth?
6 Are interest rates going to rise again?
7 Will you post this letter for me (please)?
8 Will you be going abroad for your holiday this year?

SECRET MESSAGES TO OURSELVES

FOCUS ONE   SB 25 – 26

- ■ PICTURE DISCUSSION
- ■ READING
- ■ LANGUAGE STUDY
- ☐ Small words with big meanings (*so* and *neither* to avoid repeating the sentence)

PICTURE DISCUSSION

Divide students into pairs and allow 2–3 minutes for them to try and describe the picture in their books. Now join 2 pairs together and invite students to compare their ideas. Ask different pairs to tell the rest of the class what they thought the picture was trying to express.

Keeping the same pairs, allow a further 3–4 minutes for students to interview each other by asking questions 1–4.

Now allow 1–2 minutes for each student individually to prepare a verbal description of a dream they have had (they can invent a dream if they cannot remember one!). They can make notes if they wish.

Invite students at random to describe their dream briefly. Put a list on the board of any similarities in the dreams students have had, e.g.

running   feeling afraid   falling

READING

Read out the third paragraph (students' books closed) beginning '*Elias Howe was far from . . .*'

Ask students to guess what the rest of the reading passage could be about. Tell them that the passage you read comes in the middle of the passage in their books. Ask half the class to imagine what comes **before** the passage and the other half to imagine what comes **after** the passage.

Now ask students to skim read the whole passage and see how correct their guesses were.

The multiple choice questions are more challenging in this unit. Try working through them one at a time as a class activity. Give students 3–4 minutes to skim read all the questions then ask them to try and work out

the answer to No. 1 only. Check and discuss the answer to No. 1 before going on to No. 2. Repeat this procedure for Nos. 3–5, referring every item to the relevant section of the passage and giving reasons for answers being correct or incorrect.

► Answers
   1 C   2 D   3 C   4 B   5 A

LANGUAGE STUDY

Small words with big meanings

EXERCISE A

► Answers
   1 Einstein got a lot of ideas while he was asleep, too.
   2 Carl Gustav Jung was very interested in dreams, too.
   3 Nobody else here knows how to interpret dreams either.
   4 My wife hasn't been sleeping very well lately either.

EXERCISE B

Write the example on the board and show students how the second sentence *Jung was famous for his study of them, too* can be shortened to *So was Jung*. Point out how the helping word (auxiliary) changes depending on what is in the original sentence. In pairs ask students to rewrite the second sentence in Nos. 1–8, repeating as little of the first sentence as possible and beginning with *so* or *neither*.

► Answers
   1 So did the ancient Chinese.
   2 So were the Ancient Greeks.
   3 Neither do snakes.
   4 Neither did Jung.
   5 So do cats and dogs.
   6 Neither has my dog.
   7 So will alcohol.
   8 Neither is drinking a lot of alcohol.

Revision transformations

EXERCISE C

Tell students that they will have to do this kind of exercise in Paper 3 of the exam. They will have to transform sentences without changing the meaning.

These transformations revise structures and vocabulary covered in the first three units.

Divide class into pairs. Ask students A to transform No. 1 and students B to be the 'teacher' and correct it if necessary. Reverse roles for No. 2 etc. Walk round the class listening but not correcting and making mental (or written) notes about problems you overhear. Allow 5–10 minutes for this.

Ask 2 pairs of students to compare answers and make a 'group' decision on what is correct or incorrect.

Compare answers at the end and give correct versions if students have not already done so. Comment on any problems you overheard.

► Answers

1 Not many people in England speak Chinese.
2 Do you mind posting this letter for me, please?
3 I thought the film on television was boring.
4 Please stop asking so many questions.
5 Who did you phone yesterday?
6 She has no intention of leaving.
7 Maria Elena knows very few words in English.
8 These goods are duty free.
9 Chris speaks Spanish fluently.
10 She isn't interested in music.

FOCUS TWO   SB 27 – 28

■ **LISTENING**
■ **SPEAKING**
■ **VOCABULARY**
■ **LANGUAGE STUDY**
□ Direct and reported speech ▷ GS 12.2

LISTENING 📼

EXERCISE A

Before listening to the tape, refer students to the different elements of the picture in their books and elicit descriptions from students at random. Now ask students to read through the multiple choice questions.

Play the tape twice and ask students to choose the best answer before comparing their choice with a neighbour's.

Tapescript
P = Presenter   N = Nora
P : Nora Chillingworth is the author of a popular book on dreams.
N: I read a great deal about dreams and talked to many psychiatrists and psychologists before I wrote my own book. And I also talked to almost a thousand people, some of them very famous, about their dreams.

A very successful businessman – a very rich and powerful man – told me he often dreamt he was falling from the top of some very steep stairs. Sometimes it was even a mountain peak. This, I discovered, was a symbol of his fear of failure, of losing his money and his position. He also told me he sometimes dreamt of walking into his dining-room and finding a wolf there. Now this is frequently a symbol of the fear of hunger or of being hungry. This particular businessman had at one time in his life been very poor.

Another businessman told me he had recently dreamt he was sitting in a room surrounded by a lot of people, all fully dressed. The people were looking at him and giggling. He looked down at himself and found he had no clothes on. I asked him if he had any secrets he was afraid other people would find out. At first he denied it. But then he admitted that he was being investigated by the tax officials and that he had some very large sums of money in a foreign bank. He didn't want them to find out about this money or where it had come from. A dream like that, you see, can often symbolize the fear that your secrets will be found out.

An opera singer told me that she had often had the same dream before an important performance. In it she was in a hospital, in pain. Suddenly she gave birth to a baby. The baby was perfectly formed and beautiful. The baby was a symbol of her desire to give a perfect performance.

There are two important things to understand about dreams. First of all, things never really mean what they seem to mean. The opera singer didn't want to have a baby at all. On the contrary! And you can't really understand a person's dreams unless you know a great deal about a person, about his or her secret hopes and fears. This is essential.

► Answers
   1 B   2 C   3 B   4 D   5 A

EXERCISE B

Tell students to read through Nos. 1–8 and explain that you are going to play the tape again and they should take notes **while** they are listening to the tape so that they can complete the sentences after they have finished listening.

Play the tape without pausing, then allow about 5 minutes for students to write full sentences for Nos. 1–8.

► Suggested answers

1 . . . spoke to psychiatrists, psychologists and about a thousand people about their dreams.
2 . . . his fear of failing in business and losing his money and position.
3 . . . he was also afraid of not having enough food to eat.
4 . . . he was sitting in a room surrounded by a lot of people all with their clothes on. They were laughing at him because he had no clothes on.
5 . . . his secret sums of money in foreign banks would be discovered.
6 . . . she had had a beautiful, perfect baby.
7 . . . to give a perfect performance.
8 . . . know a lot about the person and what they secretly hope and fear.

SPEAKING

Divide the class into 5 groups. Give each group one of the dreams to interpret and decide what hopes or fears they could symbolize. Allow about 5 minutes for this. Ask a member of each group to explain to the rest of the class what the group has decided.

Invite comments from the other students as to whether they agree with the interpretation or not. Write the following expressions on the board to help students:

Saying you don't entirely agree

I see what you mean but . . .
There's a lot in what you say but . . .
True, but don't you think . . . ?
Certainly that's one way of looking at it but . . .

VOCABULARY

EXERCISE A

Make two sets of 24 flash cards for all the words in Nos. 1–6. Divide the class into 2 groups. Write the example on the board:

sleep   nap   wake   dream

and ask students to tell you which is the 'odd one out'.

▶ Answer

  wake because the other three all refer to what happens when you are not (fully) awake!

Give each group of students a set of flash cards and see if they can sort out the words into 6 related groups (of three). Point out that there will be six 'odd men out' when they have finished. See which group can sort out the words first. Explain any words students do not know.

Now ask individual students to read out the word which does not belong in the exercise in their books.

▶ Answers

  1 flat   3 deny   5 cover up
  2 failure   4 admit   6 awake

EXERCISE B

Write all the words in capitals on the board. Ask students individually to make lists of as many words as possible which can be formed using the words in capitals as a stem, e.g. INVENT, *invention, inventor* and ask them to identify the parts of speech they have formed.

Ask students to copy down complete lists in their books.

In pairs, see if they can complete Nos. 1–8 with a suitable form of the word in capitals, saying what part of speech they have used.

▶ Answers

  1 invention   5 importance
  2 interpretation   6 performance
  3 solution   7 disagreement
  4 imagination   8 knowledge

Now ask students to write sentences of their own using these words.

LANGUAGE STUDY

Direct and reported speech

Refer students to GS 12 to point out the different types of reported speech and the different ways of introducing reported speech. Refer also to the various changes which occur when turning direct speech into reported speech and vice versa, e.g. pronouns, expressions of time etc.

EXERCISE A

▶ Answers

  1 'I sometimes dream I am sitting in a crowded room with no clothes on.'
  2 'Have you got/Do you have any secrets you are afraid other people will find out?'
  3 'Yes, I am being investigated by tax officials.'
  4 'Have you recently put sums of money into a foreign bank?'
  5 'Where has/did the money come from?'

EXERCISE B

▶ Answers

  1 They asked him how much money he had put into the account.
  2 He told the officials that he didn't know.
  3 The officials said that they knew more about his money than he (himself) did/he did (himself).
  4 He asked them what they meant.
  5 They told him he would find out later.
  6 He claimed that he had nothing to conceal.
  7 He insisted that everything he had told them had been true.
  8 He admitted that he had perhaps forgotten a few things.

FOCUS THREE   SB 29 – 30

- ■ USE OF ENGLISH
- ■ WRITING
- ■ LANGUAGE STUDY
- □ Review of verb forms ▷ GS 13.2
- ■ VOCABULARY
- □ Phrasal verbs (*take* and *run*)

USE OF ENGLISH

Give students 3–4 minutes to skim read the passage ignoring the blanks. Before the lesson make 3 sets of flash cards with the fifteen missing words (at the end of the passage) on individual cards.

Divide students into 3 groups to play flash card 'snap'.

Tell one student in each group to deal the cards to the students in the group.

The cards are played by students putting them face upwards on the table in turn, until a suitable word has been found to fill the first blank and then the second, and so on.

When all the cards have been played they are taken in and dealt again and the procedure is repeated until fifteen of the blanks have been filled.

▶ Answers

1	front	11	which/that
2	get	12	noise
3	want	13	run*
4	engine	14	asked
5	doing	15	told
6	see/sense*	16	was
7	stopped	17	lose*
8	had*	18	crash
9	towards	19	look
10	looked/were	20	fault*

*words supplied by students themselves

EXERCISE B

▶ Suggested answers
1 losing his girlfriend
2 aiming too high in life, by going out with a very rich girl
3 arguments
4 bad weather (a bad time in his life)
  noisy engine (lack of harmony/happiness)
  losing height (fear of failure) etc.

WRITING

Ask students if they have ever had a dream. Write on the board as many different kinds of dreams as possible, e.g. being chased, being in a strange, exotic, beautiful or frightening place, dreaming about the future etc., and discuss what these dreams could mean.

Write the following points on the board:
the scene
what happened
how did it end?
meaning

Ask students to write a composition retelling a dream that they (or someone they know) can remember. Ask them to invent a dream if they cannot remember one. Tell them to use the points on the board to help them to organize their composition. Allow 40–50 minutes for this or ask students to write the composition for homework.

LANGUAGE STUDY

Review of verb forms

▶ Answers
had, began, was sitting, noticed, were looking, were pointing, did not understand, came, was smiling, had not finished, asked, was enjoying, told, was, wanted, was smiling, were looking, stopped, asked, had forgotten, did not understand, looked, realized, had asked, had forgotten, was laughing

VOCABULARY

Phrasal verbs

EXERCISE A

Explain the meanings of the phrasal verbs with **take** in examples of your own, e.g.
Fasten your seat belts ready for take-off. The plane **takes off** *in 5 minutes.*
Your hand luggage is **taking up** *too much space. Put it on the rack, please.*
I can't **take in** *all the flight details.*
Who do you **take after**?
This airline has been **taken over** *by a larger one.*
They **took on** *too many staff.*

See if students can explain the meaning of the verbs with *take*.

Ask students in pairs to match the examples a)–f) with the meanings 1–6.

▶ Answers

1	d)	3	c)	5	e)
2	f)	4	a)	6	b)

EXERCISE B

Introduce the phrasal verbs with *run* in examples of your own and ask students to explain what they mean in the examples, e.g.

I **ran over** a football in the middle of the road the other day.
I **ran out of** petrol yesterday.
I **ran into** an old friend of mine in the supermarket this morning.
Could we **run through** the details again?
Run along and play in the garden, boys.
We **ran into** problems with the unions.

Ask students to complete Nos. 1–5 with the appropriate particle(s).

▶ Answers
1	into	4	along
2	out of	5	over
3	through		

EXERCISE C

▶ Answers
1	run over	4	run out of
2	run into	5	run along
3	run through		

FOCUS FOUR   SB 31

■ COMPOSITION (narrative)
□ Punctuation and layout of direct and reported speech ▷ GS 12

COMPOSITION

Write the following on the board:
She said . . .

See if students can think of as many words as possible to replace '*said*', e.g. *told* (someone), *asked*, *enquired* etc. Make a list for students to copy into their books.

Now write these two sentences on the board:
I said 'It's a nice morning.'
'It's a nice morning,' I said.

Ask students to comment on the word order. Stress that when using direct speech the reporting verb can come before or after the actual words.

Now ask students to turn the sentences above into reported speech, i.e. *I said (that) it was a nice morning.*

Point out that in reported speech only the above order is possible. Remind students of the changes it is necessary to make in tenses when turning direct to reported speech.

Tell students to notice also that when using the actual words, speech marks are necessary but these disappear in reported speech. Write another few examples if necessary.

EXERCISE A

Ask students to read the passage beginning '*The harbour*' . . . then in pairs discuss Nos. 1–3.

▶ Suggested answers
1 speech marks, word order, commas, new paragraph for each change of speaker
2 tenses go one tense further back in time
3 speak, said, replied, asked, answered, tell, went on to say, invited, accepted

EXERCISE B

In pairs, ask students to put the passage marked with asterisks (*) into direct speech, taking it in turns and correcting each other. Give help where necessary. When students can tackle the exercise orally ask them to write their own version in their books.

When they have finished ask them to correct each other's work.

▶ Suggested answers
'I own the boat myself so the work's quite hard. By the way, I'm going out later. Why don't you join me?'
'Oh, that would be fantastic. Thanks, I'd love to.'

or

'I own the boat myself so the work's quite hard,' he said.
'By the way, I'm going out later,' he went on to say.
'Why don't you join me?' he asked.
'Oh, that would be fantastic. Thanks, I'd love to,' I replied.

EXERCISE C

Write a class composition. Ask each student to write on a piece of paper the name of an object they bought in a shop but which does not work. Put all the pieces of paper in a hat or tin and ask one student to pull out one paper (without looking at what it says). Choose whatever is pulled out as the object the class is going to write about.

Ask students for suggestions as to
– why the object does not work
– which shop it was bought at
– what you said to the shop assistant
– why s/he refused to give you your money back
– why you asked to see the manager

– what the manager said to you
– what you said to him
– what happened in the end

Write the following on the board:
– start a new paragraph for each change of speaker
– open and close inverted commas (speech marks) for direct speech
– put a comma before a closing speech mark, e.g. '. . . ,' *he said.*

Students should now be prepared to write the composition on their own. Refer them to the suggestions for paragraph divisions in their books.

FOCUS FIVE   SB 32

■ REVISION AND EXTENSION
■ LISTENING TEST 2

REVISION AND EXTENSION

▶ Answers

1 B	6 A	11 B	16 A
2 A	7 C	12 A	17 D
3 C	8 C	13 B	18 B
4 B	9 D	14 C	19 C
5 D	10 A	15 D	20 A

LISTENING TEST 2

Tapescript

I = Interviewer   **P** = Psychologist

I: Now, could you tell us more about what you do in your department? I mean, what research are you actually doing at the moment?
P: We're trying to find out as much as we can about dreams. There's one area that we're particularly interested in at the moment . . . and that is what we call directed dreaming.
I: Directed dreaming. What is that exactly?
P: Let me explain. You know, sometimes, if you're . . . having a dream and you wake up in the middle of it, you can sometimes go back to sleep again and go back to the dream?
I: Yes.
P: Well, that is similar to what we call directed dreaming. Now, what I was talking about is a fairly common experience, but real directed dreamers are people who have almost complete control over what they dream because they actually know that they are dreaming.
I: They can dream what they want?
P: Yes . . . nearly.
I: Can anyone develop this ability?
P: Well, that's one of the things that we would like to find out. At our centre we have in fact got three people who are very reliable and who can have these directed dreams quite regularly.
I: And what sort of experiments do you do with them?

P: Well, a few weeks ago we thought it would be interesting to see if there was any way that these three regular dreamers could communicate with each other in a directed dream while they were sleeping. So one night we arranged for them all to stay at the centre. Then we asked the three of them – er, there were two men and a woman – we asked them all to meet each other in their dreams. So we told each of them to go to a pub that they all knew quite well, down by the river, and asked them, if they started dreaming, to go down there and try and find each other.
I: In the dream? Or three dreams?
P: Yes, so . . .um. . . they all went off to sleep, and the next morning we interviewed them all separately and asked them what they had seen. The two men had had dreams and could remember them, and they both said that they had been to the pub and had seen each other and had had a talk. But also, um, both of them said that they hadn't seen the woman, and we thought that was a bit, um, a bit odd. And then . . . we talked to her, and she told us that she hadn't had a dream at all that night, or she couldn't remember it anyway.
I: Fascinating. So both of the men said she hadn't appeared in their dreams and that was because she hadn't in fact been dreaming.
P: Yes, though of course it could just be a coincidence, but that's the kind of thing that we're trying to find out more about.
I: Well, thank you very much. It's been fascinating talking to you.
P: Thank you.

▶ Answers
    1 C   2 D   3 C   4 A

WORKBOOK KEY WB 13 – 16

UNIT 4

EXERCISE B

1 images	5 desire
2 insecurity	6 passion
3 symbol	7 obstacles
4 hostility	8 chasing

EXERCISE C

1 F	2 F	3 F	4 T	5 T
6 F	7 F	8 T	9 T	10 F

EXERCISE D

1 Both New York and Tokyo are important financial centres.
2 Louis Pasteur made important medical discoveries, and so did Alexander Fleming.
3 Both whales and tigers are in danger of extinction.
4 Napoleon didn't succeed in conquering Russia, and neither did Hitler.
5 Pythagoras studied geometry and so did Euclid.

EXERCISE E

1 C   2 B   3 A   4 D   5 B   6 B

EXERCISE F

1 knew
2 was feeling
3 had enjoyed
4 hadn't been feeling
5 had seen
6 had been waiting
7 had warned
8 had been wanting
9 would, could, might, should, had to, that, that day, the following day, there

EXERCISE G

I met a very interesting woman the other day. She said that her name was Vera and that she was from Russia. She had come over to England seven years ago and had been living in London since then. When she had lived in Moscow, she had been a journalist but now she was working for the BBC, and she quite enjoyed it. She was not sure if she would go back. She thought she might, because she hadn't seen her family for a long time, and she knew they wanted her to visit them.

EXERCISE H

'I was amazed to win so much money, but I won't let it change my life. I want to carry on with my job, which I enjoy, but I'll buy a new van as I need another one. I'm going to Disneyland for a holiday, which is something that I've been planning to do for a long time. When I get back, I'll go straight to work again.'

EXERCISE I

1 imagination
2 reality
3 deceiving
4 fantastic
5 illusion
6 nightmare
7 horror
8 thriller
9 terrified
10 shock

EXERCISE J

(sample answer)

I think that Janet's dream shows she is nervous about her interview; she thinks it may go wrong, like the exam she dreams about. She is also worried about money: she dreams about a mountain, showing that she has difficulties, and she wants to escape them, as shown by her flying away from her bank manager.

We can tell from Maggie's dream that she has mixed feelings about ending her present relationship and is afraid it may affect her career. Jim's death, and Maggie's falling symbolize this. She is not hurt, though, showing that she is optimistic. The fire shows that she is very attracted to Paul, but fears the passion she feels.

Jeremy's dream suggests that he is unhappy with his safe, well-paid job. The castle symbolizes a feeling of security in his job and marriage, but the thick water and powerful current in the river show he has conflicting feelings about fulfilling his ambition of becoming a film director.

FOCUS ONE   SB 33 – 34

- ■ PICTURE DISCUSSION
- ■ READING
- ■ LANGUAGE STUDY
- ☐ Ways of asking for permission

PICTURE DISCUSSION

Take in some pictures of various types of housing (or draw them on the board). Explain the difference between: *detached houses, semi-detached houses, flats, bungalows, terraced houses, town houses, cottages, tower blocks, skyscrapers* etc.

Find some housing advertisements in newspapers and ask students to choose what kind of house they would buy if they had the money.

See if students can imagine what the differences are between houses in their countries and what they imagine (or know) English houses are like.

Divide students into groups of 3–4 and allow 8–10 minutes for them to prepare answers to Nos. 1–5. Tell each student to make notes on the group's discussion. Walk round listening and helping where necessary.

Optional

Students could write up the notes of their group discussion (based on their own contribution to the discussion) to produce 'minutes' (or a summary) of what was discussed and decided.

Extension activity

Organize a project on local housing. Tell students to find out how many different types of housing there are in their own area or street and compile a statistical table of which types of housing predominate. The project can be as detailed as the students wish and can range from mere types of houses to topics such as gardens, double glazing, garages etc.

Ideally a real project should come from the students themselves so let them feel free to make suggestions about what they would like to do.

READING

Divide the class into groups of 3 or 4. Ask them to skim read the passage and write 5 questions they think they will be asked about it. Tell them not to look at the multiple choice questions after the passage. Tell students you do not want them to write multiple choice questions, simply comprehension questions. Allow about 5 minutes for this.

EXERCISE A

Now ask students to compare their questions with the information requested in the multiple choice questions 1–5 after the passage.

Ask students to choose the best multiple choice answer individually and be able to justify their choice. Allow about 5 minutes for this.

▶ Answers
   1 B   2 D   3 A   4 B   5 A

EXERCISE B

Ask students, in pairs or small groups, to build up a mental picture of what Alison and the man look like, a typical day in their lives, Alison's leisure interests and why the man has come to see Alison. See if students can also describe what kind of clothes Alison and the man might be wearing.

Extension activity

Take in some magazine pictures of people who are not famous. Divide the class into small groups. Give each group a picture of one person and allow the group 3–4 minutes to prepare a description of that person.

Collect in all the pictures and put them in the centre of a table. Ask one member from each group to describe which picture they had (without pointing it out). The other students have to guess the correct picture. This works better with as many pictures as possible, so in a small class divide the students into pairs or ask them to do the exercise individually.

LANGUAGE STUDY

Ways of asking for permission

Introduce the following ways of asking for permission in examples of your own, e.g.
*Is cycling **permitted** in parks?*
***Do you mind if** I open the window?*
***Would you mind if** I opened the window?*
***Do you object to me/my** opening the window?*
***All right if** I open the window?*

Ask students to decide if there is any difference between these ways of asking for permission. See if they can decide when they might use the different expressions, i.e. which expressions are more formal/informal. See if students can arrange them beginning with the most informal first. A suggested order of formality would be:
1 *All right if . . . ?* (most informal)
2 *Do you mind if . . . ?*
3 *Would you mind if . . . ?*
4 *Do you object to . . . ?*
5 *Is . . . permitted . . . ?* (most formal)

EXERCISE A

In pairs ask students to match Nos. 1–5 to the examples a)–f).

▶ Answers
   1 f)   2 d)   3 c) and b)   4 a)   5 e)

EXERCISE B

▶ Suggested answers
1 Do you mind if I sit here?
2 Do you object to me/my asking you a few personal questions?
   Do you mind if I ask you a few personal questions?
3 Is parking permitted here?
4 Would anybody mind if I closed this window?
   Would anybody object to me/my closing this window?
5 Are dogs permitted in here?
6 Do you object to me/my copying these documents?
7 You don't mind if I borrow this chair, do you?
8 Would it be all right if I came late tomorrow?

EXERCISE C

Ask students to decide how they would ask for permission in Nos. 1–4, using all the different expressions they have learned. Tell students that more than one answer will be possible. See how many different ways students can think of for asking for permission in each example.

▶ Suggested answers
1 Do you object to me taking/Would it be all right if I took the day off to visit my mother in hospital?
2 Would it be possible to/Would it be all right if I/I was wondering if I could put two tables together?
3 Is going outside permitted?
   Would it be possible for me to go outside?
4 I was wondering if I could have/Do you mind if I have/Would it be all right if I had a small party?

Extension activity

Give students a few minutes to prepare questions asking permission to do something in the lesson/school. They can ask you or each other their questions. They can use the following expressions:

Giving permission	Refusing permission
No, I don't (mind).	*I'm afraid not.*
No, of course not.	*Sorry, that's not*
Of course you can/may.	*possible.*
Yes, that would be fine.	*Sorry, that's out of the*
Yes, by all means.	*question.*
	I'm afraid I can't let
	you do that.

FOCUS TWO   SB 35 – 36

■ USE OF ENGLISH
■ LISTENING
■ VOCABULARY
■ PROBLEM SOLVING
■ LANGUAGE STUDY
□ Asking people not to do things
□ Asking politely
□ Reporting direct speech (reporting questions and requests/orders) ▷ GS 12

USE OF ENGLISH

Divide the class into small groups. Ask them to try and fill in Alison's part of the conversation. Tell students to read the whole conversation first, ignoring the spaces, then go back over the conversation more carefully and read what comes **after** the space to be able to predict what Alison said. Allow about 10 minutes for this. Compare answers and remember, there will be several possible answers to this exercise.

▶ Suggested answers

(2) would you mind putting your cigarette out?/ would you mind not smoking in my flat?

(3) Now, what did you want to see me/talk to me about?

(4) Oh, does it disturb/bother you?

(5) Surely it isn't too loud?/But it isn't very loud.

(6) Well, I'll (certainly) try and keep the sound down in future.

(7) No, not at all./Of course not.

(8) Who's Bruno?

LISTENING

Tapescript

A = Alison   P = Platchett

A: Excuse me, but I'm afraid I don't know your name.

P: Oh, it's Platchett. Leonard Platchett.

A: Oh, well, Mr Platchett, would you mind not smoking?

P: Oh, I'm sorry. I didn't know it bothered you. I'll put it out.

A: Thank you. Now, what . . . what was it you wanted to talk to me about?

P: Well, . . . it's about . . . uh . . . it's about the music you play in the evenings.

A: Oh, I see. What's wrong with it? Does it disturb you?

P: Yes, it does, to be frank.

A: Really? But it isn't very loud. I'm very careful about that.

P: Well, you may not think it is. But I can still hear it downstairs. The ceiling isn't very thick, you know. I can hear almost every note. Really! I'm not exaggerating.

A: I . . . I'm sorry to hear that. I'll turn it down then.

P: That's very kind of you. I . . . I hope you're not offended, by me telling you about it, I mean.

A: No, no, of course not. I'm glad you told me.

P: Good. I wouldn't complain about it if it were only me. But it disturbs Bruno, too. It really seems to upset him.

A: Who's Bruno?

P: My dog, of course! Who did you think I meant?

A: Oh, you mean *him!*

P: Yes! Perhaps he just doesn't like classical music. That *is* what you play up here in the evenings, isn't it?

A: Yes.

P: I thought so. Now, if it were rock and roll, he wouldn't mind so much. He really likes rock and roll. Particularly Elvis Presley. Excuse me.

EXERCISE A

Ask students to close their books and listen to the complete dialogue between Alison and Mr Platchett. Play the tape once without pausing. Ask students to point out any differences between the conversation on tape and their version (from memory).

EXERCISE B

Ask students to read through Nos. 1–3. Then play the tape once again, asking students to make notes as they listen to be able to answer Nos. 1–3.

Compare answers and discuss any differences of opinion.

▶ Answers

1 Really? But it isn't very loud. I'm very careful about that.

2 He doesn't like classical music.

3 He really likes rock and roll. Particularly Elvis Presley.

VOCABULARY

In groups of 3 or 4 ask students to decide which is the odd word and explain why it does not belong. Write any words students do not understand on the board and explain their meaning with synonyms or paraphrases if students cannot do so.

Ask each group to explain their reasons for their choices in one of the examples.

▶ Answers

1 amuse   3 embarrass   5 deceitful
2 bored   4 complain

Check learning: ask students to close their books. Rub all words off the board and ask students to make a list of as many words as they can remember from the exercise. Make sure students understand what the words mean and can group them according to their meanings.

Ask students to suggest headings for the groups they have made, e.g. words describing good/bad feelings, good/bad qualities etc.

PROBLEM SOLVING

Ask students if they can think of any ways of complaining politely so as not to offend somebody. Discuss why some ways would be inappropriate, e.g. *'Shut up'* (rude) or *'I'll tell the police'* (threatening) and why other ways might be more effective, e.g. *'I don't want to spoil your party/disturb your fun/be a nuisance, but . . .'* Write a list of suitable ways of complaining politely on the board.

Divide students into groups of 2–3 and allow 5–6 minutes for them to read through the information in boxes A and B, then discuss what A and B should or shouldn't do to solve their problems.

Encourage students to deal with all the solutions offered and say why they think they should or should not be adopted, e.g.

I don't think A should knock on the ceiling and shout at them because that might encourage them to make even more noise!

When students have finished, put 2 groups together and ask them to compare solutions. Did they agree?

LANGUAGE STUDY

Asking people not to do things

EXERCISE A

Introduce the examples in a)–f) orally and ask students if they can detect any difference as to when these expressions might be used, e.g.

a) an order to be obeyed
b) a polite written notice in taxis or restaurants, for example, requesting rather than ordering people not to smoke
c) a polite verbal request made by an individual to someone who is smoking when he or she is not supposed to be
d) (as c)
e) a written notice saying smoking is forbidden
f) a very polite request for someone not to do something or a reply to a request about whether smoking would be permitted.

Ask students individually to match Nos. 1–3 to their appropriate equivalent expressions in a)–f). Compare answers at the end.

▶ Answers
   1 a) and e)
   2 b) and e), possibly a)
   3 c), d) and f)

Asking politely

EXERCISE B

Write the eight sentences on flash cards. Divide the class into 8 groups. Ask each group to rephrase what is on their card politely and make a note of the sentence they have made.

Tell each group to pass its card on to the next group and repeat the procedure until each group has written a polite sentence for all the numbers. Exchange information at the end. There will be several correct answers for each example. Check that all the correct answers have been spelt correctly and make sure students realize that there are several ways of making polite requests.

Reporting direct speech

EXERCISE C

▶ Suggested answers
   1 'Do come in.'
   2 'Who does the dog belong to?'
   3 'Would you mind leaving it outside?'
   4 'Would it be all right if I smoked?'
   5 'I'd rather you didn't, if you don't mind.'
   6 'The music you play in the evenings disturbs me.'
   7 'I never play it very loud.'
   8 'Honestly, I can hear every note.'
   9 'Surely it's not that loud?'

EXERCISE D

Write the nine direct speech sentences on flash cards. Divide the class into 9 groups. Give each group one of the cards and ask them to write down what the words would be if they were in reported speech.

As in Exercise B, tell students to pass round the cards until they have written nine sentences in all. Collect in the cards and compare sentences.

▶ Suggested answers
   1 She asked him if he would mind not smoking.
   2 She asked him what he wanted to talk to her about.
   3 She insisted that she never played the music very loud.
   4 She suggested that the music might not be coming from her flat.
   5 She suggested that he might be mistaken.
   6 She insisted that the music was not coming from her flat.
   7 She ask him if he would mind getting his dog off the sofa.
   8 She told him not to bring his dog with him next time he came.
   9 She said that she was terribly sorry but she was very tired and asked him if he could leave.

Point out that there are some verbs which do not change from direct to reported speech, e.g. *would*, *could*, *might*, and that some direct speech words like *now* and *please* are not used in reported speech. Refer students to GS 12.6.

FOCUS THREE   SB 37 – 38

- ■ USE OF ENGLISH
- ■ LANGUAGE STUDY
- □ Verbs and prepositions
- ■ VOCABULARY
- □ Phrasal verbs

USE OF ENGLISH

EXERCISE A

Give students 3–4 minutes to skim read the newspaper article ignoring the blanks. Write ten of the missing words on flash cards.

Distribute the cards at various intervals to different students. Tell students either individually or in pairs or groups of 3 (depending how many students there are in the class) to fit in the word they can see to the appropriate space. Allow about 1 minute for this, then ask students to rotate the cards clockwise and repeat the procedure until they have filled in ten blanks. Give a signal for when the cards should be passed on.

Now allow time for students (in the same groups) to guess the remaining 10 words and slot in, where appropriate, any of the 10 words on flashcards still unplaced.

► Answers

1	guilty*	11	from
2	to	12	such*
3	complaining	13	except
4	which*	14	had*
5	failed*	15	way
6	unable*	16	rather*
7	accompanied	17	client
8	about	18	whose*
9	being*	19	income*
10	made	20	food

*words supplied by students themselves

EXERCISE B

Divide students into small groups and tell them to decide which of the three alternatives considered by the court would be best for Mrs Lovell. Write the following expressions on the board to help them:

Expressing approval

I'm in favour of –ing . . .
I think this is a good/an excellent suggestion.
In my opinion this is the only thing to do/course to take.

Expressing disapproval

I'm not in favour of –ing . . .
I'm totally against –ing . . .
I disapprove of –ing . . .
I couldn't possibly recommend –ing . . .

Ask groups to compare their suggestions and reach a conclusion about what should be done with Mrs Lovell.

EXERCISE C

This activity could be preceded by a group note-taking session to remind students of the points they discussed. Students could also do this for homework.

LANGUAGE STUDY

Verbs and prepositions

► Answers

1	of	5	for	8	for
2	to, about	6	from	9	about
3	to	7	with	10	in
4	from				

VOCABULARY

Divide students into 10 groups. Give each group one of the words in capitals and allow about 1 minute for them to think of as many words as possible which can be formed from their word, e.g.
complain, complaint, complaining, complained.

Now ask a 'spokesperson' from each group to read out the words the group made and ask the rest of the class to choose the correct form for Nos. 1–10. Students can then write in the words individually to reinforce learning.

► Answers

1	complaints	6	intention
2	barking	7	understanding
3	neighbourhood	8	guilty
4	defence	9	permission
5	cruelty	10	decision

Phrasal verbs

EXERCISE B

In pairs, ask students to match the explanations in Nos. 1–10 with sentences a)–j).

► Answers

1	g)	3	a)	5	b)	7	j)	9	c)
2	i)	4	h)	6	f)	8	e)	10	d)

EXERCISE C

Read out the sentences orally and see if students can supply from memory a phrasal verb which appeared in Exercise B.

▶ Answers

1 gave up	5 looked	8 broke down
2 call on	through	9 put up with
3 live on	6 look after	10 got through
4 calls for	7 turned out	

FOCUS FOUR SB 39

■ COMPOSITION (semi-formal letter)
□ A letter of complaint

COMPOSITION

Draw a sample layout of a semi-formal letter on the board.

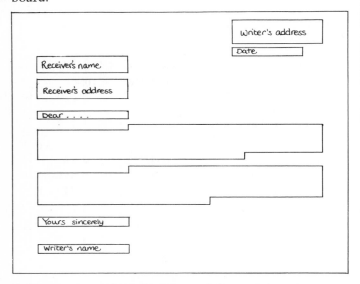

Point out that when the name of the recipient is known, the closing expression is *Yours sincerely*, but when the job title is known but not the name, the closing expression is *Yours faithfully* or *Yours truly*.

Mention the fact that layout can vary and that the form of the date 2.3.91 is confusing to Americans for whom it does not mean date, month and year but month, date and year, so it is advisable to keep to 2 March 1991.

EXERCISE A

In small groups, ask students to read through the letter in their books and give each of the three paragraphs headings. Allow about 5 minutes for this.

▶ Answers

Paragraph 1 Reason for writing
Paragraph 2 Detailed explanation of the complaint
Paragraph 3 Possible solution to the complaint

EXERCISE B

Refer students back to the sample letter in Exercise A, then ask them to rewrite the letter in their books with the correct punctuation and layout. Go round the class helping where necessary.

```
                              English Language Centre
                              84 High Street
                              Orpington
                              Hampshire

                              19 January 1991

Mr. P. J. Briggs
87 High Street
Orpington
Hampshire

Dear Mr Briggs

Thank you for your letter of 18 January concerning the disturbances created
by some of our students.

I have looked into the matter and have spoken to the students who were in
the centre that evening.  Those who were responsible for the incident have
been severely reprimanded.  In future we will take every precaution to reduce
the level of noise, and from now on all social functions will be supervised by
a member of staff.

Finally, I would like to apologize for the students' behaviour and am confident
that such an event will not occur again.

Yours sincerely

R. Vernon

R. Vernon (Headmaster)
```

EXERCISE C

Ask students to read through Nos. 1–3 and suggest words which they think they might need to write the letters.

Write the words on the board in three columns according to which letter they could be used for, e.g:

1	2	3
unwanted books	service engineer	gears
historical novels	out of order	clutch
dictionaries	endless waiting	engine
etc . . .		won't start

Divide the class into small groups. Ask each group to read the notes in the exercise carefully. Give each group one of the suggested letters to write. Allow 40–50 minutes for this. Correct the work as you go round the class.

Ask one or two students from each group to read out their letters, then give students one of the letters they have not written to do for homework.

FOCUS FIVE SB 40

■ REVISION AND EXTENSION
☐ Review of verb forms ▷ GS 13
☐ Present perfect or past simple? ▷ GS 13.1, 13.2
☐ Revision transformations

REVISION AND EXTENSION

Review of verb forms

EXERCISE A

Explain to students that it is useful to learn verbs in this way, so they will be able to remember when a verb has a different form in the Past simple and Present perfect. Ask students to supply similar examples of verbs you call out, e.g. *swim* = swam, swum.

Repeat the procedure for *rise, drink, lay, forgive, lie, blow, light* and *stick*. Go through this until students can remember the different parts of each verb.

Now ask students to complete the table in this exercise.

► Answers

swim	*swam*	*swum*
rise	*rose*	*risen*
drink	*drank*	drunk
lay	*laid*	*laid*
forgive	*forgave*	*forgiven*
lie	lay	*lain*
blow	*blew*	*blown*
light	*lit*	lit
stick	stuck	*stuck*

Now ask students if they can think of any other verbs to add to the table. It might be a good idea to compile an alphabetical list of verbs and put it on the classroom wall so that students can refer to it if they make any mistakes.

EXERCISE B

Present perfect or past simple?

Discuss the differences in usage between these two tenses. Refer students to GS 13.1, 13.2 if necesssary.

► Answers
   A: left, have travelled . . . haven't you?
   B: have lived, have visited
   A: have been
   B: was, enjoyed
   A: Did you do, were
   B: did
   A: did you go
   B: went, saw, was
   A: Have you ever been
   B: haven't had, have heard

EXERCISE C

► Answers

1 g)	3 c)	5 e)	7 b)	9 a)
2 j)	4 d)	6 h)	8 i)	10 f)

EXERCISE D

Explain the differences between *for, since* and *ago*, i.e.
for = length of time
since = from a time in the past up to now
ago = at a certain time in the past

and give examples of your own, e.g.
I've been teaching for ten years.
I taught for ten years.
I've been teaching since 1982.
It's ages since I saw him.
I started teaching three years ago.

Point out that *for* and *since* occur with the Present perfect/Present perfect progressive, but not *ago*.

In pairs, ask students to work through Nos. 1–10 discussing answers.

► Answers
   1 I haven't spoken to her since she went to London.
   2 He left school three years ago, then he worked in France for a few months before coming back to England.
   3 She has had a headache since she got up this morning.
   4 How long have you known him? Since I was ten years old.
   5 I have been here for an hour! Where have you been?
   6 He has just got a new job, and he's going to work in the States for two years.
   7 I have had this car for six years, and it has never broken down.
   8 It's two weeks since I saw him.

Revision transformations

EXERCISE E

Make a set of 20 flash cards. On 10 cards write down one of the transformations exactly as it appears in the book, e.g.
1 *'Is John having a party on Friday?' he asked.*
   He asked . . .

On the other 10 cards, write down the transformations in reverse, e.g.
1 *He asked if John was having a party on Friday.*
   'Is John . . .

Distribute all the cards to different students in the class. Ask one student to look at his/her card and try to complete the incomplete sentence. The student should say the sentence out loud. The student with the matching card should tell him if he got the sentence right, and then in turn try to complete his/her unfinished sentence. Nominate another student to do a transformation and continue until all the cards have been matched.

▶ Answers

1 He asked if John was having a party on Friday.
2 The doctor asked her why she hadn't made an appointment earlier.
3 Is smoking allowed in British cinemas?
4 He admitted that he had made a mistake.
5 Would you mind not playing your music so loudly?
6 Neither alcohol nor cigarettes are good for you.
7 They asked me how many times I had been to Spain.
8 You don't mind if I take the car this evening, do you?
9 Would it be all right if I opened the window?
10 I asked the waiter to bring me/if he would bring me another cup of coffee.

If students make mistakes in this revision exercise, refer them to the relevant section in the last two units so that they can go over it again.

WORKBOOK KEY WB 17 – 23

UNIT 5   WB 17 — 21

EXERCISE B

1 suspicious	4 deterrent
2 discreetly	5 vandals
3 residents	6 keeping a lookout

EXERCISE C

1 B   2 B   3 C   4 A

EXERCISE D

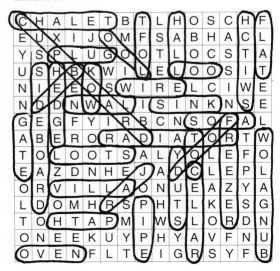

EXERCISE E

1 What is/What's your name?
2 Where have you come from?
3 What nationality are you?
4 Have you got anything to declare?
5 Did you pack everything yourself?
6 Can I have a look in your case?
7 What's in these bottles?
8 Why didn't you declare them?

a . . . what his name was.
b . . . where he had come from.
c . . . what nationality he was.
d . . . if he had anything to declare.
e . . . if he had packed everything himself.
f . . . if he could have a look in his case.
g . . . what was in the bottles.
h . . . why he hadn't declared them.

EXERCISE F

1 The boy asked the teacher if he could open the window.
2 The driving instructor told me to look in the mirror before turning right.
3 Janet asked her sister not to tell anyone the news because she wanted to keep it secret.
4 Henry told his wife not to drive so fast.
5 She asked her boss if she could come to work a little late the following day.
6 Michael asked Graham if he could borrow his tennis racquet.
7 Tim told his son to turn the music down a little.
8 He asked Mrs Robinson if he could use the phone to call his parents.

EXERCISE G

1 plumber	6 locksmith
2 architect	7 babysitter
3 carpenter	8 glazier
4 decorator	9 electrician
5 surveyor	10 gardener

EXERCISE H

1 Would it be all right if I came and stayed for a few days?
2 Is it all right if I phone my brother?
3 Do you mind if I make myself a cup of tea?
4 Would you mind if I had a bath now?
5 Do you mind if I turn on the TV?
6 Would it be all right if I took the car?
7 Would you mind if I invited a few friends over?
8 Is it all right if I read one of your books?
9 Would you mind if a few of my friends stayed?

EXERCISE I

1 C   2 F   3 A   4 B   5 D   6 E

Here are examples of possible questions:
7 Do you mind if I keep my food in my room?
8 Would it be all right if I put a record on?
9 Is it OK if I have a bath?
10 Would it be all right if I watched TV?

EXERCISE J

1   **Congratulate**
2   **At**
3   re**M**ind
4 trem**B**ling
5   f**R**om
6   **In**
7   **Depends**
8   **Get**
9 succ**E**eded

10   **For**
11   **Clever**
12   pl**E**ased

EXERCISE D

1 refusal   4 central
2 pollution   5 advisers/advisors
3 boring

EXERCISE E

1 looking   4 look
2 take   5 broke/sat
3 came

PROGRESS TEST 1   WB 22 — 23

EXERCISE A

1 A   2 C   3 C   4 D   5 C
6 A   7 D   8 D   9 A   10 C
11 D   12 C   13 C   14 D   15 A

EXERCISE B

1 few	8 after	15 for
2 whose	9 would	16 charge
3 who	10 find/consider	17 which/that
4 in	11 up	18 if/whether
5 and	12 for	19 has
6 at	13 qualifications	20 would
7 he	14 for	

EXERCISE C

1 Daisy told her chauffeur not to drive so fast.
2 Jane asked me if she could bring a friend along to the party.
3 He stopped smoking when he was thirty.
4 There aren't many people in Ireland who speak Gaelic/many people who speak Gaelic in Ireland.
5 Neither of my sisters speaks Spanish.
6 It must be expensive to run a big car like that.
7 Jennifer has been teaching for six years.
8 What interests you most about the film?
9 John's mother asked him what had happened to his knee.
10 I thought what he said was amazing.

6 DOES HONESTY ALWAYS PAY?

FOCUS ONE — SB 41–42

- **PICTURE DISCUSSION**
- **READING**
- **LANGUAGE STUDY**
  - □ *I wish* and *If only* ▷ GS 14.1

PICTURE DISCUSSION

Give students 1–2 minutes to look at the pictures in their books, then ask them to describe the people in the pictures (refer students to the vocabulary given in Unit 4, Focus One if necessary). The man covering his mouth with his hand is Richard Nixon, former President of the United States of America. He had to resign from that position after admitting that he had lied to the people of the United States about his part in the Watergate affair. In pairs, ask students to decide what is happening in the pictures. Put all the suggestions on the board and decide which is the most likely. Write these expressions on the board to help students say what they think.

Saying what is most likely

It's most probably . . .
I (should) think it's more likely to be . . .
The most likely/probable explanation is that . . .

Now ask students, still in pairs, to try and describe how these people are feeling. Conduct a 'brainstorming' session of vocabulary connected with feelings and put all the suggestions on the board, e.g.

worried, relaxed, happy, bored, interested, embarrassed, etc.

Ask students to give the characters in the 'policeman' picture an identity by attributing some of these feelings to each one. Now ask them to imagine a conversation between them. Tell students to be prepared to read/act out their conversation for the rest of the class. Choose several pairs of students to do this and compare the different conversations students have written.

Now divide students into groups of 3. Appoint one student as the teacher/examiner and tell this student to ask the others in turn Nos. 1–5 in the book.

Topics for further discussion

1 Attitudes towards the police in different countries
2 The role of the police in modern society
3 Should the police be armed?
4 Should politicians be honest?

READING

With students' books closed, ask one student to read one paragraph of the passage and the other students to take notes on the passage content. Now ask another student to read the second paragraph and so on until the passage has been covered in full. Repeat the procedure with different students reading a second time, giving students a second chance to add to their notes.

From the notes they have written, ask students to piece together the content of the passage orally so that they have a clear picture of what the passage is about.

EXERCISE A

Now ask students in pairs to decide which is the best multiple choice answer to Nos. 1–4 in the exercise.

▶ Answers

  1 C   2 A   3 B   4 A

EXERCISE B

▶ Answers

1 borrow	4 skilled (at)	7 squirm about
2 debts	5 itch	8 the context
3 fulfil	6 be taken as proof	

EXERCISE C

▶ Answers

1 lend	3 scratching	5 win
2 itching	4 gain	6 borrow

LANGUAGE STUDY

I wish and *If only*

EXERCISE A

Give students examples of your own using *I wish*, *I want* and *If only*, e.g.
1 **I wish** I were rich!
2 **I want** to be successful.
3 **If only** I had a lot of money!

See if students can explain your feelings when you use each of the above examples. Ask students to say which of the examples expresses the feeling that you are sorry about something (1 and 3).

Now read out the pairs of sentences in the book (students' books closed) and ask which sentence, a) or b), expresses the idea that the speaker is sorry that something is not so. Refer students to GS 14.1 if necessary.

▶ Answers

  1 b)   2 b)   3 b)   4 b)

EXERCISE B

Write the first sentence on the board and show students how it can be transformed, e.g.
I'm sorry I can't speak English perfectly.
I wish I could speak English perfectly.

Now ask students to do the same for Nos. 2–7.

▶ Answers

  1 I wish I could speak English perfectly.
  2 If only I had a lot of money.
  3 I wish I knew the answer to that question.
  4 If only I didn't have to work in this terrible place.
  5 I wish I could help you.
  6 If only I were rich.
  7 Don't you wish you could drive?

FOCUS TWO   SB 43 – 44

- ■ READING
- ■ SPEAKING
- ■ WRITING
- ■ VOCABULARY
- ■ LANGUAGE STUDY

READING

Divide the class into two groups. Ask students to work in pairs. Tell students in group 1 to read the review of 'The Sting' and prepare to talk to the rest of the class about the film.

Ask students in group 2 to read the review of 'Eyes of Laura Mars' and do the same. Allow about 6 minutes for this.

Now ask students in group 1 to tell the rest of the class about the film they read about, then ask students in group 2 to do the same for their film.

Take a vote to see which film the students prefer.

SPEAKING

Ask students to match Nos. 1–4 with A–D in their books, then in pairs, ask each other the questions they have made. Tell students to reverse roles so that they both have an opportunity to ask and answer the questions.

▶ Answers

  1 C   2 D   3 A   4 B

WRITING

Write a selection of words connected with films on flash cards and their definitions on other flash cards. Give each student a card. Ask one student to read out his/her word. The student with the corresponding definition should read it out.

Suggested words are:

producer	*director*
location	*script*
starring	*special effects*
thrilling	*scenes*
shot	*camera work*
photography	*acting*
theme music	*plot*
dialogue	*moving*

Write on the board:
The film is called . . . and stars . . .
It takes place in . . .
The story/plot of the film concerns . . .
The film's good/bad points are . . .

Give students 20–30 minutes to write a review of a film they have seen. Tell them to use the expressions on the board to help them and to write about 50–80 words. Go round the class helping where necessary.

Ask several students to read out their reviews at the end and put some of the reviews on the wall for other students to read.

VOCABULARY

EXERCISE A

▶ Answers

  1 e)   3 f)   5 g)   7 c)
  2 d)   4 a)*   6 a)*   8 b)

* have the same meaning

See if students can use the words in Nos. 1–8 in sentences of their own.

EXERCISE B

In pairs, ask students to choose one of the words in Exercise A to complete Nos. 1–7. Tell different pairs of students to compare answers.

▶ Answers

1 been deceiving	5 take you in
2 pass himself off as	6 betrayed
3 cunning	7 tricks
4 cheats	

LANGUAGE STUDY

Read out the sentences, leaving a gap where the preposition should be, and ask students to jot down quickly in their books what they think the missing preposition is.

Read the sentences again and ask students to shout out their answers. Correct any mistakes.

Now ask students individually to write in the correct prepositions for Nos. 1–9.

▶ Answers

1 on	4 by	7 by/at
2 for	5 on	8 of
3 in . . . out of	6 at	9 on

FOCUS THREE   SB 45 – 46

- ■ USE OF ENGLISH
- ■ LISTENING
- ■ SPEAKING
- ■ LANGUAGE STUDY
- □ Regrets with *wish* ▷ GS 14.1
- ■ VOCABULARY
- □ Word combinations

USE OF ENGLISH

EXERCISE A

Give students 3–4 minutes to read the passage, ignoring the blanks, and to look at the picture in their books.

In pairs, ask students to fill in the ten words they are given and try to guess the missing ten words. Go round the class explaining the meanings of any words students do not understand and helping where necessary.

Ask students for a verbal summary of the subject matter of the passage. Ask a few check comprehension questions if necessary, e.g.
What's the passage about?
What are the advantages of the Liebuster?

▶ Answers

1 thanks*	11 tell*
2 out	12 dishonest
3 looks*	13 home*
4 fact/reality*	14 away*
5 than	15 before
6 addition	16 available*
7 bigger*	17 yours/one
8 whether*	18 last
9 far	19 wait/delay
10 means	20 without*

* answers supplied by students themselves.

EXERCISE B

▶ Suggested answers

1 Yes, I'm terribly sorry I'm late.
2 It is the second time this has happened in the last two weeks.
3 I know. I hope you'll forgive me.
4 Well, why are you late this time?
5 The boss asked me to work late again.
6 Well, why didn't you phone me?
7 I tried to but it wasn't possible.
8 What do you mean? Are you trying to tell me that there are no phones in your office?
9 Of course there are phones in the office but there is something wrong with them.

LISTENING

EXERCISE A

Tell students that they will hear a complete version of the conversation between Peter and Jenny. Ask them to suggest what the real situation might be. Ask students if they believe Peter and if not, why not?

Now ask them to read through Nos. 1–8 **before** listening to the tape. Tell them they will have to decide whether the statements are true or false while they listen. They will hear the passage twice.

Tapescript
J = Jenny **P** = Peter

J : So you got here at last, Peter.
P: Yes, I'm terribly sorry I'm late.
J : It's . . . it's the second time this has happened in the last two weeks.
P: I know. I . . . uh . . . I hope you'll forgive me.
J : Well, why are you late this time?
P: Uh . . . the boss asked me to work late again.
J : Well, why didn't you phone me?
P: I . . . uh . . . I tried to but it wasn't possible.
J : What do you mean? Are you trying to tell me there are no phones in your office?
P: Of course there are phones in the office but . . . but . . .
J : Yes? Go on!
P: Well, there's something wrong with them.
P: That's strange.
J : What's strange?
P: I keep hearing a . . . a . . . buzzing noise.
J : Let's eat. I've put the dinner out.

P: Don't you hear it, too?
J: What?
P: That strange buzzing noise.
J: I don't know what you're talking about.
P: There it is again.
J: Come on! Let's have something to eat!
P: This is a lovely meal, Jenny. Uh . . . did you have a busy weekend?
J: Yes.
P: It's a pity you have to go away so often on business at the weekend.
J: Is it?
P: Of course it is!
J: Why?
P: Because . . . because . . . we could have more time together if you didn't have to work at the weekend so often. What's wrong with you this evening?
J: And what did you do?
P: What?
J: What did *you* do last weekend?
P: I . . . uh . . . well, uh . . . not very much.
J: Tell me about it.
P: Oh, I saw . . . saw some friends.
J: Which friends?
P: You don't know them.
P: What *is* that noise? Where's it coming from?
J: Friends, eh?
P: Yes.
J: So you didn't see Carla again?
P: Carla? Of course not! That was over ages ago.
J: You didn't by any chance have dinner with her on Saturday evening?
P: What are you getting at?
J: Answer my question!
P: No, of course I didn't see her.
J: Oh, I wish you wouldn't lie to me like that!
P: Now I know where it's coming from!
J: What?
P: That strange buzzing noise! It's that watch of yours!
J: What are you talking about?
P: I've never seen you wearing that watch before! Is it new?
J: Don't change the subject!
P: Let me see it. It . . . it's one of those new ones they're advertising, isn't it? Ah ha, so it *is* a *Liebuster*!
J: I . . . I . . .
P: You've been giving me a lie-detection test, haven't you?
J: No, I haven't!
P: There! That proves it!

Play the tape once without pausing, then after a brief interval (about 1 minute) play the tape again without pausing. Students should now have decided whether the statements are true or false and should be able to give reasons for their answers.

▶ Answers

1 False	4 True	7 False
2 False	5 True	8 True
3 True	6 False	

EXERCISE B

Ask students to read through questions 1–5. Play the dialogue again and ask them to take notes if necessary to be able to discuss the questions later. Divide students into small groups and ask them to discuss the answers to the questions and come to a conclusion as to what is really going on between Peter and Jenny.

▶ Suggested answers

1 a watch
2 she thinks he has another girlfriend
3 – working late
  – trying to phone
  – something wrong with the phones
  – seeing friends at the weekend
  – Jenny doesn't know the friends
  – not seeing Carla (relationship over)
4 an ex-girlfriend
5 the watch buzzes when she says something about not giving him a lie-detector test

SPEAKING

Divide students into groups of 3–4 and allow 4–5 minutes for them to discuss the answers to Nos. 1–6 in their books, then join 2 groups together and allow time for them to compare answers.

LANGUAGE STUDY

Regrets with *wish*

EXERCISE A

Refer students to GS 14.1 if necessary. Introduce your own examples of wish + *would* and *had*, e.g.
I wish you wouldn't make so much noise.
I wish you hadn't made so much noise.

Ask students to explain exactly what the meaning of these two sentences is, e.g. 1 Somebody is making a lot of noise and you want them to stop, 2 Somebody made a lot of noise in the past.

Now ask students in pairs to match Nos. 1–4 with the explanations a)–d) in their books.

▶ Answers
  1 c)   2 d)   3 b)   4 a)

EXERCISE B

▶ Answers
  1 I wish I hadn't done that.
  2 I wish you wouldn't do that!
  3 I wish I had got here earlier.
  4 I wish you wouldn't make that noise!
  5 I wish you wouldn't say things like that!
  6 I wish you hadn't said that.
  7 I wish you hadn't done that.
  8 I wish I hadn't asked that question.
  9 I wish you hadn't asked that question.
  10 I wish you wouldn't ask so many questions.

VOCABULARY

EXERCISE A

▶ Answers

1 inspector	4 actor	6 visitors
2 loser	5 sailors	7 murderer
3 thinker		

Word combinations

EXERCISE B

Ask students to read out each of the examples and try and explain what the combinations mean.

EXERCISE C

Now show students with an example on the board how words can be formed from phrases, e.g. a machine that washes dishes = *a dish-washer*.

Ask students in pairs to try and make word combinations for Nos. 1–8 in the same way.

▶ Answers

1 a pressure-cooker	6 a tin-opener
2 a paint-thinner	7 a carpet-sweeper
3 a paint-remover	8 ant-powder/ant-killer
4 a hair-dryer	9 a cork-screw
5 hair-restorer	10 a bottle-opener

See if students can think of any other examples or find any others in their dictionaries.

FOCUS FOUR — SB 47

■ COMPOSITION (formal speech)

COMPOSITION

Either photocopy or type out the paragraphs of the speech on a separate sheet.* Cut out separate cards and stick paragraphs A–E on different cards. Make several sets according to the number of groups you wish to have in the class.

With books closed, give each group a set of jumbled paragraphs and ask them to put them in the correct order. When they have decided on the order of the paragraphs, compare answers and ask students to tell you what the speech is about. Ask a few check comprehension questions if necessary, e.g.
Who is speaking? What is the occasion? Who is leaving? Where is he going?

* You may make photocopies of page 47 of the Student's Book for classroom use (but please note that copyright law does not normally permit multiple copying of published material).

Ask students to supply their own headings for the paragraphs.

EXERCISE A

Now ask students to open their books, and match the headings given there (1–5) with the paragraphs A–E.

▶ Answers

1 B	2 E	3 D	4 A	5 C

Ask students to compare their headings with those in their books.

EXERCISE B

Before students begin to prepare their speeches, discuss what wedding speeches would be like in their own country (if they are made at all) and what they might be like at a British wedding.

Then in pairs, ask students to read the notes in the book carefully and then write their own notes together about what they are going to say in each of the paragraphs suggested in their books. Go round the class giving help where necessary. Remind students that the occasion is a wedding and ask them what they think the tone of the speech should be, e.g. sad, happy, funny, serious etc.

As each pair of students finishes, ask students to write their speeches on their own. Invite several students to read out their speeches as if a wedding were taking place and put as many speeches up on the walls round the classroom as possible for the rest of the class to read.

FOCUS FIVE — SB 48

■ REVISION AND EXTENSION
■ LISTENING TEST 3

REVISION AND EXTENSION

Set students a timed revision 'test' in exam conditions, i.e. no talking, or referring to books (dictionaries etc). Allow them 15–20 minutes working entirely on their own. Ask them to write their answers in this way, giving the question number and the letter of the correct answer only, e.g. 1 B, on a separate piece of paper. Collect in the papers and give students a mark out of 20. This will give them some idea as to what it will be like to do an exercise like this in a formal exam atmosphere. Tell them that their marks at this stage will bear little resemblance to what they might get in the exam but will give them an idea as to the progress they have made so far in studying the material.

▶ Answers

1 B	6 B	11 C	16 D
2 A	7 A	12 D	17 A
3 C	8 D	13 B	18 C
4 C	9 C	14 A	19 D
5 D	10 B	15 C	20 B

Check learning: go over answers in class and explain any mistakes students made. Refer them to relevant sections in the GS or in their books where necessary.

LISTENING TEST 3

Tapescript

Ladies and Gentlemen, it gives me great pleasure to be here tonight to announce the overall winner of the 'Product of the Year' award. I am very glad, too, to see so many of you here tonight, as I know many of you have travelled a long way to be here with us. But first of all, what I would like to do before I announce the winner, is to thank everyone – all the scientists, engineers and chemists – who have worked so hard and put in so many entries to the competition.

As you know, there are four finalists, and each of them have already come first in their own category. Now I would just like to remind you of the four products which impressed the judges so much.

There was, firstly, from the Home and Leisure Category, the idea of a music plug. It allows the user to play music in any room in the house by simply plugging a speaker into an ordinary electrical socket. The second, from the Computer Category, was the telephone imager – and this allows photographs to be sent down a normal telephone line using a special mathematical system. Our third finalist, from the Transport Category, was the powered parachute. This is a small aeroplane made from a parachute and small motor which can carry one or two people. And our last finalist, from the Engineering Category, came up with the plastic fold-away concrete mixer. This machine is suitable for home use and for small buildings, and can be carried easily.

Before I announce the winner, I would like to say a few words of praise for not only those scientists, engineers and designers who have reached the final, but also for all of the others whose excellent ideas were sent to the judges. An inventor's life is not an easy one, as I am sure you are well aware. The public have an image, I think, of the mad professor whose ideas come in a flash of inspiration.

The reality, however, is very different from that. An inventor needs, above all, to work hard and work long hours. Ideas don't fall from the sky – they are more often than not the result of years of concentration. The inventor might perhaps be trying to change the design of a product that already exists; now this involves experiments, testing it, making it perhaps, working out how well it works, then starting again from the beginning, always trying out new ideas and approaches. And that, of course, is not the end of the line – when a good new idea or new design has been thought out, the inventor has to persuade a manufacturer to use the invention; he or she has to be a scientist, a diplomat, an accountant, a salesman – all these things in one.

And so we hope that this award will help tonight's winner with the development of his or her invention, and may make it a little easier to bring these excellent products to the market. And now, if I may, I would like to open this envelope to announce the winner. And the winner of the 'Product of the Year' competition is Mr Henry Medway, for the Medway powered parachute.

▶ Answers

1 T	2 F	3 F	4 T	5 T
6 F	7 F	8 F	9 T	10 F

WORKBOOK KEY WB 24 — 27

UNIT 6

EXERCISE B

tactfully   bluntly   to be open
unreliable   to play fair   to keep one's word
to tell a lie

EXERCISE C

1 I wish I had a different job.
2 If only I didn't have to do military service.
3 I wish that dress didn't cost so much.
4 If only I didn't feel so ill.
5 I wish I was studying at Oxford too.
6 If only I didn't have to get up so early.
7 I wish the dog didn't eat so much/didn't cost so much to feed.
8 If only she was going out with me.

EXERCISE D

(sample answers)

1 I wish I hadn't said that.
2 I wish I hadn't sold those shares.
3 I wish I had worn gloves during the robbery.
4 I wish I had been better prepared.
5 I wish I had bought a better one.
6 I wish I hadn't left the map behind.

EXERCISE E

Across:

1 OF	10 WORRIED	18 GOOD
3 CAPABLE	11 AT	20 NO
7 BY	13 AFRAID	22 SORRY
8 PLEASED	16 KIND	23 WITH
9 UP	17 AT	

Down:

2 FULL OF	12 OF	17 ABOUT
3 CLEVER	13 AT	19 BY
4 ABOUT	14 RUDE OF	21 ON
5 BY	15 IN	
6 EXCITED	16 KEEN	

EXERCISE G

1 If only I hadn't resigned.
2 I wish you wouldn't make phone calls during the morning.
3 If only you would listen to what I say.
4 If only you had been at the concert.
5 I wish you were here; the weather's lovely.
6 If only she would phone me.
7 I wish we could see you a bit more often.
8 If only it would stop raining.
9 I wish I had never started to smoke.
10 If only I was twenty years younger.

7 LETTERS TO AN ADVICE COLUMN

FOCUS ONE   SB 49 – 50

- ■ READING
- ■ LANGUAGE STUDY
- ☐ Is it still going on? (Present perfect, Present perfect progressive, Past simple) ▷ GS 13.1, 13.2
- ■ VOCABULARY

READING

EXERCISE A

Take into the lesson some 'problem' pages from magazines if available. Give small groups of students different letters to read and see if they agree with the answers given in the magazine.

Now divide the class into two groups. Ask group 1 to read and make notes on the first letter and group 2 the second. Allow 5 minutes for this. Ask students from each group to explain what their problem was and discuss solutions.

Ask students, in the same groups, to choose the best answer to Nos. 1–4. Students will have to skim read the letter they did not prepare to be able to answer all the questions.

▶ Answers
   1 B   2 D   3 C   4 A

EXERCISE B

Extension activity

After students have done Nos. 1–6 in the book, ask them to conduct a face-to-face role play in pairs with Student A explaining one of the problems in the reading passage and Student B giving advice. Write these expressions on the board to help them:

Giving advice

If I were you I'd . . .
You'd better . . .
I think you should . . .

Ask students to reverse roles when they have finished.

LANGUAGE STUDY

Is it still going on?

EXERCISE A

Read out the pairs of sentences with students' books closed and ask students to explain any difference they can between them, i.e. in b), c) and e) the event or situation is over, but in a), d) and f) the event or situation still exists. Refer students to GS 13.1, 13.2 if necessary.

Ask students to write sentences of their own showing that an event or situation a) is over and b) is still going on, using similar tenses.

EXERCISE B

▶ Answers

   1 went out
   2 has been going
   3 was, died
   4 have been living
   5 have you had
   6 did you have
   7 began, lasted

   8 began, has been going on
   9 A Have you ever been
      B went
      A Did you like
      B did, liked

VOCABULARY

Using your own examples explain what the words mean, e.g.

money = what is used as a means of exchange
pay = money paid for a job done
cash = coins, notes etc.
salary = fixed payment at regular intervals for (professional) services
wages = money paid to an employee, usually on an hourly, daily or weekly basis

Now ask students to use one of the words to complete Nos. 1–5.

▶ Answers

   1 salary   3 pay   5 cash
   2 money   4 wages

Ask students to make sentences of their own using these words.

FOCUS TWO   SB 51–52

- ■ USE OF ENGLISH 1
- ■ SPEAKING
- ■ USE OF ENGLISH 2
- ■ VOCABULARY
- □ *Lend* or *borrow*?
- □ *Fault, error* or *mistake*?
- ■ LANGUAGE STUDY
- □ Conditionals ▷ GS 4.1, 4.2

USE OF ENGLISH 1

▶ Answers

1 Since	8 having*	15 short*
2 fault*	9 result	16 would*
3 was*	10 up*	17 reason
4 going*	11 told*	18 borrowed*
5 interfere*	12 wish*	19 forgive*
6 made*	13 like*	20 advice
7 after	14 broken*	

* words supplied by students themselves

SPEAKING

EXERCISE A

Ask students in pairs to ask and answer questions about the four topics in the books.

▶ Suggested answers
  Q: What was the cause of the quarrel?
  A: The writer's father criticized her boyfriend and she thought her father had no right to interfere in her private life.
  Q: Why does the writer need money?
  A: To buy a new car.
  Q: What is she afraid her father will think if she asks for the money?
  A: That this was the only reason she had contacted him again.

USE OF ENGLISH 2

Guided discussion and writing

Tell students to look at the pictures and read the descriptions of Tony, Harry and Alice.

EXERCISE A

Divide students into groups of 2–3 and allow 2–3 minutes for them to discuss answers to Nos. 1–4. Now tell students to write out their answers in complete sentences. Join 2 groups together and ask them to compare answers.

EXERCISE B

In pairs, tell students to write out a dialogue of at least eight lines between Tony and Harry. Allow 4–5 minutes and help if necessary. Students could read/act out their dialogue for the rest of the class.

EXERCISE C

Tell students to write out a similar dialogue of at least eight lines between Tony and Alice. This could be done either in class or for homework.

VOCABULARY

lend or borrow?

EXERCISE A

Ask students to study the dictionary definitions in their books. Allow about 2 minutes for this.

Now ask them individually to complete Nos. 1–6 by writing in the appropriate word.

▶ Answers

1 borrow	3 lent	5 borrowing
2 lend	4 borrow	6 lending

fault, error or mistake?

EXERCISE B

Ask students to refer to the dictionary definitions, then choose the appropriate word to complete Nos. 1–5, pointing out that in one example both *error* and *mistake* could be used.

▶ Answers

1 mistake	3 error	5 error/mistake
2 fault	4 mistake	

Now see if students can use these 3 words in sentences of their own.

Dictionary skills

Use this opportunity to encourage students to use dictionaries and to train them in dictionary skills.

Point out that words in dictionaries are listed in alphabetical order for each letter in the word, not merely the first letter, e.g. *movement* would come after *month* because *v* comes after *n* in the alphabet. Tell students that some dictionaries also give page headings showing the first and last words listed on each page, e.g. *movement/much*.

Give students a dictionary task. Ask each student to note down on a piece of paper the page heading words for two pages of their dictionary and then twelve words taken at random from the dictionary but all beginning with the same letter.

Ask each student to pass his/her paper and dictionary to another student. Tell students to begin. The winner is the first student to find and correctly note down the page numbers in the dictionary for all the words they have been given.

LANGUAGE STUDY

Conditionals

EXERCISE A

► Answers

There is a difference in meaning between 2a) and b). 1a) and b) mean the same thing. 2b) can be rephrased 'I won't visit you because I haven't enough time.'

EXERCISE B

► Answers

1 I would see you tomorrow if I had enough time.
2 People would go to that restaurant if the prices weren't so high/were lower.
3 Jack would have a chance of passing the exam if he studied.
4 I would go in the water if it were warm/were not so cold.
5 They would interview you for the job if you spoke Spanish.
6 We would let those fans come here if they were not so violent/were less violent.

EXERCISE C

► Answers

1 is	3 paint	5 came
2 would look	4 will buy	6 were

FOCUS THREE   SB 53 – 54

- ■ LISTENING
- ■ USE OF ENGLISH
- ■ LANGUAGE STUDY
- ☐ *still*, *yet* or *already*?
- ☐ Another look at reported speech (offers, promises, thanks, apologies, requests)
  ▷ GS 12.2

LISTENING

EXERCISE A

Give students about 1 minute to read through the application form. In pairs, ask them to predict what the tape will be about.

Now tell students that while they are listening they have to fill in as many details as possible from the conversation. Play the tape once without pausing then, after a short interval, play the tape again without stopping.

Tapescript

A: Now, er . . . Miss . . . Miss
B: Allen. Jean Allen.
A: How do you spell that, by the way? A–L–L–A–N or A–L–L–E–N?
B: With an 'e'.
A: I see . . . now, we have your address, of course.
B: Not my new one. I've just moved.
A: Oh, I see. What is your new address?
B: 97, Bristol Gardens.
A: 97, Bristol Gardens. Which part of London is that? I mean, have you got the postal code?
B: Yes, NW12 CR3.
A: NW12 CR3. Now, you're 31 years old, is that correct?
B: Yes.
A: Uh huh . . . and, you're a journalist, I believe.
B: Yes. For the *North London News*.
A: I see. The *North London News*. Interesting job, is it?
B: Yes, very.
A: Uh . . . by the way, what's the address of the *North London News*?
B: York Square, London NW12.
A: York Square, London NW12.
B: Yes. I'm afraid I don't know the rest of the postal code . . . can't remember it.
A: It doesn't matter . . . uh, how long have you been with the paper, by the way?
B: Let's see . . . I started in November, '86.
A: Since November, '86. Yes . . . uh . . . I'm sorry to have to ask you all these questions but . . . how much do you earn a year?
B: Almost £11,000 . . . well, £10,500 to be exact.
A: £10,500. Now . . . this car you'd like to buy . . . uh . . . how much will it cost?
B: £5,400.
A: And how much exactly do you want to borrow?
B: Uh . . . let's see . . . I haven't worked out the exact figure yet. About . . . hmmm . . . I've saved about £2,000 and my father has offered to lend me another £1,000 . . . uh . . . £2,400 . . . no, I'd like £2,600. I'll probably need an extra £200 for road tax and insurance.

A: You already have a car, haven't you?
B: Yes.
A: Won't you get anything for it if you trade it in?
B: Very little, if anything, I'm afraid. It broke down a few weeks ago and can't be repaired.
A: I see. Well, now, I think it may be possible . . .

▶ Answers

LOAN APPLICATION

Name *Miss Jean Allen*

Address *97 Bristol Gardens,*
London NW12 CR3

Age last birthday *31*

Occupation *Journalist*

Employer's name and address *The North London News, York Square, London NW12*

How long employed there *Since November 1986*

Present income per annum *£10,500*

Amount of loan required *£2,600*

Purpose of loan *To buy a car*

EXERCISE B

Tell students to listen to the sentences in a)–h) and silently read them as they are listening. Ask them to notice how the stress changes with words like *break 'up/ 'break-up* etc.

Tapescript

a) Lovers often break UP.
b) What caused the BREAKup?
c) Why do cars break DOWN?
d) What caused the BREAKdown?
e) When did the plane take OFF?
f) Let's go and watch the TAKE-off.
g) I'm going to take OVER your job.
h) I'm responsible for the TAKE-over.

Tell students to think of each part of combinations like these as A and B, e.g. *break* (A) *up* (B) or *break* (A) *down* (B) and ask students to say which part is stressed when the combination is a noun (b), d), f) and h)) and

which part is stressed when the combination is a verb (a), c), e) and g)). They will notice that part A is stressed for the nouns and part B for the verbs.

EXERCISE C

Ask students to listen to Nos. 1–10 on the tape, then take it in turns to read the sentences aloud to each other.

Tapescript

1 I'll pay my bill when I check OUT.
2 I'll pay at the CHECK-out.
3 How did the robbers get AWAY?
4 How did they make their GET-away?
5 One boxer knocked the other one OUT.
6 He won by a KNOCK-out.
7 He tries to impress people by showing OFF.
8 He's a terrible SHOW-off.
9 I hope you won't let me DOWN.
10 It was a big LET-down.

EXERCISE D

▶ Answers
1 let . . . down (9)
2 let-down (10)
3 get away (3)
4 get-away (4)

▶ Suggested answers for other combinations
1 leave
2 a desk/cash register where accounts are settled
5 punched him so that he lost consciousness
6 a punch which made him unconscious
7 doing things to attract attention
8 a person who does things to attract attention

USE OF ENGLISH

▶ Suggested answers
1 I have already discussed a further loan with my bank manager.
2 He has offered/offered to lend me £2,600.
3 Now it seems there is/will be no problem about buying the car.
4 I have not yet decided exactly which car to buy/ I am going to buy.
5 However, one of my friends has suggested that I (should) buy a Fiat Uno.
6 She bought one several years ago and is/has been very satisfied with it.
7 Another friend suggested/has suggested that I (should) buy a Volkswagen.
8 He says/said he has had one for six years and it is still going very well.
9 I will let you know as soon as I have decided which car will be/is the best for me.

LANGUAGE STUDY

still, *yet* or *already*?

EXERCISE A

▶ Answers

1 yet	4 yet	7 still
2 already	5 still	8 already
3 still	6 already	

Another look at reported speech

EXERCISE A

▶ Answers (there may be several correct answers)

1 'I'll lend you £1,000 for the car.'
2 'I'll send/I promise to send it to you immediately.'
3 'Thanks (very much) for offering to lend me the money.'
4 'I'll pay the money back within a year (I promise).'
5 'We can let you have/We'll give you a loan of £2,600.'
6 'Could you increase the offer by £500?'
7 'No, there is no possibility of that.'/'We couldn't possibly do that.'
8 'I'm really very sorry that we cannot offer you any more.'

EXERCISE B

▶ Answers

1 My father refused to lend me a penny.
2 My mother offered to give me the money.
3 Ronald promised Julia that he would take her out the following day.
4 Julia's brother threatened to kill Ronald if he ever saw his sister again.
5 Allan promised to be there on time/that he would be there on time.
6 The next/following day he apologized for being late again.

FOCUS FOUR SB 55

■ COMPOSITION (argument)
☐ Expressing an opinion

COMPOSITION

EXERCISE A

Before opening their books, tell students that they are going to read a passage giving reasons against having a death penalty for serious crimes. Ask them if they can predict any of the arguments the author will use.

In small groups ask students to skim read the composition on the death penalty ignoring the blanks and see if any of their predicted arguments were mentioned. Students should then discuss which of the alternatives in Nos. 1–10 would best complete the composition. Students can then write in the answers on their own. Discuss any unknown vocabulary.

▶ Answers

1 C	3 A	5 D	7 B	9 A
2 C	4 B	6 D	8 C	10 B

EXERCISE B

▶ Answers

Paragraph 1 = Introduction
Paragraph 2 = Innocent people should never be killed
Paragraph 3 = The death penalty does not prevent all crime
Paragraph 4 = Society should set an example
Paragraph 5 = Conclusion

EXERCISE C

Ask students to read through the notes and write a composition on one of the suggested subjects in class. Go through the points with the students before they start writing to make sure they do exactly what is required of them.

Ask students who have chosen the same subject to work in a group together and prepare a 'group' composition which they all copy down. Go round the class giving help and advice where necessary. Ask students to write one of the compositions they have not done in class for homework.

FOCUS FIVE   SB 56

■ REVISION AND EXTENSION
□ Conditional 1 ▷ GS 4.1
□ Conditional 2 ▷ GS 4.2
□ Conditional 1 or 2?
□ Revision transformations

REVISION AND EXTENSION

Conditional 1

EXERCISE A

In pairs, ask students to read out the conversation to each other taking a role each and supplying the correct form of the verb in brackets. Ask one of the pairs to read out the conversation to the rest of the class.

▶ Answers
A: does, will be, misses, will have
B: will he get, takes
A: will be, is, may
A: gets, can, is, put, has already eaten, will not be
B: will he do, am, gets
A: are not, arrives, will have to
B: go, will leave, can

Conditional 2

EXERCISE B

In pairs, ask students to decide what they would do in the situations mentioned in Nos. 1–5. Explain that all their answers should contain 'If I . . . , I would . . .'

Ask students to tell the rest of the class what their decisions were.

EXERCISE C

In groups of 3 or 4 tell students to imagine on what conditions they would do the things mentioned in Nos. 1–5. Ask them to begin their sentences with 'I wouldn't . . . unless . . .'

Compare answers when students have finished.

Conditional 1 or 2?

EXERCISE D

▶ Answers
1 If I were you, I would apply for a job as soon as possible.
2 If I spoke perfect English, I would not need to take the exam.
3 If he were taller, he would be able to join the police.
4 You will/would be rich if you win/won the pools.

5 You will not be able to travel next week unless you get a visa.
6 If the weather is nice next weekend, they will go to the country.
7 Unless you hear otherwise, I shall/will come at 8.15.
8 If I were the Prime Minister, I would change a lot of things.
9 If the bus leaves/has left by the time I arrive, I will get a taxi.
10 If my headache does not go/has not gone away soon, I'll take an aspirin.

Revision transformations

EXERCISE E

▶ Answers
1 If she were not so busy, she could come to the party.
2 John asked if he could borrow some money from Mary.
3 He apologized for not replying to his/her/my last letter.
4 I wish you wouldn't complain all the time.
5 He has had his car for five years.
6 She has been learning English for three months.
7 I wish I didn't have to do so much work.
8 If I could afford it I would go on holiday.
9 I wish I lived in a big house.
10 She threatened to take him to court if he didn't stop following her.

WORKBOOK KEY WB 28 – 32

UNIT 7

EXERCISE A

1 C   2 B   3 C   4 D   5 A

EXERCISE B

1 borrow   5 borrowing, lends
2 loan   6 lent
3 loan   7 loan
4 borrowed   8 borrow

EXERCISE C

Sentence b suggests that something might happen.
Sentence c (being taller and joining the Police Force) is highly improbable.
Sentence a tells you that something is always true.
1 will/'ll go (type b)
2 smoke (type a)
3 turns (type a)
4 get (type b)

5 would/'d give (type c)
6 wasn't/weren't; were not (type c)
7 'll/shall report (type b)
8 would you choose (type c)

EXERCISE D

1	mistake	5	mistake
2	fault	6	offence
3	error	7	error
4	offences	8	faults

EXERCISE E

1	taken over	6	break up
2	show off	7	check out
3	let me down	8	get away
4	took off	9	knocked out
5	broke down	10	get away

EXERCISE F

1 We arrived last week.
2 What have you been doing since you got back?
3 We've been trying to organise the house and the children.
4 Did you want to come home after being away for so long?
5 We loved being abroad but we were glad to come home.
6 What did your wife do while you were working?
7 Well, she was very busy because she managed to get a part-time job.
8 Have you started looking for a job in this country yet?
9 No. I haven't had a minute since we got back.
10 Is that the time? I must dash. (Do) Give us a ring and we'll arrange a night for you to come to dinner.

EXERCISE G

1	cost	7	banknotes
2	currency	8	pay
3	change	9	cash
4	wealth	10	fees
5	expenses	11	wages
6	salaries	12	coins

EXERCISE H

1 haven't done it yet/still haven't done it.
2 already shown it to me/already shown me it.
3 haven't arrived/come yet/still haven't arrived/come.
4 haven't read/finished it yet/still haven't read/finished it.
5 hasn't done it yet/still hasn't done it.
6 haven't had a reply from him yet/still haven't heard from him.
7 had already left.

EXERCISE I

Where were you on the night of the robbery?
I was out for the evening with some friends.
What were you doing?
We went to see a film and then went for a drink in a local pub.
What time did you get back home?
I can't remember exactly.
Do you think any of the neighbours might have heard you coming home?
No, I'm sure they didn't – I was very quiet. I didn't want to wake up my father, who has to get up very early in the morning to go to work. I'm sorry (that) I can't prove it but all my friends have disappeared/gone abroad on holiday.

EXERCISE J

Tom suggested (that) the police should talk to the owner of the pub, who would remember him.
The police officer replied that they had already done that. They had shown the owner of the pub Tom's photograph but he hadn't been able to remember him at all.
Tom told the police officer that it had been very busy that night, so perhaps the owner (just) hadn't noticed him.
The police officer asked Tom to put his coat on and accompany him to the police station. He said that they would have to continue their enquiries there.
Tom said that he would get his coat and come quietly. He swore that he hadn't done/committed the robbery. He threatened that if he was sent to prison he would make life very difficult for him later.

EXERCISE K

(sample answer)

Prepare yourself for giving up smoking by deciding when temptation is greatest. Then you can change your routine so that these 'temptation times' do not arise. You should also set a definite day for giving up smoking.

On your chosen day just stop completely – don't smoke at all. As the days go by, encourage yourself by thinking how much better you feel, and how much better off you are.

Anyone who has tried to give up smoking and failed should try to decide what caused their failure and how they can best avoid it in future. They should also remember that the craving to smoke will eventually go: every day is a step on the way!

8 SPACE WARRIOR MADNESS

FOCUS ONE   SB 57 – 58

- ■ PICTURE DISCUSSION
- ■ READING
- ■ LANGUAGE STUDY
- □ Three types of past action (*was about to, was doing, had done*) ▷ GS 13.2, 13.3

PICTURE DISCUSSION

Give students 2–3 minutes to study the pictures and make a list of everything they can see in both pictures. Input vocabulary if necessary, e.g.

slot machines   neon signs   stools   betting

Put a master list of vocabulary on the board, then allow a further 3–4 minutes for students in pairs to prepare answers to Nos. 1–4 in their books. Invite different students to tell the rest of the class about one of the answers they decided on.

Topics for further discussion

1 Do you approve of games/activities like these? Why? Why not?
2 How do young people spend their free time in your country?
3 Can you think of any ways in which games/activities like these might be dangerous?

Extension activity

Write the following expressions on the board:

Explaining how to do something
First you take/put . . .
Then you turn/twist/insert . . .
Next you push/pull . . .
Finally you . . .

Ask students to prepare a short talk explaining how to make, do, play or cook something. Tell them to use the expressions on the board (or adapt them) if they wish. Allow 6–8 minutes and help if necessary, then choose several of the students to give their talks in the lesson. (The preparation could be done for homework.) Other students could give their talks in a later lesson. Allow time at the end of each talk for questions.

READING

EXERCISE A

Type out the reading passage or photocopy it onto separate sheets.* Cut the passage in half straight down the middle.

Divide students into groups of 4 or 6. Give one half of the students the left-hand part of the passage and the other group the right-hand part. Ask them to try and complete the missing half, by discussing and asking each other questions and making notes about the missing information.

Now let students see the whole passage and skim read it, before answering Nos. 1–5.

▶ Answers
   1 B   2 A   3 D   4 C

EXERCISE C

▶ Answers
   1 Even if he *wanted to stop playing the games he could not stop.* But he *does not want to stop.*
   2 He had taken a ten-pound note out of *my handbag* and was just about to put *the note* in his pocket.
   3 I always thought *electronic games* were harmless enough but Nick has been going *to a big amusement arcade* every day after school.

LANGUAGE STUDY

Three types of past action

EXERCISE A

Read out examples a)–c) and ask students to explain the difference between them if they can, e.g.
a) he was going to do it but he hadn't done it yet
b) he was in the process of doing something
c) the action was already completed

Now ask students to match Nos. 1–3 to the examples.

▶ Answers
   1 c)   2 a)   3 b)

* You may make photocopies of page 57 of the Student's Book for classroom use (but please note that copyright law does not normally permit multiple copying of published material).

EXERCISE B

▶ Answers (several correct answers may be possible)

1 He was just about to close the café.
2 It was just about to land.
3 He was just about to blow his whistle.
4 He was just about to kiss her.
5 She was just about to dive.
6 It was just about to spring/jump up at the bird.
7 They were just about to start their exam.
8 She was just about to cry.

Ask students to write some examples of their own using *(just) about to . . .*

FOCUS TWO   SB 59 – 60

- ■ USE OF ENGLISH
- ■ LANGUAGE STUDY
- □ *so* or *such?* ▷ GS 6.1
- ■ VOCABULARY
- □ *ache* or *pain*?

USE OF ENGLISH

EXERCISE A

Divide the reading passage into roughly 4–5 sections and ask individual students to read aloud one of these sections in turn, missing out the blanks. Tell the others to listen and make a mental note of what the passage is about (books closed). Discuss the subject matter of the passage before asking students to skim read the whole passage themselves.

Ask students in pairs to fit the five words after the passage into the appropriate spaces and supply the other fifteen themselves.

▶ Answers

1 lights*		11 movement*	
2 planets*		12 so*	
3 on*		13 call*	
4 done		14 pains	
5 striking/hitting		15 case	
6 enthusiastic*		16 had*	
7 spend*		17 than*	
8 marked*		18 play/use*	
9 pressure		19 consciousness*	
10 heal*		20 examined*	

* words supplied by students themselves

LANGUAGE STUDY

so or *such*?

EXERCISE A

▶ Answers

1 such   2 so   3 so   4 such

EXERCISE B

▶ Answers

1 The film was so amusing that I couldn't stop laughing.
2 This was such an interesting book that I could hardly put it down.
3 The programme was so terrifying that I had bad dreams after watching it.
4 This is such a dangerous game that children shouldn't be allowed to play it.
5 This is such a difficult problem that nobody can solve it.
6 This problem is so easy that even you can solve it.
7 You are speaking so quickly that I can't understand you.
8 You are such a good student that you could easily pass the Proficiency examination.

VOCABULARY

EXERCISE A

▶ Answers

1 common	4 kick	7 break
2 know	5 painless	8 ignore
3 fed up	6 muscle	

Explain any words students may not know.

EXERCISE B

▶ Answers

1 assumption	4 play	7 repairs
2 grip	5 movement	8 flashes
3 damaged	6 pressure	

ache or *pain*?

EXERCISE C

Introduce the meanings of the words with examples of your own, e.g.

ache = verb, to cause pain, e.g. *my tooth aches*; noun, a dull, continuous pain, used with *tooth*, *ear*, *head*, *stomach* and *heart*, e.g. *toothache*.

pain = noun, physical suffering in general, often more severe than 'ache', used with parts of the body, e.g. *a pain in my leg*, *arm*, *shoulder* etc.

It is possible, but unusual, as a verb, and it is more usual to say 'my stomach hurts' or 'my stomach aches' rather than 'my stomach pains me'.

Now ask students to complete Nos. 1–6 with *ache* or *pain*.

▶ Answers

1 ache	3 pain	5 ache
2 pain	4 ache	6 pain

FOCUS THREE   SB 61–62

- **SPEAKING**
- **LISTENING**
- **LANGUAGE STUDY**
- ☐ *used to do* or *be used to doing*? ▷ GS 13.2.2
- **VOCABULARY**
- ☐ Phrasal verbs (*hang* and *count*)

SPEAKING

EXERCISE A

Divide students into groups of 3–4 and ask them to read through the scene-setting paragraph in their books. Refer them to the prompts below and tell them to use these to help them to reach a conclusion. Allow 3–4 minutes and help if necessary, then invite one member from each group to report back to the class with their decision. Were the decisions the same?

Optional

Students could write up the minutes of their discussion and explain what decision was made and how it was reached.

EXERCISE B

▶ Suggested answers

a) On a space invader machine.
b) Where do I insert the money?
   What do I do when the enemy spaceship appears?
   How do I fire the rocket?
   How do I win?
   How many shots do I get for 10p?
c) any suitable answer acceptable

EXERCISE C

Conduct a brainstorming session based on the picture in the book for language which will be useful for a role play of the situation. Some of the following expressions might be suggested:

Asking politely

I wonder if I could . . . ?
Do you think I could possibly . . . ?
I really think you should refund my money.

Explaining/Complaining

Well, the thing is . . .
You see I . . . and nothing happened
I'm afraid I've just lost some money . . .

Saying something is true

Well, of course I did.
Why should I lie to you?
You must have heard/seen me . . .

In pairs, ask students to prepare the role play as suggested in their books. Allow 3–4 minutes for this. Ask several pairs of students to act or read out their versions to the rest of the class.

LISTENING 📻

Give students a timed listening test to complete on their own. Allow 2–3 minutes for students to read through the instructions and multiple choice questions Nos. 1–5. Play the tape once without pausing. Allow an interval of about 1 minute then play the tape again without pausing. Collect in answer sheets (prepare separate answer papers) and mark them (at home) before returning them to students later. Give a mark for the answer out of 10 (2 marks for each correct answer).

Tapescript

I come from a big family . . . three brothers and a sister . . . and we all work in the family business. My mother runs it now. We specialize in baking cakes . . . fruit cakes, wedding cakes, that kind of thing . . . we used to have a small shop that sold the bread and other things we baked, but now we just concentrate on the baking side and deliver bread and cakes to shops here and in Bristol.

My father started the business, but he died six years ago and, as I said, my mother runs it now. She is used to doing the accounts and that kind of thing. Even before he died, when she was looking after the children and running the house, she helped him a lot with the business. So that when dad fell ill . . . he was ill quite a lot in those last few years . . . it wasn't difficult for her to take over from him. My older brother, George, was already doing a lot of the baking by then, and I used to help out at weekends, too, even when I was a kid.

I . . . I have to start work very early six days a week . . . always up by four . . . except Sundays, that is, . . . but when I'm not working, I do the usual things . . . watching television if there's a good football game on, . . . things like that . . . but what I really like is to get out if the weather's good . . . can't bear to be indoors when the sun's shining . . . and walk or go fishing. That's the good thing about living in a small town like this . . . it doesn't take long to get out in the country . . . just a few minutes, and there are several rivers around which are really good for fishing . . . they haven't been killed off by the pollution you get in lots of rivers . . . that's what I really like doing . . . fishing and walking. For a time I used to make furniture . . . there's a big workshop down in the basement. It's what my dad liked to do in his spare time but I just don't like to be indoors that much . . .

Of course, in the evenings, as I say, I watch television now and then but . . . well . . . frankly, I'm so busy during the day, . . . have to get up so early . . . that I just doze off if I sit down in front of it for very long . . . can't concentrate . . . I begin to yawn and the next thing I know I'm asleep. I'm usually in bed by 8 anyway . . . except on Saturdays.

► Answers

   1 B   2 B   3 D   4 C   5 A

LANGUAGE STUDY

used to do or *be used to doing*?

EXERCISE A

Make sure students understand that *run* here = manage.

Write the examples on the board and ask students to explain the difference between them, e.g.

used to run = did in the past but does not now
used to running = accustomed to doing this (it's nothing new)

Now ask students to match a) and b) with Nos. 1 and 2 in their books.

► Answers

   1 b)   2 a)

EXERCISE B

► Answers (Sentence 1 should be rephrased using a negative form.)

   1 I'm not used to hearing bad language.
   2 I used to smoke a lot.
   3 I'm used to travelling long distances to work.
   4 Julia used to see Ronald every day.
   5 I used to work in that shop.
   6 English people are used to driving on the left.

VOCABULARY

Phrasal verbs

EXERCISE A

► Answers

   1 b)   2 d)   3 a)   4 c)

EXERCISE B

► Answers

   1 hang about   3 hang on to
   2 hung up   4 hang on

EXERCISE C

► Answers

   1 on   2 up   3 in   4 out

EXERCISE D

► Answers

   1 count up   3 count out
   2 count in   4 count on

FOCUS FOUR   SB 63

■ COMPOSITION (describing people)

COMPOSITION

Take in some magazine pictures of famous people. Give each pair of students one of the pictures and ask them to describe their character to the rest of the class without saying who it is. The other students have to guess the identity of the person.

EXERCISE A

► Answers

   1 h)   3 d)   5 e)   7 a)   9 i)
   2 f)   4 b)   6 g)   8 c)

EXERCISE B

Ask students to study the pictures in their books and notice how Margaret is described. Ask them to note which descriptive words are used with the verb *be* and which with the word *have*. Ask students on their own to write a description in class of one other character and another for homework. Tell students to use the description of Margaret as a model.

EXERCISE C

Discuss the meanings of the words used to describe people's characters, then ask students in groups of 3 or 4 to divide the words into what they consider to be 'good' and 'bad' qualities. Encourage them to give reasons for their answers, e.g. *competitive* – is this a good quality in your private life or at work? At work it can be a good quality because . . .

Compare answers when students have finished.

EXERCISE E

Describe a friend of yours to the students and ask them to draw a rough sketch of what your friend might look like. Make sure you have a photograph of your friend to show students when they have finished drawing their rough sketch. Compare what your friend really looks like with the sketches of the students.

Now ask students to read the instructions and write a description of a friend of theirs, following the paragraph plan given in the book. Ask students to exchange compositions when they are finished and have been corrected and ask them to draw a rough sketch of what their partner's friend might look like.

FOCUS FIVE SB 64

■ REVISION AND EXTENSION
■ LISTENING TEST 4

REVISION AND EXTENSION

► Answers

1 C	6 C	11 D	16 D
2 C	7 D	12 A	17 B
3 B	8 B	13 A	18 C
4 A	9 A	14 D	19 A
5 D	10 B	15 B	20 B

LISTENING TEST 4

Tapescript

P = Presenter   B = Brinks   L = Lawson

P: There has been an armed robbery this morning at the Halifax Building Society's branch in Edward Street. John Brinks is at the scene with Detective Sergeant Henry Lawson.

B: Detective Sergeant, can you tell us what you know about the robbery?

L: Yes, the raid took place this morning shortly after 11.30, when a man accompanied by a woman went into the offices of the, er, Building Society and asked to see the manager. Er, there were no other customers in the building at the time. They were let into the manager's office, and the woman produced a gun from her handbag. Then they took the manager back out of his office and made him tell the cashiers to hand over all the money they had in the tills and in the safe. Er, it came to about £25,000.

B: Presumably you have a number of witnesses.

L: Yes, we have a good description of both of them. Er, the man was about one metre eighty centimetres, around 35 years of age, with blue eyes and short curly red or ginger hair. He was wearing jeans, a green sweater and a three-quarter length blue coat. When he spoke to the cashier when he came in he called himself Mr Ericson, but we doubt whether that is his real name. But we do know that twice during the robbery, the woman called him Eddy, and that may be his real first name. He also speaks with a strong Scottish accent, which may help us to trace him.

B: And what about the woman?

L: Now, she is in her early twenties, slim, and quite tall – about one metre seventy centimetres. She was wearing a long white raincoat, which was quite loose-fitting and which she didn't take

off, and she had a beige handbag, which is what they used to hide the gun in. She's got straight, shoulder-length blonde hair, blue eyes and, like the man, has a noticeable accent.

B: Do you have any other information?

L: Yes. The car they used was seen by two or three people – and it's a blue or dark blue Ford Escort and we have the registration number . . . and it's G595 ERI. I'll say that again, it's G595 ERI. Now, the car was stolen from Bishopstone just over a week ago, so if anyone has seen it in the last week, we would like to hear from them. We also know that the car's front left headlight was broken when it was stolen, and is still broken, we think.

B: So you would like information from the public about the car.

L: Yes, and the people. We are appealing to anyone who thinks they may recognize the two robbers or knows anything about the car. We've set up an incident room in Swindon, and the telephone number is Swindon 774529. So we would like people to ring us if they have any information, er, and, of course, all calls will be dealt with in the strictest confidence.

B: Thank you very much.

L: Thank you.

B: And the phone number again if you have any information is Swindon 774529. And now back to the studio.

► Answers

1 (shortly after) 11.30 a.m.
2 Edward
3 £25,000
4 1.8m
5 35
6 blue
7 short, curly red or ginger
8 jeans
9 three-quarter length blue coat
10 Mr Eddy Ericson
11 Scottish
12 1.7m
13 early twenties
14 blue
15 straight, shoulder-length blonde
16 long white (loose-fitting) raincoat
17 blue or dark blue
18 registration
19 front left, broken

WORKBOOK KEY WB 33 – 36

UNIT 8

EXERCISE A

1 F	2 T	3 F	4 T	5 T
6 T	7 F	8 T	9 F	10 F

EXERCISE B

irritable: angry or bad-tempered
frustration: disappointment or dissatisfaction
dreadful: awful or terrible
on the go: busy
trigger: cause to happen
drag: pull
sneak: slip away without being noticed
gripped with: seized by
rebelled: fought back
on a knife edge: in a tricky or dangerous situation

EXERCISE C

1 peculiar	6 heart
2 ignore	7 mend
3 keen	8 reject
4 kiss	9 repair
5 medicine	10 refund

EXERCISE D

1 Sheila was just having a bath when there was a knock at the door.
2 Ann had been just about to ring the bell when she noticed that the door was half open.
3 Ann had just closed the door (behind her) when she dropped her handbag.
4 Sheila had just finished her bath when she heard a noise.
5 Ann was just picking up her handbag when she knocked over a chair.
6 Sheila was just deciding to phone the police when she heard another noise.
7 Ann had just shouted for Sheila when she noticed Sheila standing by the phone.
8 Sheila was just dialling 999 when she heard a familiar voice shouting her name.
9 She had just put down the phone when she saw her friend Ann standing in the doorway.

EXERCISE E

1 The students were so enthusiastic . . .
2 It was such an expensive car . . ./The car was such an expensive one . . .
3 The rent was so high . . .
4 It was such a crowded city . . ./The city was such a crowded one . . .
5 The football players were so good . . .
6 The coffee was so strong . . .
7 It was such a long journey . . ./The journey was such a long one . . .
8 They were such naughty children . . .
9 The film star was so talented . . .
10 The company was so successful . . .

EXERCISE F

1 count . . . in	6 hang up
2 hang on	7 hanging about
3 hang on to	8 counted up
4 count . . . out	9 count on
5 counting on	10 Hang on to

EXERCISE G

toothache	stomach-ache
earache	backache
headache	

EXERCISE H

1 I used to smoke . . .
2 When I was a teenager, I used to go to a lot of dances.
3 I hate living here but I'll get used to it eventually.
4 I'm used to working hard . . .
5 Although the job was difficult at first, he soon got used to it.
6 We used to have lots of friends . . .
7 Peter used to be difficult . . .
8 When you buy a new car, you need some time to get used to it.
9 I'll never get used to living in a cold climate.

EXERCISE I

tall:a	dark hair: a
short: b	fair hair: c
average height: c	shoulder-length hair: a
thin: a	short hair: c
slim: c	curly hair: c
of medium build: b	balding: b
male: a,b	in her teens: c
female: c	in his early twenties: a
well dressed: b,c	middle-aged: b
shabbily dressed: a	
bearded: b	
clean shaven: a	

The person you are looking for is a tall thin man in his early twenties with shoulder-length dark hair. He is clean-shaven but his clothes are shabby.

THE FACE BEHIND THE MASK

FOCUS ONE — SB 65 – 66

- ■ PICTURE DISCUSSION
- ■ READING
- ■ LANGUAGE STUDY
- □ *although* and *despite* ▷ GS 6.4

PICTURE DISCUSSION

Write the following words on the board while students are looking at the pictures in their books: *carnival, ball, dance, disco, party, wedding, funeral, christening, coming-of-age party, tribal celebration, fancy dress party, costume ball.*

Ask students to choose the most appropriate setting for the pictures. Discuss any unknown vocabulary. Ask students to work in pairs and prepare a description of one of the people in the pictures and say what the person is wearing. Invite different students to tell the rest of the class what their character is wearing or dressed up as.

Now tell students, in pairs, to interview each other, asking and answering Nos. 1–4 in their books. Allow 2–3 minutes, then choose several pairs to act out their interview for the rest of the class.
Topics for further discussion

1 Describe a party you have been to.
2 Do you enjoy or hate occasions like these? Explain why.
3 Describe your dream party. What would it consist of?

READING

Ask students to read only the first two paragraphs of the story in the newspaper. Allow about 5 minutes for them to plan what they think the rest of the passage will consist of. Compare answers before asking students to skim read the rest of the passage in their books.

EXERCISE A

Ask students in small groups to choose the best answer **without** referring back to the passage. When they have made their decisions, write the answers on the board.

Now allow students 2–3 minutes to check their answers by referring back to the passage, and count how many changes they made after doing this. Give the class the correct answers and count how many answers students guessed correctly **before** and how many **after** referring to the passage.

▶ Answers
1 B   2 D   3 A   4 B

EXERCISE B

▶ Answers

1 a lack of	4 bruise
2 draining fluid	5 a fake
3 patient	6 regular

EXERCISE C

▶ Answers

1 the doctors who were away on holiday
2 standing around, watching
3 regular examination and treatment by psychiatrists
4 psychiatrists

LANGUAGE STUDY

although and **despite**

EXERCISE A

▶ Answers
1 b)   2 a)

Point out that 1b) is followed by a noun and 2a) by a subordinate clause.

EXERCISE B

▶ Answers

1 Although	3 Despite	5 Although
2 Despite	4 although	6 despite

EXERCISE C

▶ Answers

1 Despite the good weather, we stayed indoors.
2 Although the price of petrol is high, big cars are still popular.
3 In spite of his pleasant manner, he isn't a good doctor.

4 Even though she was ill, my mother always had a smile on her face.

5 Although the weather is terrible, tourists keep coming here.

6 In spite of your strange sense of humour I like you.

7 Despite the fact that they quarrel regularly,/their regular quarrels, Jack and Mary still say they love each other.

8 Even though they love each other, they have broken up.

FOCUS TWO   SB 67–68

- ■ READING
- ■ SPEAKING
- ■ VOCABULARY
- ■ USE OF ENGLISH 1
- ■ LISTENING
- ■ USE OF ENGLISH 2

READING

Tell students to open their books and skim read the passage. Allow 1–2 minutes for this. Now tell students to close their books and tell you as much as possible about the passage.

With books open, ask students in pairs to ask each other whether statements 1–5 are true or false and refer to evidence in the passage for their answers.

▶ Answers

1 False	3 True	5 False
2 False	4 True	6 True

SPEAKING

Students might find the following expressions useful:

Asking for advice

What do you think I ought to do?
Could you give me any useful advice?
Do you think I should/ought to . . .
Do you think I'd feel better if . . .

VOCABULARY

▶ Answers

1 fitness	3 relaxation	5 easily
2 tiredness	4 medical	6 risky

USE OF ENGLISH 1

▶ Suggested answers

1 Well, now, what seems to be the problem?

2 Could you tell me what kind of a pain it is?/Can you describe this pain to me?

3 When do you feel it most?/When do you get it/this pain?

4 How long have you had it?

5 And where do you (usually) feel it? Where does it usually affect you?

6 When did it start hurting a lot?/When was the last time you felt it/this pain?

7 Does it hurt now?

8 How long did the pain last?

LISTENING

EXERCISE A

Ask students to read through Nos. 1–5 before listening to the tape. Play the tape once without pausing, then ask students to discuss the answers in small groups.

Tapescript

D = Doctor   P = Patient

D: Hmm . . . now you say this pain affects you after meals.

P: Yes.

D: Only after meals?

P: Yes.

D: After all meals? Or after certain meals in particular?

P: Yes. After dinner. It doesn't seem to bother me so much after breakfast, for some reason.

D: And lunch? What about after lunch?

P: Well, you see, I rarely eat lunch . . . in fact, I never do, except when I'm not working.

D: Why is that?

P: Well . . . uh, you see, when I'm working I haven't the time.

D: What do you do?

P: My job, you mean? I'm a motor-cycle despatch rider.

D: A what?

P: A motor-cycle despatch rider . . . I deliver parcels and things like that on my bike. All over London.

D: Really? Tell me, is there a lot of stress involved with the job?

P: Yes, there is. A lot of stress. I'm always in a rush . . . there's always another job to do . . . and the traffic's very heavy most of the time.

D: How long have you had this job?

P: For about . . . uh . . . four months now . . . no, a little longer . . . almost five months.

D: Did you ever have this pain in your stomach before then?

P: No . . . never had any problems like that at all until three months ago.

D: I see. Hmm.

▶ Suggested answers

1 a motor-cycle despatch rider

2 delivering parcels all over London on his motor-bike

3 almost five months ago

4 before the stomach pains began

5 yes—stress—always in a rush—no time to eat lunch—heavy traffic, so dangerous driving conditions

EXERCISE B

Explain the content of the tape for Exercise B and ask students to fill in the card while they are listening. Play the tape once without pausing. Allow about 1 minute then play the tape again (still without pausing).

```
NAME: .PETER. CLARKE.........
DATE OF BIRTH: January 21st, 1963
ADDRESS: 44 Ventnor Road.....
. . . . . . . . . . . . . . . . . . . . . . . . .
TEL: 445-0121...............
DOCTOR: Dr. MORTIMER........
```

Tapescript

R = Receptionist   **P** = Patient

R: Could I have your name, please?
P: Peter Clarke. That's with an 'e' on the end.
R: C–L–A–R–K–E?
P: Yes.
R: Date of birth?
P: January 21st, 1963.
R: And your address?
P: 44 Ventnor Road
R: 44 . . . what?
P: Ventnor Road. V–E–N–T–N–O–R.
R: Have you got a telephone number?
P: 445–0121
R: 445–0121
P: Right.
R: Doctor's name?
P: Dr Mortimer. M–O–R–T–I–M–E–R.
R: Thank you. Now if you'll just take a seat, I'll tell you when the specialist is ready to see you.
P: Thank you.

USE OF ENGLISH 2

▶ Suggested answers

1 Two months ago I was in your hospital for a stomach operation.
2 The day after the operation I was examined by a young doctor who said his name was Dr. Simon.
3 I was in pain so he gave me an injection.
4 Although his manner was very pleasant there was something strange about him.
5 Yesterday I read an article in the newspaper about a fake doctor practising in your hospital.
6 I am certain that this 'doctor' and the young man who gave me the injection are/were the same person.

7 How can/is it possible for such people to avoid detection?
8 I hope in future you will be able to prevent such things (from) happening in your hospital!

Now see if students can write this letter from memory on their own. Tell them it does not have to be exactly the same as this letter but must convey the same message.

FOCUS THREE   SB 69 – 70

- ■ LISTENING
- ■ VOCABULARY
- □ *avoid* or *prevent*?
- □ Phrasal verbs
- ■ LANGUAGE STUDY
- □ *mustn't* or *don't have to*?, (*needn't, don't need to*) ▷ GS 7.8, 7.9, 7.11

LISTENING

Ask students in pairs to read through the multiple choice items and guess which might be the correct answer. Now ask them to listen and choose the correct answer on their own. Play the tape once without pausing, then after a short interval (about 1 minute) play the tape again without pausing and tell students to tick the correct box as they listen.

Tapescript
P = Presenter   **R** = Reporter

P: If you live near Poole Park, you must be relieved to know that the strange 'gorilla attacks' that took place there between June and September have finally been brought to an end. But who or what was really responsible for them? Well, the mystery was finally explained in a courtroom here in Poole when a 39-year-old librarian called Rodney Bunting confessed to everything. Our reporter, Janet Freetown, was at the trial.
R: Bunting was described as a deeply disturbed man whose mother had prevented him from having normal social contacts. In particular, she objected to him going out with women. It was shortly after her death six months ago that he began his gorilla attacks.
  'I got the idea from watching a film on television. It was about a man who dressed up as a gorilla and wandered about the streets, terrifying people. I managed to get hold of a gorilla's costume and learned how to imitate them by studying their habits in the zoo,' Bunting said. Then, one night in June, Bunting put on his costume and crept out of his house into nearby Poole Park, where he sat in a tree until a young couple came into the park and sat down on a bench. 'When they started kissing, I jumped down and ran towards them, beating my chest and roaring. They were terrified and ran away. It gave me a strange sense of power,' Bunting admitted.
  Four more attacks occurred, the last on the evening of September 16th when Mrs Della Winters, a 69-year-old widow,

was taking her pet poodle, Samson, for a walk. When Bunting leapt out from behind a bush she did not run away but hit him over the head with her umbrella. When Bunting tried to get away, the poodle ran after him. So did a policeman, who had heard Mrs Winters' shouts. Bunting fell from a fence he was trying to climb and was arrested.

Mrs Winters later said that when she saw Bunting she didn't think he was a gorilla. 'Oh, he grunted like one, and had the same strange movements, but what gave him away was his tennis shoes. They were white and I could see them underneath all that hair. I realized he couldn't possibly be a gorilla. Gorillas just don't wear tennis shoes, do they?'

Bunting was given a six-month sentence and ordered to undergo regular psychiatric treatment for the next two years.

▶ Answers

1 B   2 A   3 D   4 B   5 D

VOCABULARY

avoid or *prevent*?

EXERCISE A

Refer students to the dictionary definitions in their books and ask them to complete Nos. 1–6 using either one or the other of these words.

▶ Answers

1 prevent   3 avoid   5 prevent
2 avoid   4 prevent   6 avoid

EXERCISE B

▶ Suggested answer

–prevent the prisoners from escaping

Phrasal verbs

EXERCISE C

▶ Answers

a) gave . . . away   e) went after
b) give up   f) stand for
c) pass himself off   g) got on with
d) taken in   h) passed away

Now ask students to match the explanations in Nos. 1–8 with the phrasal verbs in a)–h)

▶ Answers

1 e)   3 a)   5 c)   7 d)
2 g)   4 h)   6 f)   8 b)

EXERCISE D

▶ Answers

1 out   4 up   7 away
2 away   5 out   8 in
3 up   6 in

Ask students which sentences could be written with *off* or *on*.

▶ Answers

5 and 6

LANGUAGE STUDY

mustn't or *don't have to*?

EXERCISE A

▶ Answers

b), c) and d) mean more or less the same thing.
a) would be used to speak to a young child.

EXERCISE B

▶ Answers

Sentences 2, 3, 4 and 6 could be rephrased using *You mustn't . . .*
2 You mustn't park here.
3 You mustn't take guns with you on the plane.
4 You mustn't talk to each other during the exam!
6 You mustn't give anybody else this information.

The other sentences could be rephrased as:
1 You needn't/don't have to do this homework.
5 You needn't/don't have to leave a tip but you can if you want to.
7 You needn't/don't have to wait for me if you want to leave.

FOCUS FOUR   SB 71

■ COMPOSITION (informal letter)

COMPOSITION

Students could be asked to bring envelopes and writing paper for this lesson.

EXERCISE A

▶ Answers

1 A   3 B   5 A   7 A
2 B   4 C   6 B   8 C

EXERCISE B

▶ Answers

1 Things which are similar — the address of the writer, paragraphs.
2 Things which are different — the informal beginning, ending and contractions.

EXERCISE C

▶ Answers

1 thanks
2 congratulation
3 refusing an
   invitation
4 sympathy
5 making an
   invitation
6 apology

Ask students to think of situations when these types of letters might be written, e.g. the birth of a new baby (congratulation), failing a driving test (sympathy) etc.

EXERCISE D

Allow students 40–50 minutes to read through the instructions for the letter inviting a friend to stay and to write the actual letter as if they were going to send it, i.e. put it in an envelope with an address on the front. When the letters have been checked, ask students to exchange letters and write a suitable reply to each other imagining that they are Stuart.

Students themselves can decide whether they are going to accept or refuse the invitations.

Extension activity

Ask students to write genuine letters to each other inviting their partners to a party or on an outing. Tell students to exchange letters, and write suitable replies to each other.

FOCUS FIVE   SB 72

- ■ REVISION AND EXTENSION
- ☐ Changing nouns to adjectives
- ☐ Adjectives to nouns

REVISION AND EXTENSION

Changing nouns to adjectives

EXERCISE A

▶ Answers

1 a) and c) are nouns.
2 b) and d) are adjectives.

EXERCISE B

In groups of 3–4, ask students to supply the missing words in Nos. 1–12 and use some of the words they have made in sentences of their own.

▶ Answers

NOUN FORM	ADJECTIVE FORM
1 care	*careful*
2 *cheer*	cheerful
3 grass	*grassy*
4 *noise*	noisy
5 health	*healthy*
6 *fun*	funny
7 peace	*peaceful*
8 *smoke*	smoky
9 hope	*hopeful*
10 *use*	useful
11 salt	*salty*
12 *shame*	shameful

Adjectives to nouns

EXERCISE C

▶ Answers

1 high, patient
2 height, patience

Now ask students to complete Nos. 1–6.

▶ Answers

1 depth
2 strength
3 importance
4 possibility
5 Honesty
6 intelligence

EXERCISE D

▶ Answers

ADJECTIVE	NOUN
1 difficult	*difficulty*
2 *real*	reality
3 sincere	*sincerity*
4 *lonely*	loneliness
5 sad	*sadness*
6 *long*	length
7 wide	*width*
8 *wise*	wisdom
9 soft	*softness*
10 *violent*	violence
11 free	*freedom*
12 *young*	youth

EXERCISE E

▶ Answers

1 comfortable
2 sandy
3 windy
4 expensive
5 complaint
6 greasy
7 hungry
8 difficulty
9 beauty
10 kindness
11 boredom
12 sleepy
13 thankful
14 noisy

Discuss any vocabulary unknown to the students.

WORKBOOK KEY WB 37 – 40

UNIT 9

EXERCISE A

1 C   2 B   3 D   4 D   5 A

EXERCISE B

1 preserve
2 running down
3 shortage
4 consumption
5 vague
6 implant

EXERCISE C

1 despite/in spite of
2 although/even though
3 although/even though
4 despite/in spite of
5 despite/in spite of
6 despite/in spite of
7 despite/in spite of
8 although/even though
9 despite/in spite of
10 although/even though

EXERCISE D

1 must
2 mustn't
3 can
4 mustn't
5 can
6 must
7 needn't
8 have got to
9 must
10 needn't/don't need to
11 needn't/don't have to
12 must

EXERCISE E

1 disease
2 epidemics
3 spread
4 victim
5 symptoms
6 died
7 cure
8 infected
9 serious
10 protect
11 vaccinate
12 immune
13 virus
14 treatment
15 eradicated
16 recovered

EXERCISE F

(The clauses in most of the sentences can be transposed, sometimes with adjustment of pronouns/ nouns.)
2 Despite the fact that Agatha comes from a very rich family, she is not really happy.
3 Even though he has a university degree in German, he can't speak it.
4 Although she never practises, she plays the piano well.
5 In spite of hurting his foot before the race, he managed to win it.
6 Despite working very hard, Henry didn't pass the exam.

EXERCISE G

1 avoid
2 prevent
3 avoid
4 avoiding
5 prevent
6 prevent

EXERCISE H

1 won't be allowed to
2 will have to
3 had to
4 mustn't
5 didn't have to
6 won't need to
7 was allowed to
8 didn't need to/didn't have to

EXERCISE I

1 gave . . . away
2 get on with
3 gave up
4 taken in
5 got off
6 gave up/in
7 stand for
8 got on

10 WORDS AND FEELINGS

FOCUS ONE SB 73 – 74

- ■ PICTURE DISCUSSION
- ■ READING
- ■ SPEAKING
- ■ LANGUAGE STUDY
- □ Comparisons ▷ GS 1.3

PICTURE DISCUSSION

Ask students to write down three adjectives which they feel describe their own character. Ask them to write at least one 'bad' quality they think they have and one 'good' quality. Write all the adjectives on the board and discuss the meaning of any unknown words.

Initiate a discussion on how body movements can reveal personality traits, e.g. shyness, impatience etc.

In groups of 3–4 ask students to compare the feelings and gestures shown in the two pictures in their books. Invite one member of each group to tell the rest of the class what the group decided.

Now divide students into pairs and ask them to interview each other, taking it in turns to ask and answer Nos. 1–4 in their books. Invite several pairs to act out one of their interview exchanges.

Tell each student to prepare **one** example to answer No. 5, then, in groups of 3–4, ask students to compare answers. Were any of the students' ideas the same? How were they different?

Topics for further discussion

1 What kinds of things make you angry? How do you show your anger?
2 Would you ever take part in a demonstration?

READING

Ask individual students to read two or three sentences aloud. Ask check comprehension questions at the end, e.g.
What gestures or emotions are common in any language?
What do experiments in America suggest about our ability to express or recognize feelings?
What have psychologists such as E. G. Beier shown?

Divide the class into groups of 3 or 4 and ask them to discuss Nos. 1–6, make a note of their answers and report back to the rest of the class on their findings.

▶ Suggested answers
1 b) and d)
2 a), c), e) and f)
3 'He opened his eyes wide' suggests anger in Chinese but surprise in English.
4 Because some people are more sensitive/more emotional themselves/more observant.
5 People want to show they are interested but give the impression they don't care.
6 We communicate our feelings through sounds we can make, e.g. exclamations of surprise.

SPEAKING

EXERCISE A

Read out Nos. 1–3 and ask students to decide what emotions are being described.

▶ Answers
1 sadness   2 anger   3 happiness

EXERCISE B

In pairs, ask students to choose one of the people in Nos. 1–3 and prepare a description for the rest of the class which does not say exactly which person is being described but which explains only what s/he does to express the emotion. The other students have to guess which one has been chosen from the description of the person's actions.

LANGUAGE STUDY

Comparisons

EXERCISE A

▶ Answers
1 are   2 find   3 at   4 than

EXERCISE B

Write the first example on the board, then ask students to finish Nos. 2–8 in the same way without changing the meaning of the sentence in their books.

▶ Answers

1 Fear and anger are easier to express than disgust and contempt.
2 Most people find it more difficult to express disgust and contempt than (to express) fear and anger.
3 Old people are better at interpreting body language than young people.
4 My husband finds it easier to conceal his emotions than to express them.
5 It is easier for him to talk about work than to do it.
6 It is easier to criticize than to make good suggestions.
7 You find it easier to criticize than to make good suggestions.
8 It is easier for me to understand English than to speak it.
9 Did you find this exercise more difficult to do than the last one?

FOCUS TWO   SB 75 – 76

- ■ SPEAKING
- ■ VOCABULARY
- □ *give, cause, make* or *bring*?
- ■ USE OF ENGLISH
- ■ SPEAKING

SPEAKING

Divide students into small groups and ask them to describe which feeling they think each picture illustrates. Invite students to agree or disagree with each other about their interpretations of the pictures.

Extension activity

Conduct a class survey on feelings. Write the following grid on the board and ask students to complete it.

How often do you experience these emotions?
Tick (√) the appropriate box.

	pleasure	happiness	sadness	anger	fear	nervousness
often						
fairly regularly						
rarely						

Ask students to interview each other then total the number of ticks in each column and draw conclusions about the emotions experienced the most.

VOCABULARY

EXERCISE A

Read out the words in capitals and ask students to shout out as many words as possible that can be made from them. Now ask students to fill in the appropriate form of the words in Nos. 1–10. Discuss any unknown vocabulary.

EXERCISE A

▶ Answers

1 pleasure	6 embarrassing
2 happiness	7 surprised
3 boredom	8 painful
4 bitterness	9 enjoyable
5 excitement	10 pleasant

EXERCISE B

▶ Answers

1 of	4 about	7 at/by
2 with	5 in/with	8 by
3 with	6 in	9 To

EXERCISE C

▶ Answers

1 ashamed	5 boring	9 doubt
2 delight	6 funny	10 surprise
3 frighten	7 disgusting	
4 bored	8 humorous	

give, cause, make or *bring?*

EXERCISE D

▶ Answers

1 make   3 bring
2 give   4 cause

Ask students to write sentences of their own using
make . . .angry, give . . . pleasure,
bring . . . happiness, cause . . . pain.

USE OF ENGLISH

▶ Answers

1 movement   11 closer
2 connection   12 members
3 in   13 aspect
4 sound   14 between
5 by   15 to
6 hand   16 apart
7 same   17 seems
8 make   18 acceptable
9 less   19 express
10 to   20 farther

SPEAKING

In groups of 3–4 ask students to discuss what the gestures in Nos. 1–4 mean in their country. Compare answers, e.g.

shake hands	= greeting/making some kind of agreement
kiss on the cheek	= greeting/affection
stand up	= form of respect
pat on head	= display of affection etc.

FOCUS THREE   SB 77–78

■ LISTENING
■ ROLE PLAY
■ VOCABULARY
☐ Phrasal verbs (*get*)
■ LANGUAGE STUDY
  Preferences (*I prefer, I'd rather*) ▷ GS 14.2

LISTENING 📼

Ask students to read through Nos. 1–4 before hearing the tape.

Play the tape once without pausing and ask students to choose the correct answer while they are listening. After a short interval (about 1 minute) play the tape a second time without pausing and ask students to fill in any answers they did not complete the first time.

Tapescript

I = Interviewer   **C** = Carl

I : What . . . what kind of things make you feel happy?
C: Happy?
I : Yes. Are there certain times when something happens or for some other reason you feel happy?
C: Yes, of course . . . but I don't think there's a particular reason . . . at least, if there is, I don't know what it is.
I : Well, what about the weather, for instance?
C: . . . Well, I suppose like everybody else I prefer good weather to bad weather . . . I mean, I'd rather look at a sunny blue sky than a cloudy grey one . . . but. . . well . . . uh . . . I'm not really that sensitive to it . . . I mean, bad weather doesn't really get me down.
I : Are you happy all the time?
C: Of course not. I have my ups and downs like everybody else.
I : Well, then, could you describe the things that make you feel happy, you know, reading, lying on the beach, watching T.V. . . . ?
C: Well . . . I prefer cycling to just about everything else. I like being out in the open . . . active . . . not sitting around.
I : What about when you feel unhappy? Do you usually know what causes that?
C: Yes.
I : Well, can you give me an example?
C: Yes . . . like the argument I had with my girlfriend a few weeks ago.
I : What was the argument about?
C: Well . . . uh . . . she accused me of being cold and reserved towards her . . . she criticized me for not showing my feelings. She said I was a 'typical Englishman' and that I was deliberately hurting her.
I : Is she English herself?
C: No. She's Australian.
I : But why did this argument make you feel so unhappy?
C: Well . . . uh . . . it wasn't so much the fact that we had an argument. She apologized later . . . it was . . . uh . . . something else.
I : I don't think I understand.
C: Well . . . uh . . . you see, I was sitting with her in a coffee-shop and . . . uh . . . I wasn't saying very much because . . . well . . . you see, she'd borrowed some money from me and hadn't paid it back. And . . . anyway . . . suddenly she said 'Why are you sitting there like that? What's bothering you, for God's sake?'
I : And what did you say?
C: I didn't say anything.
I : But . . . why couldn't you tell her about what was really bothering you?
C: I just don't know. I find it very difficult to talk about money, particularly to a woman. I'd rather die than say something like 'Where's that £50 you owe me?'.

▶ Answers

1 B   2 D   3 A   4 C

ROLE PLAY

Divide students into pairs and give them a role each (A or B). Allow 3–4 minutes for them to prepare their roles then ask several pairs to read or act out their conversations for the rest of the class.

Write the following expressions on the board to help them:

Asking what's wrong

Is anything wrong?
What's the matter?
You're not your usual self today.
Have I done anything to upset you?

Reminding someone tactfully

Look, I hate to mention it but . . .
Remember that (book) I lent you?
Oh, by the way, . . .
Have you by any chance (finished that book) . . . ?

Apologizing

I'm really very sorry . . .
I do apologize . . .
I'm always forgetting things . . .
How forgetful of me . . .

VOCABULARY

Phrasal verbs

EXERCISE A

a) gets . . . down   d) gets out of
b) get by   e) get over
c) gets on   f) gets round to

Tell students to open their books and match the explanations in Nos. 1–6 with the examples a)–f).

▶ Answers

1 d)   3 a)   5 b)
2 f)   4 c)   6 e)

EXERCISE B

▶ Answers

1 round to   3 out of   5 down
2 over   4 by   6 on with

LANGUAGE STUDY

Preferences

EXERCISE A

▶ Answers

a) good weather   c) being outdoors
b) being active   d) work

▶ Suggested answers

1 would
2 I would prefer (to)/I would prefer not to

EXERCISE B

▶ Answers

1 I prefer Rome to Paris.
2 Marie prefers French food to Italian.
3 I prefer cooking my own meals to eating in restaurants.
4 Would you rather work for me or starve?
5 I'd rather not answer that question.
6 We'd rather read a story than do this exercise.
7 Do you prefer studying examples to analysing grammar rules?
8 Most people would rather spend money than earn it.

FOCUS FOUR   SB 79

■ COMPOSITION (narrative)
☐ Writing a story

COMPOSITION

EXERCISE A

Ask students to read the sample composition silently, then read it again and in pairs, put the events in Exercise A into the correct order.

▶ Answers

1 He set out on the journey.
2 He noticed the weather was good.
3 He decided to take a short cut.
4 The weather changed.
5 He realized he had gone the wrong way.
6 It got completely dark.
7 He collapsed by a rock.
8 He heard a car.
9 He found himself on a track.
10 He saw the car.

EXERCISE B

In different pairs, ask students to list the tenses used to describe the events in A, B and C and find two examples of each.

▶ Answers

A was doing (Past progressive), e.g. was falling, was getting etc.
B had done (Past perfect), e.g. had set out, had been etc.
C did (Past simple), e.g. stood up, set off etc.

EXERCISE C

▶ Answers

1	was sitting	8	had put
2	was pretending	9	had given
3	trying	10	talked
4	was	11	were
5	was	12	took
6	had taken	13	gave
7	had chosen	14	was

EXERCISE D

Play a class composition game. Take in some sheets of A4 paper and give one to each student. Tell them to write down answers to the information you require, fold over the paper and pass it on to the next student who will then write down the answer to the next piece of information, fold over the paper and pass it on. At the end each student will have a complete composition with each part written by a different student.

First set the scene for the composition by reading the introduction in the students' book. Then dictate the points to be mentioned:
– describe the weather
– the time of day
– how your friend felt
– what he could hear and see
– what he was doing
– how the situation occurred
– what he did before he was rescued
– how he was rescued

Then ask students to write down a sentence or two describing the weather. They should then fold over their papers and pass them on to the next student, who writes down a sentence or two about the time of day, and so on until all the information has been given.

Ask students to read out the version of the composition they end up with. Some of the versions should be very funny!

Students can be asked to write a similar composition for homework choosing a situation of their own. Here are some suggested topics:

1 Driving through a long tunnel in the mountains your car suddenly stops . . .
2 While out riding on the moors alone your horse suddenly goes lame . . .
3 While cycling in a remote part of Scotland you suddenly get a puncture in your tyre . . .
4 While on a motoring holiday with your family you find that all the hotels are full for the night . . .

FOCUS FIVE SB 80

- ■ REVISION AND EXTENSION
- ■ LISTENING TEST 5

REVISION AND EXTENSION

Allow students about 10 minutes to complete this section on their own choosing the best answer to Nos. 1–20. Ask them to count their totals at the end and decide on any areas where they feel additional practice might be needed.

▶ Answers

1 C	6 A	11 C	16 B
2 B	7 B	12 D	17 C
3 C	8 C	13 B	18 A
4 D	9 A	14 A	19 D
5 A	10 C	15 D	20 D

LISTENING TEST 5

Tapescript

J = Jenny   P = Peter

J: I don't, I don't really know that it's all that useful. I mean, what's the point, Peter, of teaching people about life-saving? The thing is . . .

P: Come on, Jenny, what's wrong with that?

J: Well, when you learn it, the whole situation is just so unrealistic. They teach you how . . . they teach it in a swimming pool, don't they? And the point is, the only time you're ever likely to need it is in an entirely different situation, in the middle of the sea or something like that.

P: I did it at school and I've used it.

J: When did you ever save anyone's life?

P: I did, really.

J: Where?

P: In Australia, with Chris.

J: When?

P: It was, um, during one of the holidays . . . I can't remember when exactly, but . . .

J: Wait a minute . . . I think I remember him telling me something about it. I take it all back. What happened exactly?

P: Well, we were on holiday, and there were . . . I don't know . . . about five or six of us, and Katie was there, and Jane I think . . . and a few others. Anyway, we were travelling up the east coast, and we stopped at this hotel which was really nice, and it was right by the beach. And there was this extraordinary man called Brian, I think, that used to run it and shout at everybody all the time. Anyway, in the morning we were all on the beach, and we wanted to have a swim. It wasn't a particularly nice day – I mean, the sun wasn't shining and it was a bit grey and windy, and the sea was quite rough, actually, and Brian had warned us about the sea and had said it was dangerous. But the thing was that it was the first time on the holiday that we'd actually been to the sea, because we'd spent the first few days in the mountains and then, then a couple of days seeing some people, so we really wanted a swim . . . and we were pretty good at swimming anyway.

J: Or you thought you were.

P: But they had these really big waves, and they looked so tempting because we wanted to go bodysurfing. Have you ever done any?

J: What? Surfing?

P: No, bodysurfing . . . it's like surfing, except you don't have a board, and what you do is . . . you've got to swim out, and when a wave comes along, you've got to start swimming really fast, just at the right moment, before it breaks . . . and if you get it right, then you can come all the way in, and the wave pushes you all the way up to the beach . . .

J: Oh, I know.

P: Now, that's fine as long as you get it right. But what happened was that Chris and I were in the water, and this big wave came along, and he didn't quite get it right, he was a bit too late, and the wave pushed him right under the water, right to the bottom, and he must have hit a rock or something . . .

J: Oh, no.

P: And they're so strong when you get them wrong, these waves, and it's absolutely impossible to do anything about it. I had missed that wave, so I was OK, but I couldn't see him . . . and he didn't come up for ages . . . and then I heard him . . . and he couldn't swim . . . so I went over to see, see what was happening . . . and he was in real trouble, because he'd broken his arm so he couldn't swim properly . . .

J: How awful.

P: It was pretty bad, because we were quite a long way out, and it was difficult to swim at the best of times, with the waves and everything. But that was when I remembered about this life-saving business, and I got him to basically lie on his back in the water, and then I got in front and put my arm sort of round his neck, and then just started swimming back to the shore. It took a long time, mind you, but if I hadn't actually learned how to do that, I wouldn't've known what to do.

J: And you got back?

P: Yes, and then we went off to hospital and got him fixed up. But the point is that it *is* useful to learn about first aid and emergencies and things like that when you're at school, because you never know when you might need it.

J: Yes, I suppose so. Maybe you're right.

▶ Answers

1 F	4 T	7 T	10 T
2 F	5 T	8 F	11 F
3 F	6 F	9 F	12 T

WORKBOOK KEY WB 41 – 46

UNIT 10 WB 41 — 44

EXERCISE A

1 C 2 A 3 D 4 C 5 B

EXERCISE B

bored: interested
tolerant: intolerant
even-tempered: quick-tempered/bad-tempered
patient: impatient
brave/courageous: cowardly
sensitive: insensitive
unashamed: ashamed
sincere: insincere
observant: unobservant
important: unimportant
legible: illegible
obedient: disobedient

EXERCISE C

Unfavourable	Open	Favourable
shock	surprise	happiness
boredom	astonishment	contentment
fear	amazement	pleasure
disgust		approval
contempt		amusement
sadness		delight
anger		joy

1 surprise	6	sadness
2 amusement/pleasure	7	fear
3 boredom	8	pleasure
4 approval	9	happiness/contentment
5 anger	10	contempt

EXERCISE D

good	better	best
easy	easier	easiest
much/many	more	most
interesting	more interesting	most interesting
fast	faster	fastest
bad	worse	worst
large	larger	largest
thin	thinner	thinnest
hard	harder	hardest
unusual	more unusual	most unusual
pretty	prettier	prettiest
expensive	more expensive	most expensive

1 easier	6	more interesting
2 more expensive	7	most difficult
3 larger	8	thinner
4 most unusual	9	worse
5 hardest	10	fastest

EXERCISE E

1 I prefer TV to the cinema but I'd rather go to the cinema tonight.
2 I prefer flying to driving but I'd rather drive to Manchester tomorrow.
3 I prefer the country to the town but I'd rather spend this weekend in town.
4 I prefer a cold climate to a hot climate but I'd rather have a holiday in the sun this year.
5 I prefer meat to fish but I'd rather have the fish this evening.
6 I prefer smart clothes to casual clothes but I'd rather wear jeans at the weekend.
7 I prefer large cars to small cars but I'd rather buy a small car to start with.
8 I prefer long hair to short hair but I'd rather have short hair in the summer.

EXERCISE F

make sad: get (someone) down
manage or cope: get by
be good friends with: get on with
manage to avoid doing: get out of
recover from: get over
make or find time to do: get round to

1 I don't think he'll ever get over the shock of his wife's death.
2 Doing the same thing every day really gets me down.
3 Although he's unemployed, he manages to get by.
4 They don't get on with each other, I'm afraid.
5 He always gets out of doing the washing-up.
6 I must get round to taking that film to be developed.
7 I found an excuse for getting out of the meeting.
8 It often takes a long time to get over an unexpected shock.

EXERCISE G

had arrived, were waiting, to say, would depart, were looking, trying, began, announced, would be delayed, decided, were just arriving, having struggled, stuck, saying, knew, would be

EXERCISE H

1	make	5	cause
2	bring	6	make
3	caused	7	bring
4	give	8	gives

PROGRESS TEST 2   WB 45 — 46

EXERCISE A

1 C   2 D   3 D   4 A   5 D
6 D   7 A   8 C   9 B   10 A
11 A   12 B   13 B

EXERCISE B

1 comes
2 in
3 their
4 although/though
5 had
6 that
7 rather
8 or
9 as
10 have
11 should/must
12 have/take
13 where
14 been
15 used
16 other
17 to
18 have/need
19 so
20 than

EXERCISE C

1 It was such a good play that she went back to see it again; It was so good a play that she went to see it again.
2 It's two years since Nella and I (last) saw each other.
3 In spite of having terrible pains in her legs, Ann climbed the mountain.
4 You don't need/have to wear a tie to eat at the restaurant.
5 If I had a partner I would go to the dance.
6 The floods prevented them from getting home.
7 She is not used to staying at home all day.
8 I don't go to the dentist as often as I should.
9 I wish I had kept in touch with her.
10 Michael apologised to Daphne for breaking the vase.

EXERCISE D

1	medicine	4	cured
2	fit	5	ill
3	operation		

EXERCISE E

1	loan	4	receipt
2	gifts/presents	5	borrow
3	lend/loan		

EXERCISE F

1	stars/starred	4	cinema
2	scene	5	screen
3	plot		

FOCUS ONE   SB 81–82

- ■ PICTURE DISCUSSION
- ■ PASSAGE FOR COMMENT
- ■ LISTENING
- □ *wedding* or *marriage*?
- ■ VOCABULARY
- ■ USE OF ENGLISH

PICTURE DISCUSSION

Ask students to look at the cover of the novel *Secretary Wife* and in pairs, write four questions which they think the examiner might ask them about it. In different pairs, ask them to ask and answer the questions.

EXERCISE A

Still in pairs, ask students to take it in turns to ask and answer Nos. 1–4 and compare answers with those of another pair.

EXERCISE B

Extension activity

Ask students to prepare a short talk (3–4 minutes) about their favourite book or short story, or about a set book for FCE if one is being studied. Ask students in turn to give their talks and encourage the others to ask questions about the book if they wish.

PASSAGE FOR COMMENT

Preteach difficult vocabulary, e.g. *crippled, walked out on*.

Ask students to read through the passage about the novel and in groups of 3–4 write four questions that they might be asked about a passage like this in the exam.

Ask groups to exchange questions and find suitable answers.

In pairs ask students to interview each other asking the questions in Nos. 1–5.

▶ Suggested answers
1 Laura is in love with Carl, Carl still loves Rosemary.
2 Carl's ex-fiancée
3 He was crippled in an accident and Rosemary walked out on him.
4 feeling sorry for himself, a reaction after losing Rosemary, needing someone to look after him
5 whether Carl really loves Laura or not

LISTENING 📼

Ask students to read through the order form before they listen to the tape. Now play the tape twice without pausing and tell students to fill in as many details as possible while listening to the tape.

Tapescript

A: I've been trying to get hold of the book for some time.
B: Well, I'm sorry we haven't got it . . . uh . . . but we can order it for you.
A: How long should it take to get it?
B: Only a few days.
A: All right.
B: Now, what was the title, again?
A: *Never Say Never.*
B: Uh huh . . . uh . . . do you happen to know the name of the author?
A: Yes. It's Claudia Jameson.
B: Jameson?
A: Yes. J–A–M–E–S–O–N.
B: Yes, yes . . . uh . . . and the publisher was Mills and Boon?
A: Yes. Mills and Boon.
B: Just let me look in the catalogue for the ISBN number.
A: The what?
B: The ISBN number . . . it's a kind of code number. It makes it much easier to order the book . . . uh . . .let's see . . . yes . . . here it is . . .
A: Could I have it, too?
B: Yes. O, dash, two six three, dash, seven four two eight two, dash, two.
A: Thank you . . . I just wanted to make a note of it myself . . . er . . . just in case . . . uh . . .
B: Now, could I have your name, please?
A: Yes. Anne . . . that's with an 'e' on the end . . . Parker.
B: Anne Parker. And your address?
A: 25 Lewes Road . . . that's L–E–W–E–S not –I–S.
B: 25 Lewes Road . . . and can I have your telephone number, as well?
A: Seven Three Seven Five O Six.
B: Thank you very much. As soon as it comes in, I'll ring you or drop you a card.
A: Thank you very much.

► Answer

CUSTOMER'S NAME	ANNE PARKER
ADDRESS	25 LEWES ROAD
	Tel. 737506
TITLE OF BOOK	NEVER SAY NEVER
AUTHOR	Claudia Jameson
PUBLISHER	MILLS AND BOON
ISBN NO.	0-263-74282-2

VOCABULARY

EXERCISE A

► Suggested answers

Men = handsome,
Women = beautiful, sweet, lovely, pretty
Both = attractive, good-looking, ugly, handsome

wedding or **marriage?**

EXERCISE B

Ask students to read through the dictionary definitions in their books and decide which definition is being explained.

► Answers

1 wedding   2 marriage

Dictionary skills

Tell students that most dictionaries contain an index of the abbreviations used in the text, e.g. (F) = French, *inf* = infinitive, *suff* = suffix. Point out to students that if they know the meaning of these abbreviations, it will make their task of understanding words they look up much easier.

Ask students if they know or can guess the meaning of the following abbreviations:
n, adj, vi, vt, adv, abbr, cf, Lat, sing, Gk

Dictionary definitions also give information on how to pronounce a word. As phonetic symbols may vary it is worth going through a phonetic list with students to show them how to apply the symbols to help pronunciation, e.g.

cry /kraɪ/ phonetically would be as follows in the list of symbols:
k as in *cat* /kæt/
r as in *red* /red/
aɪ as in *five* /faɪv/

Symbols such as /'/ also indicate where the stress comes on the word, e.g. *cardboard* /'kɑ:dbɔ:d/, in this case on the first syllable.

EXERCISE C

► Answers

1 married	9 beautifully
2 marriage	10 better-looking
3 engaged	11 best-looking
4 engagement	12 kindness
5 attracted	13 kindly
6 attractive	14 sweetly
7 attraction	15 sweeten
8 beautiful	

EXERCISE D

► Answers

1 in, with	5 for	8 on
2 at	6 by	9 after, with
3 to	7 in	
4 to		

USE OF ENGLISH

Guided discussion and writing

Allow 1–2 minutes for students to read the summary of another romantic novel and in groups of 2–3 allow a further 6–7 minutes for students to discuss answers to Nos. 1–6. Tell students to keep a note of their answers. Help and advise where necessary.

Now allow 10–12 minutes for students to write out their answers using their notes to remind them what their group's answers were. This task could be set for homework if time is running short in class.

FOCUS TWO   SB 83 – 84

■ READING
■ SPEAKING
■ LANGUAGE STUDY
  ☐ Gerund (*going*) or infinitive (*to go*)?
  ▷ GS 5.1, 5.2

READING

Ask students to skim read the passage twice, then in small groups decide what had happened before this extract and what will probably happen after it. Compare answers and decide which is the most likely explanation.

EXERCISE A

Keeping the same groups ask students to choose the best answers to Nos. 1–5.

▶ Answers

1 B 2 A 3 D 4 C 5 D

EXERCISE B

▶ Answers

1 C 3 C 5 A
2 A 4 C 6 B

LANGUAGE STUDY

Gerund (*going*) or infinitive (*to go*)?

EXERCISE A

Refer students to GS 5.1, 5.2 if necessary. Point out that certain verbs are followed by the gerund, others by the infinitive and some by either the gerund or the infinitive. Tell students there is a list of these verbs in the Grammar Summary.

In pairs, ask students to decide which is the correct form in Nos. 1–12.

▶ Answers

1 working
2 changing
3 working
4 thinking
5 to stay ('staying' is possible)
6 to apply
7 filling
8 thinking
9 applying
10 spending
11 to stay
12 working

EXERCISE B

▶ Answers

a) can be rephrased as *I'm tired so/I'm so tired that I'm not going to do this exercise.*
b) can be rephrased as *I'm bored with this exercise and don't want to do it any more.*

Ask students to rephrase Nos. 1–6 using either *too tired to . . .* or *tired of -ing*.

▶ Answers

1 I'm too tired to pay attention.
2 I'm tired of reading this book.
3 Jane was tired of typing letters.
4 Jane was too tired to cook a meal for herself.
5 Adam was tired of travelling all over the world.
6 He was too tired to read the report.

FOCUS THREE   SB 85 – 86

■ USE OF ENGLISH
■ LISTENING
■ LANGUAGE STUDY
☐ *who*, *which* or *that*? ▷ GS 11
☐ More kinds of comparisons ▷ GS 1.3
■ ROLE PLAY

USE OF ENGLISH

EXERCISE A

▶ Answers

1 expected	7 for	14 which
2 so/two	8 which/that	15 back
3 clear/mental	9 were	16 only
4 could	10 moment	17 would
5 seemed/	11 consider	18 whose
appeared	12 about	19 looking
6 way	13 more	20 dressed

EXERCISE B

▶ Answers

C is the correct description. A and B do not apply because Adam Francis is young and more attractive than Jane had expected.

LISTENING 📼

Tapescript
J = Jane   A = Adam

J : Hello, Mr Francis. I'm Jane Winters. We've often spoken over the phone.
A: Hello. Nice to meet you.
J: I have the documents you asked me to br . . .
A: They can wait. Where's the car?
J : Outside. I've hired a Rolls Royce for you, just as you asked me to. And I've also arranged for Mr Johnston to be your driver. I believe he knows you very well.
A: Here he is now. Hello, Johnston.
Jo: Hello, sir. Good to see you again. Let me take those bags for you.
A: Thanks.
Jo: I'll take them to the car. Just wait outside the terminal. I'll pick you up in about five minutes.
A: Thanks, Johnston.
J : Uh . . . did you have a good flight?
A: Hmm? Pardon?
J : Was it a pleasant flight?
A: Oh, not bad. Nothing out of the ordinary.
J : You . . . you must be tired.
A: No, not really. I'm looking forward to getting to the hotel and having a shower, though. Then we'll have dinner.
J : Dinner? But . . .
A: Yes, we'll have dinner first. Then we'll discuss business matters.
J : But . . . I thought you would have had dinner already.

A: Huh? Where?
J: On the plane.
A: On the plane! I never eat that kind of plastic food, Miss . . . Miss . . . uh . . .
J: Winters.
A: And what was your first name again?
J: Jane.
A: Good. I'll call you that, then . . . if you don't mind.
J: No. Of course not.

▶ Answers

1 C   2 C   3 B   4 A

LANGUAGE STUDY

who, *which* or *that*?

EXERCISE A

▶ Answers

1 who (*that* is not possible because this is a non-defining relative clause)
2 which (*that* is not possible after the preposition *in*)
3 who/that
4 who (*that* is not possible–see 1)
5 which/that
6 which (*that* is not possible–see 1)
7 who (*that* is not possible–see 1)
8 which/that

More kinds of comparisons

EXERCISE B

There is no difference in meaning between sentences a) and b) in the examples.

▶ Answers

1 The weather is colder than (everybody) expected.
2 Jane hadn't expected Adam to be so attractive.
3 I didn't think prices here would be so high.
4 I had planned to get here later.
5 The meeting ended later than we had planned.
6 I didn't think you would be so beautiful.
7 We didn't think the meal would be so expensive/cost so much.
8 This exercise is more difficult than I had expected.

ROLE PLAY

Divide the class into pairs. Ask one student to prepare role A, the other role B.

Put the following phrases on the board to help students:

Role A	**Role B**
rather tired	*good flight?*
quite exhausted	*family all well?*

I'd like to . . . if you don't mind.
Would you mind if I . . .?

Shall we discuss this over a drink?/dinner?
I expect you've already eaten on the plane.

Allow 2–3 minutes for students to prepare their roles, then invite several pairs of students to read or act out their conversations for the rest of the class.

FOCUS FOUR   SB 87

■ COMPOSITION
□ A talk

COMPOSITION

EXERCISE A

Read out the introduction of the talk and ask students to notice as they read the composition how the points mentioned in the introduction are repeated throughout the talk.

Now read the conclusion and ask students once again to notice how the points mentioned in the introduction and paragraphs 2, 3 and 4 are brought back in the conclusion.

Students should now be able to complete the reference table in their books.

▶ Answers

	Paragraph 1	Paragraph 5
Paragraph 2 (Travel arrangements)	*how you can get to Scotland*	*good value for money*
Paragraph 3 (Hotels)	*what sort of accommodation*	*a wide range of excellent hotels*
Paragraph 4 (Activities)	*what you can do when you are there*	*a varied and interesting programme of activities*

EXERCISE B

Divide the class into 4 groups. Each group should choose a famous person who is still alive, and, following the instructions given in their books plan what they would say in the 'Balloon Game'. Students should then write down the talk individually.

Ask several students to read out their talks when they have finished. The class can then vote to decide who should stay in the balloon.

Students can choose another of the talks to do for homework.

FOCUS FIVE   SB 88

■ REVISION AND EXTENSION
☐ Infinitive with or without *to*? ▷ GS 5.2
☐ Gerund (*going*) or infinitive (*to go*)? ▷ GS 5
☐ Changes in meaning ▷ GS 5.3
☐ Revision transformations

REVISION AND EXTENSION

Infinitive with or without *to*?

EXERCISE A

▶ Answers

to get, to stay, do, do, to take, to look after, to stay, worry, to do, to cook.

Gerund (*going*) or infinitive (*to go*)?

EXERCISE B

▶ Answers

say, get, going, living, make, being, practise, coming, see.

EXERCISE C

Ask students to read the dialogue to each other taking either part A or B and put the verbs into the correct forms as they are reading. Check answers, then ask students to write in the correct forms on their own.

▶ Answers

A: to tell
B: to do
A: to say, being
B: feeling, to be, to have
A: to give, seeing, to listen
B: to consider putting off getting, trying
A: to marry, to learn to live, talking, to meet, to be

Changes in meaning

EXERCISE D

▶ Answers

1 to get	4 to do	7 going
2 to send	5 opening	8 to say
3 eating	6 talking	

Revision transformations

EXERCISE E

▶ Answers

1 I hadn't expected the train to arrive so late.
2 I'd rather not go to Scotland for the summer.
3 There was something about her which/that reminded him of his mother.
4 The classroom in which our lessons were held was very cold.
5 Would you mind opening the window?
6 Riding a motorbike is more dangerous than driving a car.
7 It was such a difficult exam that I couldn't finish it.
8 He is better at football than I am.
9 Despite their dislike of him/Despite the fact that they disliked him, they agreed to help.
10 The meal was more expensive than I had realized.

WORKBOOK KEY WB 47 – 50

UNIT 11

EXERCISE A

1 B	2 B	3 D	4 B	5 B

EXERCISE B

1 were introduced	8 got engaged
2 found her attractive	9 got married
3 chatting her	10 drifted
4 have a date	11 split
5 going out with	12 living
6 fall in love	13 got divorced
7 proposed	

EXERCISE C

1 being	9 to make
2 travelling	10 to go
3 thinking	11 to visit
4 to be	12 to stay
5 coming	13 to get
6 telling	14 to write
7 to risk	15 seeing
8 making	

EXERCISE D

1 When I was in hospital we were allowed to have visitors every day.
2 The police officers made him sign the confession.
3 She advised me to complain to the manufacturers.
4 The fisherman warned us not to swim in the sea.

5 I know my brother wants me to go on holiday with him.
6 I was taught to read Latin at school.
7 John's parents let him smoke at home.
8 When I was in the army, I was forced to go on runs every day.
9 I shall never forget the night when we went to the opera and heard Pavarotti sing in *Tosca*.
10 My friend encouraged me to telephone John as/ because I wanted to see him again.

EXERCISE E

1 b	2 a	3 a	4 b
5 a	6 b	7 b	8 a

EXERCISE F

1 cleaning		6 meeting	
2 to buy		7 raining	
3 to say		8 to escape	
4 to get		9 feeling	
5 to understand		10 to go	

EXERCISE G

1 wedding	5 reception
2 bride	6 best man
3 bridesmaids	7 honeymoon
4 groom	

EXERCISE H

good	**good or bad**	**bad**
tolerant	extrovert	aggressive
amusing	intellectual	stingy
attractive	predictable	proud
entertaining	conventional	
faithful	wealthy	
patient	shy	
reliable	impulsive	
sensitive		
easy-going		
sensible		
responsible		

12
A STUDY IN CONTRASTS

FOCUS ONE   SB 89 – 90

- ■ READING
- ■ SPEAKING
- ■ VOCABULARY
- ■ LANGUAGE STUDY

READING

Divide the class into two groups. Tell one group to read the passage about Aaron and Candy Spelling, the other to read the passage about Martin and Rebecca Granger, and write about 10 questions to ask the other group. Students can work in groups of 3–4 to write the questions.

Ask each group to skim read the passage they have not prepared, then answer the questions put to them by the other group.

Now ask students individually to choose the best answer to Nos. 1–7.

▶ Answers

   1 C   2 A   3 D   4 D   5 C   6 B
   7 D

SPEAKING

In pairs, ask students to prepare their answers to Nos. 1–3 in as much detail as possible, perhaps even drawing rough sketches. Write these expressions on the board to help students:

Expressing preferences

I'd rather live . . .
I would prefer to live . . .
I would like . . . better than . . .

Compare sketches and ideas.

VOCABULARY

▶ Answers

1 shabby	3 partial	5 repair
2 cottage	4 relaxing	6 shower

LANGUAGE STUDY

EXERCISE A

▶ Answers

The b) sentences suggest most clearly that there is something unusual and surprising in the statement.

EXERCISE B

Ask students to rewrite Nos. 1–8 beginning with *Not only . . .* and ending with *as well.* Point out the inversion of subject and verb after *Not only.*

▶ Answers

  1 Not only can I sing, but I can dance as well.
  2 Not only is he a thief, but he is a killer as well.
  3 Not only does* he lie, but he steals as well.
  4 Not only will you pass your exam, but you will get a very good mark as well.
  5 Not only is the room I live in cold, but it smells as well.
  6 Not only does* the roof leak, but there is a ghost in the house as well.
  7 Not only is this computer expensive, but it's useless as well.
  8 Not only did* we have to clean the house, but we had to repair the roof as well.

Point out that we need *does/did* in examples like 6 and 8. Refer students to GS 6.7 if necessary.

FOCUS TWO   SB 91 – 92

- ■ PROBLEM SOLVING
- ■ VOCABULARY
- □ *lie* or *lay*?
- □ *bring, fetch, take, carry* or *wear*?
- ■ LANGUAGE STUDY
- □ *have something done* ▷ GS 8.3, 15.1.1

PROBLEM SOLVING

Divide students into groups of 4–5. Appoint one student in each group to look at one of the pictures in the book. The others should keep their books closed and have to guess what is in the picture by asking questions. The questions can only be those which require a 'yes' or 'no' answer. Allow 20 questions to see if students can build up an accurate description of what is in the picture without actually seeing the photograph themselves.

Supply any vocabulary students may need to describe the pictures in their books, e.g.
croft, camper van, harbour, canal,
then divide students into pairs and tell them to prepare a brief description of each picture. Invite different pairs of students to describe one of the pictures for the rest of the class.

Divide students into groups of 3–4 and explain that the people in their books are looking for somewhere to stay for a few weeks in the summer. Students must decide which type of accommodation would be most suitable for the people mentioned.

Allow 3–4 minutes then join 2 groups together and tell them to compare answers. Did they agree?

VOCABULARY

lie or *lay*?

EXERCISE A

▶ Answers

1 lay	4 lay	7 lain
2 lay	5 laid	8 lied
3 lying	6 laid	

bring, take, fetch, carry or *wear*?

EXERCISE B

▶ Answers

1 take	3 bring	5 carry
2 wear	4 fetch	6 bring/take

LANGUAGE STUDY

have something done

EXERCISE A

▶ Answers

1 a) She delivered it herself.
   b) She paid or asked someone to deliver it for her.
2 a) I shall repair it myself.
   b) I will pay somebody to repair it for me.
3 a) You should take the scissors and cut your hair.
   b) You should go to the hairdresser's for a hair-cut.

EXERCISE B

▶ Answers

1 They are going to have it torn down.
2 He is going to have several new suits made.
3 She is going to have her hair cut.
4 He is going to have the film developed.

EXERCISE C

▶ Answers

1 Candy had the house torn down.
2 The businessman had several new suits made.
3 The actress had her hair cut.
4 He had his film developed.

EXERCISE D

▶ Answers

1 Candy has had a new house built.
2 You should have your house redecorated.
3 I must have this film developed.
4 You can have your shoes repaired in an hour.

FOCUS THREE   SB 93–94

- ■ LISTENING
- ■ VOCABULARY
- ☐ Phrasal verbs (*keep*)
- ■ LANGUAGE STUDY
- ☐ Who is *they*?
- ☐ The passive ▷ GS 8

LISTENING

EXERCISE A

Before reading through the multiple choice questions ask students to look at the picture in their books and write down four things they think they are going to hear on the tape. Make a list of the different ideas on the board.

Now ask students to read through Nos. 1–5 and decide if their original ideas will appear on the tape or not. (Allow about 5 minutes for this.)

Play the tape through twice with a short interval between each play and ask students to choose the correct answer as they listen.

Tapescript

N = Narrator   Di = Diana   Do = Donald

N : When Linda de Vere-Hardy died three days ago, she had been almost completely forgotten. But she was one of the most unusual women of her generation. Lady Diana Cusard went to school with her . . . .

Di: I remember how she shocked us all when she told us she had a boyfriend in the town who was a car mechanic . . . they didn't do such things in those days . . . just after the First World War. Daughters of aristocrats didn't go out with car mechanics, I mean. She got him to teach her all about cars, and things like that. She had no time for all the usual things girls in those days were supposed to be interested in . . . French and History and cooking, and that sort of thing.

N : In the early '20s, Linda de Vere learned how to fly. She was one of the first women to qualify as a pilot in Europe . . . or anywhere else in the world.

Do: She wanted to do the same thing Lindberg had done . . . fly solo across the Atlantic, but she couldn't find the right sort of plane for that, so she decided instead to fly solo all the way from London to Delhi all alone. But on the way, when she was over the desert, she ran out of fuel and almost crashed. Somehow she persuaded a camel-driver to travel across the desert and back to get her some petrol, and she flew on, and eventually got there . . . to Delhi. A lot of people would have given up and returned to England, but she didn't. She was determined to finish it . . . and she did.

N : That was Donald Winstone, who also knew her well.

Do: I was a young architect at the time. We had a kind of . . . uh . . . I suppose you would call it a love-affair . . . but we never got married. It wasn't that she wasn't fond of me or that I wasn't fond of her . . . but the fact, really, that she didn't want to start a family. And I did.

N : In 1934, Linda de Vere spent six months in Hollywood, Lady Diana Cusard again . . .

Di: She met Clark Gable there, the film star. They say that he was deeply in love with her. I didn't think the stories were true at first. But now I'm not so sure. She always refused to talk about it.

▶ Answers

1 C   2 B   3 B   4 D   5 A

EXERCISE B

Ask students to read through Nos. 1–8 before listening to the second part of the tape. Play the second part of the tape twice with a short pause in between and ask students to take notes as they listen and finish the sentences from their notes.

Tapescript

N = Narrator   Di = Diana   Do = Donald   I = Ian

N : After the Second World War, in which she flew bombers across the Atlantic from the United States to Britain, Linda de Vere married Angus Hardy, an international banker. Lady Diana knew Hardy, as well.

Di: He was ten years younger than she was . . . that caused quite a sensation, too.

N : Was it a happy marriage?

Di: Oh, very much so. They shared a love of fiction and he encouraged her to write those detective novels which were so popular in the '50s and early '60s. Her books aren't read very much any more, but at the time, you know, they gave her a prize for one of them. I . . . uh . . . I don't think she ever got over the shock of his death in that terrible car crash in 19 . . . when was it . . . 1962.

N : For about the last twenty-five years of her life, she lived alone on a small island off the coast of Scotland.

I : I visited her a few times when I was younger, but . . . there was nothing for me to do there, all alone with her in that house.

N : This is her only child, Ian de Vere-Hardy speaking.

I : I felt terribly lonely there and stopped going. That's one reason I never got to know my mother. We just didn't keep up any kind of relationship. I . . . I rather wish we had, now. She seemed to live almost entirely in the past. We had nothing to say to each other.

N : Let Donald Winstone have the last few words about her.

Do: She was a most unusual woman. They used to say she was a bit crazy, back in the '20s, simply because she decided to live her own life in the way she wanted to. I'm proud to have known her. She was brave and had a great spirit of adventure. The world would be a much poorer, much less interesting place without people like her.

▶ Suggested answers

1 he was 10 years younger than she was.
2 fiction.
3 killed in a terrible car crash.
4 lived alone on a small island off the coast of Scotland.
5 he had kept up some kind of relationship with her.
6 he felt terribly lonely there.
7 she was brave and had a great spirit of adventure.
8 would be a much poorer, less interesting place without people like her.

VOCABULARY

EXERCISE A

▶ Answers

1 delivery
2 popularity
3 safety
4 security
5 encouragement
6 argument
7 bravery
8 beauty

Phrasal verbs

EXERCISE B

▶ Answers

a) keep up . . . with
b) kept on
c) keeping back (from)
d) keep up with
e) Keep off

Tell students to read the explanations in Nos. 1–5 and match them to the phrasal verbs in a)–e).

▶ Answers

1 e)   2 b)   3 c)   4 a)   5 d)

EXERCISE C

▶ Answers

1 keep up with
2 keep off
3 Keep up
4 keeping back from
5 keep on

LANGUAGE STUDY

Who is *they*?

EXERCISE A

▶ Answers

1 b) and c)   2 a)

The passive

EXERCISE B

▶ Answers

1 I will be given a prize if I can learn this.
2 Perhaps one day a cure for the common cold will be found.
3 Perhaps one day an easier way to learn English will be found.
4 Once I was told that I could learn English in my sleep.
5 English is said to be easy to learn.
6 It is spoken all over the world.
7 English books are sold in that shop.
8 My car is being repaired.

FOCUS FOUR   SB 95

■ COMPOSITION (argument)
☐ For and against

COMPOSITION

EXERCISE A

▶ Suggested answers

FOR
– animals do not suffer unnecessarily
– if the trade were made illegal, hunters without licences would cause greater suffering to animals
– banning the trade would mean more unemployment
– people would lose their freedom of choice

AGAINST
– animals do suffer unnecessarily
– killing animals for their coats is a luxury
– an animal has more right to live than a human being has to wear its coat
– the manufacture of artificial fur could create jobs and satisfy the demands of fashion

Extension activity

In addition to writing the composition suggested in Exercise D, students could also be asked to design a poster which tries to persuade people either for or against one of the topics mentioned in the Focus. These posters could be displayed on the classroom walls.

FOCUS FIVE   SB 96

■ REVISION AND EXTENSION
■ LISTENING TEST 6

REVISION AND EXTENSION

▶ Answers

1 D	6 A	11 D	16 C
2 A	7 B	12 A	17 B
3 B	8 B	13 B	18 C
4 C	9 B	14 C	19 D
5 A	10 A	15 A	20 C

LISTENING TEST 6

Tapescript

A: We hear a lot these days about whales and the need to protect them – but when did this interest start, because people have been hunting whales for centuries, haven't they?
B: Yes, for at least a thousand years, and there were no real problems until this century, really. What happened was that fishing technology became much more efficient and the ships were much faster, so more and more whales were caught. In the 1960s the main whaling countries were killing more than sixty thousand whales a year, and I think everyone began to realize that something had to be done.
A: When did the killing begin to slow down?
B: It was quite a slow process, and it was environmental groups like Greenpeace that really made things change. I mean, they set out to make people aware of the fact that whales were fast becoming extinct. But even now we don't know if all this interest has come too late. If you take the great blue whale for example, which at thirty to forty metres long is the biggest animal there has ever been – now there are perhaps about two thousand or so left. In fact they have been protected for quite a long time, but there is still no sign that the population is growing.
A: Am I right in thinking that killing whales is against the law?
B: Yes. In fact there was an international agreement to stop killing whales, but there are three countries which still catch whales, and they are Iceland, Norway and Japan. In fact, under the international agreement, they are allowed to catch whales for scientific research, and they use this as an excuse to carry on as they did before.
A: What do they use the whales for?
B: In Japan it's quite a popular kind of food, and it's very traditional . . .

► Answers

1 technology	4 blue whales	7 Norway
2 faster	5 protected	8 Japan
3 extinct	6 Iceland	9 scientific research

WORKBOOK KEY WB 51 — 54

UNIT 12

EXERCISE A

1 B   2 B   3 C   4 D   5 D

EXERCISE B

retired: having stopped work at the age of 60 or 65
enormous: very big
weeds: unwanted plants
commute: to travel to town to go to work every day
wander: to walk around with no particular destination
awful: terrible
hire: to employ
gossip: news and talk about what people are doing
charity: organisation that collects money for the poor
incredibly: unbelievably

EXERCISE C

1 isolated	4 lonely
2 only	5 single
3 alone	

EXERCISE D

lie	lying	lied	lied
lie	lying	lay	lain
lay	laying	laid	laid

1 lay	6 lay
2 lays/laid	7 lie
3 have laid	8 lied
4 lie	9 lying
5 lying	10 lain

EXERCISE E

1 . . . not only were the beaches wonderful, but the weather was lovely as well.
2 . . . not only was the train delayed, but there were long traffic jams as well.
3 . . . not only do they kill many young riders, but they are dangerous for other road users as well.
4 . . . not only had he burned a house down, but he had killed three people as well.
5 . . . not only can I speak the language, but I have lived in Moscow as well.
6 . . . not only has she had several years' experience, but she is good with children as well.
7 . . . not only can she speak excellent French, but she can speak perfect German as well.
8 . . . not only does it have plenty of rooms, but it has a nice garden as well.
9 . . . not only did he break his leg, but he twisted his wrist as well.
10 . . . not only was the food very bad, but the waiters were rude as well.

EXERCISE F

1 take	6 wears
2 fetch	7 taking/taken
3 fetch	8 wear
4 bring	9 bring
5 carry	10 bring

EXERCISE G

1 I have all my suits made at Savile Row.
2 I normally have my photos developed by 'Trueprint'.
3 She's going to get the whole of the house repainted.
4 Have you ever had your eyes tested?
5 Where did you have your car repaired?
6 You ought to get these documents checked by a lawyer.
7 He had his letters forwarded.
8 My father had this desk made a few years ago.

EXERCISE H

1 Where did you have it done?
2 When did you have it taken?
3 Do you know where I can have them dry-cleaned?
4 When was the last time you had it serviced?
5 . . . they have had central heating installed.
6 . . . he had had his back teeth taken out.
7 . . . I would have them fixed properly.
8 . . . I have my shirts ironed by a lady in the village.

EXERCISE I

1 KEEP ON	7 TAKE AFTER
2 GET ON	8 GET
3 HANG AROUND	9 TAKE ON
4 KEPT BACK	10 GET OVER
5 ROUND	11 KEEP UP
6 RUN	12 COUNT ON

EXERCISE J

1 Coal is dug out by miners.
2 Eyes are tested by opticians.
3 Food is cooked by chefs.
4 Books are written by authors.
5 Letters are typed by secretaries.
6 Horses are ridden by jockeys.
7 Portraits are painted by artists.
8 Money is lent by bankers.
9 Planes are flown by pilots.
10 Criminals are caught by detectives.

£ 13
A SHOPPER'S NIGHTMARE

FOCUS ONE SB 97–98

- ■ READING
- ■ ROLE PLAY
- ■ LANGUAGE STUDY
- ☐ Relative clauses without *who* ▷ GS 11.1.2

READING

Ask students to look at the picture in their books and in pairs try to explain what is happening and what the passage might be about.

Write these expressions on the board to help students:

Speculating

It looks as though . . .
They seem to be . . .
She/they might have . . .

EXERCISE A

Students read through Nos. 1–4 **before** they read the passage. Allow 3–4 minutes for students to read the passage and answer the multiple choice items.

▶ Answers

1 A   2 D   3 C   4 B

EXERCISE B

▶ Suggested answers

1 she wanted to exchange a jumper she had been given for her birthday for a larger size.
2 they had no jumpers in her size.
3 she was grabbed by a man and a woman.
4 did not believe it was really her receipt for the jumper.
5 find the shop assistant she had spoken to earlier.
6 apologized for what had happened.

EXERCISE C

▶ Answers

1 C	3 C	5 A	7 A	9 C
2 B	4 A	6 C	8 A	10 B

Now read out the key words with students' books closed and see if students can remember the words they were identifying, e.g. What's another word for *go quickly*? Answer = *dash* etc.

ROLE PLAY

Divide the class into pairs or groups and ask them to discuss Nos. 1 and 2 and prepare a conversation to read or act out in class.

The following expressions might help students:

Store manager

I'm dreadfully sorry about . . .
I can't apologize enough for . . .
How can we express our regret for . . . ?
On behalf of the store I would like to apologize for . . .

Customer

I've never been treated like that before . . .
It's disgraceful . . .
Picking on innocent people . . .
Being made to feel like a common criminal . . .
You'd better make sure it doesn't happen again.

LANGUAGE STUDY

Relative clauses without *who*

EXERCISE A

Ask students to study the pairs of sentences in a)–d) and decide why *who* is necessary in the transformed sentences in b) and d).

▶ Answer

who is necessary in b) and d) because it is the subject of the following verb, i.e. *spoke* and *arrested*

EXERCISE B

▶ Answers

1 The shop assistant I spoke to was very polite.
2 The shop assistant who spoke to me was very polite.
3 The man who grabbed my arm was a store detective.
4 The woman who grabbed the other arm was a store detective, too.
5 The man they took me to see was their boss.
6 The shop assistant they went to find was the girl I had spoken to before.
7 The man who came to see me later was the manager.
8 The man I saw later was the manager.

FOCUS TWO   SB 99—100

- ■ PICTURE DISCUSSION
- ■ LISTENING
- ■ SPEAKING
- ■ WRITING
- ■ LANGUAGE STUDY
- □ *what* clauses
- ■ VOCABULARY

PICTURE DISCUSSION

Ask students in small groups to look at the pictures and list as many objects as possible which are visible in both pictures.

In pairs ask students to take it in turns to ask each other to describe exactly where the object is in the picture, e.g. *in the middle, in the top right hand corner, at the side* etc.

Now ask students, still in pairs, to discuss Nos. 1—4 and compare their answers with another pair.

Topics for further discussion

1 Describe what the shops are like where you come from.
   Compare opening hours with those of shops in England.
2 What do you think shops will be like in the future? Will the little corner shop survive?

Extension activity

Ask students to conduct a survey of the shops etc. in the main street of the place where they are studying. Find out what kind of shops there are and what other services are offered, e.g. banks, post office etc. Ask students to produce a map showing what kind of shops there are and where they are located.

LISTENING   📼

Tapescript

I = Interviewer D = Detective

I : Is there such a thing as a typical shop-lifter?

D: Uh, not really . . . but there are certain categories most shop-lifters fall into. Three categories, I would say.

I : Tell me more about these three categories.

D: Well . . . uh . . . people in the first category are what I call 'the sudden impulse type'. They see something and just can't . . . uh . . . resist the temptation to steal it. The strange thing about this first category is that the people in it are often well off and could easily afford to buy the thing. Sometimes they don't even need it . . . and often they're emotionally disturbed in some way . . . middle-aged women, for example, whose husbands have left them, or perhaps older men whose wives have recently died.

I : What about the second category?

D: Well, those are people who are really . . . uh . . . petty thieves. They work alone, and know exactly what they want before they go into the store. These days a lot of them, but by no means all, are teenagers who steal things they can't afford. Leather jackets. Watches. Expensive cosmetics. Things like that.

I : And the third category? What kind of people do you find in the third category?

D: Ah, yes, they're what I call 'the professionals'.

I : Why?

D: Well, first of all, because they're highly organized. And secondly because they do it for a living. They usually operate in gangs of three or sometimes four, and they're extremely difficult to catch.

I : In gangs of three?

D: Yes. The first person is called 'the spotter'. The spotter is really the brains behind the operation. He . . . or she . . . decides what should be stolen and when. The spotter also keeps an eye open for store detectives, but never does the actual stealing. That's the hand's job.

I : 'The hand'?

D: Yes, that's what he's called. The spotter communicates with the hand through special signals. The hand does the stealing but never takes the goods out of the store. That's the job of the third person, who we call 'the catcher'. Each person in the team or gang has a special job, you see. They work together but they do entirely different things.

I : Can they make a lot of money that way?

D: Oh, yes. Yes, they're very well off, believe me . . . much better off than a store detective . . . or even a journalist!

▶ Answers
   1 D   2 A   3 A   4 B   5 C

LANGUAGE STUDY

what clauses

▶ Answers
   1 I didn't hear what you said.
   2 You never agree with what I say.
   3 I never buy what I can't afford.
   4 Did you understand what I said to you?
   5 What the boss said made everybody laugh.
   6 What you did at the party was terrible.
   7 Did what I said to you at the party offend you?
   8 Was what I asked you to do so difficult?

VOCABULARY

EXERCISE A

▶ Answers
   1 *decision* – the other three words mean 'to want something'.
   2 *surrender* – the other three words mean 'not to give in'.
   3 *disgust* – the other three words mean 'to feel a liking for something'.
   4 *well-off* – the other three words mean 'to be poor'.
   5 *significant* – the other three words mean 'not important'.

EXERCISE B

▶ Answers

1	resistance	5	hunger
2	refusal	6	significance
3	disgusting	7	decisive
4	attractive	8	innocence

FOCUS THREE   SB 101–102

■ USE OF ENGLISH
■ ROLE PLAY
■ READING
■ VOCABULARY
□ Phrasal verbs (*try, look, take, miss*)

USE OF ENGLISH

▶ Suggested answers

1 Can I help you?
2 Why weren't you satisfied with them?/What's wrong with them?
3 How often/How many times did you wash them?
4 And how did you dry them?
5 Have you got a receipt?
6 I'm afraid I can't do anything at all/exchange them/give you your money back unless you've got a receipt.
7 It's the policy of the store, I'm afraid.
8 Well, he's in a meeting/busy/out at the moment.

ROLE PLAY

Divide students into pairs or small groups and ask them to look at the picture in their books and study the two roles A and B. Allow about 5 minutes for students to prepare the conversation between A and B to read or act out for the rest of the class. The following expressions may be useful:

A

Excuse me . . .
I wonder if you could help me?
I'd like to . . .
Would it be possible to . . . ?
I'm afraid I haven't got . . .

B

Certainly . . . Let's see . . .
Normally we would be only too happy to exchange . . .
I'm afraid it isn't our policy to . . .
It looks as if it has been worn . . .
You see we couldn't possibly exchange . . .

READING

▶ Answers

Group 1	a)	d)	f)	g)	i)
Group 2	c)	e)	h)		
Group 3	b)				

VOCABULARY

EXERCISE A

▶ Answers

1 b)   2 d)   3 a)   4 c)

See if students can find less formal ways of saying Nos. 5–8.

▶ Suggested answers

5 are asked not to smoke
6 for soiled or damaged goods
7 ask one of our sales staff for help
8 with adults

Phrasal verbs

EXERCISE B

▶ Answers

1	look it over	4	try . . . on
2	look around	5	take . . . back
3	miss out on		

FOCUS FOUR   SB 103

■ COMPOSITION (describing places)
☐ Using adjectives

COMPOSITION

EXERCISE A

▶ Suggested answers

- too short
- no introduction
- sentences very short
- no paragraphs
- hardly any descriptive adjectives
- no explanation of why the place was important or how the writer felt about it

EXERCISE B

▶ Suggested answers

1 Identifying the place
  Describing the setting of the house
  Describing the inside of the house and its atmosphere
2 – hardly any (only 2) in the first composition
  – about 10 in the second composition
3 The second, e.g. favourite place, looked forward to, freedom, those happy days, a homely atmosphere etc.

Using adjectives

EXERCISE C

▶ Answers

1 I have got an old tennis racket which has/with a broken string.
2 She is a pretty girl who has got/with blue eyes.
3 He is a lazy student who never does any work.
4 It is an old school which has/with a good reputation.
5 I've got an electric typewriter which was quite expensive.

EXERCISE D

Ask students to read through the notes in their books and write a description of a place they know well. Give students a choice of three places, one of which they may choose to write a similar composition about for homework, e.g.
– A place which made you sad.
– A place you visited recently.
– Your dream home.

FOCUS FIVE   SB 104

■ REVISION AND EXTENSION
☐ The passive ▷ GS 8.2
☐ Forming opposites

REVISION AND EXTENSION

The passive

EXERCISE A

▶ Answer

b) would be better in a newspaper because what happened to the people is the important news and the people come first in passage b).

In pairs, ask students to discuss the answers to Nos. 1–3.

▶ Suggested answers

1 b) by putting the people first and the explosion second
2 *It is believed* because we do not have to mention people at all.
3 No, because *arrested* means taken into custody by the police.

EXERCISE B

▶ Answers

1 Yesterday afternoon two people were killed and three others (were) injured in a fire which occurred at a café in George Street.
2 It is believed that the fire was started deliberately.
3 A young man was seen running from the café shortly before the fire began.
4 A number of other fires have been reported in the area in the last month.
5 It is believed that the same young man may be responsible for all these fires.

Forming opposites

EXERCISE C

The prefixes mentioned change the meanings of the words by making them into the opposite, or negative. These prefixes are used with verbs and adjectives.

Now ask students to complete the tables in their books with the correct opposite of the words given.

▶ Answers

VERB	OPPOSITE
like	*dislike*
spell	*misspell*
agree	*disagree*

believe	*disbelieve*
understand	*misunderstand*
cover	*uncover*
dress	*undress*
connect	*disconnect*
please	*displease*

ADJECTIVE	OPPOSITE
able	*unable*
possible	*impossible*
capable	*incapable*
necessary	*unnecessary*
patient	*impatient*
proper	*improper*
correct	*incorrect*
conscious	*unconscious*
complete	*incomplete*
polite	*impolite*

Read out all the words with the students' books closed and see if students can remember how to form the opposites of the words from memory.

Point out that *il-* and *ir-* are also used to form the opposites of some adjectives. Refer students to the two dictionary definitions in their books for *illegal* and *irregular*.

Dictionary skills

Ask students to look at the two definitions for *illegal* and *irregular*, and to tell you about the order in which information about words is given, e.g.
1 phonetic symbols and stress
2 part of speech, e.g. noun, verb
3 meaning + example
4 other meanings + examples

Notice that the order may change according to the dictionary used.

Ask students to write a dictionary definition for a word, to include these four types of information, and then to check it against a definition in an actual dictionary.

WORKBOOK KEY WB 55 – 58

UNIT 13

EXERCISE B

1 No   2 No   3 Yes   4 Yes   5 No
6 Yes

EXERCISE C

1 stroll	6 merciful
2 tender	7 sturdy
3 gentle	8 carefree
4 cunning	9 suspicious
5 eager	10 surprised

EXERCISE D

1 at	6 in
2 on	7 on
3 upon/with/on	8 for
4 from	9 with
5 in	10 up

EXERCISE F

1 The woman who spent fifteen minutes measuring the kitchen talked to the Priors.
2 The plans the woman drew up were for a new kitchen.
3 The units the Priors were interested in would (have) cost £9,000.
4 The dishwasher on special offer that month was not needed by the Priors.
5 The piece of paper the Priors signed entitled them to a discount of £2,000.
6 The deposit the woman asked for was £100.
7 The man the woman worked for would have been furious if she had not obtained the order.
8 People who are not so strong-minded would probably place an order.

EXERCISE G

1 What you said was untrue.
2 Did what she said upset you?
3 I haven't thought about what I ought to do./I ought to do something but I haven't thought about what (it should be).
4 What they suggested was very practical.
5 Was what they did to you terrible?
6 I don't understand what made him do it.

EXERCISE I

unpack	unexpected
disagree	misspell
improper	impossible
unlikely	independent
nonsense	unusual
illegal	uncooked
irregular	improbable
unlucky	incorrect

14 MYSTERIES OF MEMORY

FOCUS ONE SB 105 – 106

- ■ PICTURE DISCUSSION
- ■ READING
- ■ LANGUAGE STUDY
- ■ VOCABULARY
- □ Words connected with memory (*memory, recall, remember, remind*)

PICTURE DISCUSSION

Tell students, in groups of 2–3, to discuss Nos. 1–3 then compare answers with another group. Allow 5–6 minutes.

Now tell each student individually to answer No. 4. Choose students at random to tell the class about one of their earliest memories.

READING

Introduce the passage by asking students if they have a good memory or not. Discuss what kinds of things they find easy or difficult to remember.

Ask them to skim read the passage in pairs and underline what they consider to be the main points. Allow about 5 minutes for this.

Allow 4–5 minutes for pairs to choose the best answer to Nos. 1–4.

► Answers
  1 D   2 C   3 B   4 A

LANGUAGE STUDY

EXERCISE A

► Answers
  1 b)   2 d)   3 a)   4 c)

EXERCISE B

► Answers
  1 I can't remember meeting you before.
  2 Can you remember posting that letter?
  3 Can you remind me to post this letter?

  4 Please remember to pay these bills.
  5 I don't remember you lending me the money.
  6 I'll remind you to do these things tomorrow.
  7 I must remember to phone my mother tomorrow.
  8 Don't you remember me lending you £50 last week?

VOCABULARY

Words connected with memory

Ask students to write down as many words connected with memory that they can think of. Put them all on the board and talk about the meanings of the words and how they can be used in sentences.

EXERCISE A

Ask students to study the definitions of the words in their books. With their books closed, now see if they can explain the words in their own way to the rest of the class.

Ask them to complete Nos. 1–6 with a suitable word and decide which sentence could contain either *remember* or *recall*.

► Answers
  1 memory   4 remember
  2 recall/remember   5 remind
  3 remind   6 memories

FOCUS TWO SB 107 – 108

- ■ LISTENING
- ■ USE OF ENGLISH 1
- ■ VOCABULARY
- ■ LANGUAGE STUDY
- □ *should have, must have,* or *might have*? ▷ GS 7.4, 7.5, 7.8
- □ *who, whose, which* or *that*? ▷ GS 11
- ■ USE OF ENGLISH 2

LISTENING

EXERCISE A

Tapescript
B = Barbara

B: I don't remember anything about the accident at all. Apparently . . . so I'm told . . . there must have been some ice on the road because the car suddenly spun out of control and I hit a tree. I might have been killed . . . I was lucky. But because I wasn't wearing a safety-belt . . . I should have been but I wasn't . . . I was thrown through the windscreen. My head and face were all cut up . . . my nose was broken . . . luckily the cuts have healed now. I've still got the scars, of course. Fortunately my daughter wasn't in the car at the time. I'd just taken her to school, and I must have been in a hurry to get to work . . . but I don't think I was driving very fast.

What really worries me isn't the scars . . . I can live with those . . . no . . . it's the fact that since the accident I can't . . . can't concentrate as well as I used to. And my memory plays strange . . . tricks . . . on me. As I say, I can't remember the accident itself, or taking my daughter to school . . . but apparently that's quite normal. But even after I got out of hospital I was . . . how shall I say it . . . forgetful. Yes. Forgetful. Far more than before. And I still am. I sit down to do things and then can't remember what it was I wanted to do. A few days ago, for instance, I had just started to write a letter to a friend . . . I wanted to thank her for sending me a book for my birthday . . . and then the phone rang. When I came back and saw the piece of paper lying there I couldn't remember why I was writing the letter or even who I was writing to . . . it was several hours before I suddenly remembered again.

I've seen a specialist several times since the accident and she tells me not to worry . . . that that will only make it worse . . . and that in time my brain will somehow find a way of functioning as well or nearly as well as it did before. There's no permanent damage, you see . . . as I say, I was lucky . . . but I still worry about it. It's almost as if when the accident happened I lost an important part of my life which I'll never get back.

▶ Answers

1 B   2 D   3 C   4 B

USE OF ENGLISH

▶ Suggested answers

1 It was very nice of you to send me that lovely book for my birthday.
2 I have not had time to read much (of it) but it seems very interesting.
3 Since the accident I have had some problems with my memory but now I'm beginning to feel almost normal again.
4 I still have some scars on my face but they are not as bad as before.
5 My daughter Sarah is doing very well at school and hopes/is hoping to go to university next year.
6 How are you and your family?
7 I hope to hear from you soon.
8 Thanks again for the wonderful book and give my love to everybody.

VOCABULARY

EXERCISE A

▶ Answers

1 on   5 under   8 in
2 in   6 to   9 with
3 by   7 of   10 In . . . to
4 to

EXERCISE B

▶ Answers

1 apparently   6 Luckily
2 memory   7 recovery
3 injury   8 satisfactory
4 concentration   9 specialist
5 forgetful   10 thankful

EXERCISE C

Prepare a list of objects and people which could be *injured*, *damaged*, *harmed*, *hurt*, *spoilt* or *ruined*. Ask students to group the objects and people under the verbs they could be used with.

Suggested list to write on the board of people and objects for grouping:
child, *old man*, *woman*, *pedestrian*, *motorist*, *property*, *fence*, *telephone box*, *politics*, *war*, *indoctrination*, *leg*, *arm*, *foot*, *feelings*, *rain*, *fun*, *outing*, *carpet*, *building*, *chances*.

Discuss the general meaning of the words and the shades of differences between them, e.g.

injury = physical harm, used for people or reputations
damage = harm resulting in a loss of value, e.g. to property
harm = often a moral wrong or evil. Note: *to come to no harm* = avoid damage or injury
hurt = to cause pain or injury to
spoil = to damage or injure so as to make useless or valueless
ruin = to bring about the downfall or destruction of a thing or person

Ask students to complete Nos. 1–6 with a suitable word.

▶ Answers

1 hurt   4 injure
2 damage   5 harm
3 spoil/be ruined   6 ruin/spoil

LANGUAGE STUDY

should have, must have or **might have?**

EXERCISE A

► Answers

a) a duty which was not carried out
b) a reasonable conclusion made about something in the past
c) a possible explanation for something in the past

1 a)   2 c)   3 b)

EXERCISE B

► Answers

1 I might have been killed.
2 I must have been driving at a safe speed.
3 I must have been wearing a safety-belt.
4 I should have been working at that particular time.
5 I should have been helping my boss.
6 I might have been listening to the car-radio when the accident happened.
7 I must have been thinking of something else.
8 I should have been concentrating on my driving.

who, whose, which or **that?**

EXERCISE C

1 who/that   4 which/that
2 which   5 which
3 whose   6 whose

USE OF ENGLISH 2

Guided discussion and writing

Ask students, in groups of 2–3, to read the instructions and information in their books and discuss answers to Nos. 1–4, making notes on their decisions. Allow 6–7 minutes, then tell 2 groups to compare answers. Did they agree?

Tell students to write up their note-form answers to Nos. 1–4 in complete sentences, either in class or for homework.

FOCUS THREE   SB 109–110

■ USE OF ENGLISH
■ VOCABULARY
□ Word combinations

USE OF ENGLISH

EXERCISE A

► Answers

1 to   11 single
2 would   12 consists
3 sense   13 purposes
4 short   14 ways
5 dead   15 split/divided
6 seem/appear   16 In
7 losing   17 have
8 capable   18 wrong
9 possible/so   19 more
10 answer   20 had

EXERCISE B

► Answers

1 long-term, short-term and sensory
2 a) sensory   b) short-term   c) long-term

VOCABULARY

Word combinations

EXERCISE A

► Suggested answers

1 a place where you can park for a short time only
2 a place where you can park for a long time if you wish
3 someone who cannot see things at a distance
4 a runner who takes part in races over long distances
5 a speech which is tiresomely long
6 a politician who is not extreme in his views

EXERCISE B

► Answers

1 a long-sighted person
2 a short-term loan
3 a long-term loan
4 a middle-class person
5 a middle-aged person
6 a short-sleeved shirt
7 a three-legged dog
8 a medium-sized house

FOCUS FOUR SB 111

■ COMPOSITION (giving directions)

COMPOSITION

EXERCISE A

▶ Answer

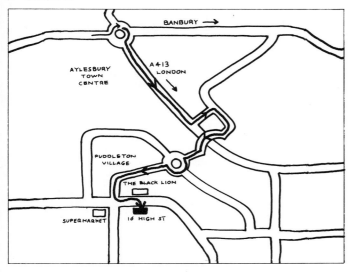

EXERCISE B

▶ Answers

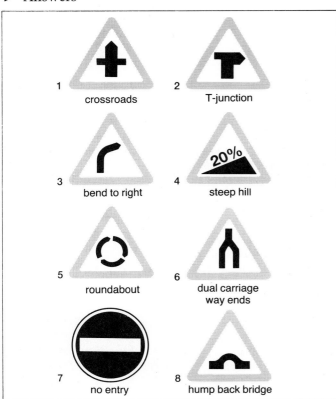

1 crossroads	2 T-junction
3 bend to right	4 steep hill 20%
5 roundabout	6 dual carriage way ends
7 no entry	8 hump back bridge

FOCUS FIVE SB 112

■ REVISION AND EXTENSION
■ LISTENING TEST 7

REVISION AND EXTENSION

Ask students to try and correct another student's work before discussing the correct answers in class.

▶ Answers

1 C	6 D	11 A	16 C
2 A	7 D	12 B	17 B
3 B	8 D	13 A	18 A
4 B	9 B	14 D	19 C
5 A	10 C	15 D	20 D

LISTENING TEST 7

Tapescript

J = Jane   **H** = Harry

H: Hello?

J: Harry. Hello.

H: Jane. How are you?

J: Fine. I haven't seen you both for ages. What are you doing on Saturday?

H: What . . . this Saturday?

J: No, next Saturday . . . the 13th.

H: Hang on a second – I don't think we're doing anything, but I'll just have a look . . . um no, that's fine.

J: Good. Now, can you come to dinner?

H: Yes, that'd be lovely, but you've moved, haven't you?

J: Yes, I'm in north Oxford now. Have you got a pen?

H: Yes.

J: OK. I'll tell you how to get here. Will you be coming from Witney?

H: Long Hanborough probably.

J: All right . . . then you take the A34 from Long Hanborough up to the Peartree Roundabout.

H: Uh uh . . .

J: Then you turn left at the roundabout, OK? . . . and you go along the ring road . . . then you get to the Kidlington roundabout, it's a couple of miles.

H: Right.

J: Now, you could come from the other way but you'd have to cross the traffic, so it's better from Kidlington . . .

H: Yes. I know the road.

J: Anyway, when you get to the roundabout you take the third exit . . . and you go down that road . . . it's called North Road I think . . . and you go on over the flyover . . .

H: Where they're building the motorway . . .

J: Yes. Do you know the North Oxford Golf Club?

H: Yes, I think so.

J: Well, it's about 250 metres after the flyover, on the right, and the turning you need is about another fifty metres after the golf course, on the left.

H: OK, yes, I think I've seen it. There's a sign that says Water something . . .

J: Yes, to Water House Farm. So you go along there, basically through the farm. It's quite a long drive, about a mile, so don't think you've got lost because you haven't.

H: Uh uh.

J: Go past the farm, that's the main building on the right with a stone wall round the garden, and just carry on, and the farm we're in is called Middle Farm – it's a Georgian farmhouse – and it's about half a mile on down the same road. It's got a white fence all the way round, so go through the gate round to the back because we don't use the front door. Oh, and be careful of the speed ramps . . . they're quite hard to see, but they're on the road between the farms and you'll ruin your suspension if you hit them hard.

H: OK . . . what time would you like us there?

J: 7.30 to 8.00? Shall I give you my number just in case you get lost or anything?

H: Er, yes, might as well.

J: It's 350984.

H: OK. See you on Saturday then.

J: Lovely. Bye.

H: Bye

▶ **Answers**

1 left	4 golf course	7 white fence
2 third	5 Water House Farm	8 speed
3 North	6 stone wall	

WORKBOOK KEY WB 59 – 62

UNIT 14

EXERCISE A

I remembered to post the letter: I didn't forget to post the letter.
I remember posting the letter: I recall that I posted the letter.
I remember you posting the letter: I recall that you posted the letter.
I reminded you to post the letter: I told you to post the letter.
I forgot to post the letter: I didn't post the letter.
I've forgotten posting the letter: I posted the letter, but I don't recall it.

1 I apologize for forgetting your birthday.
2 Mother reminded me to send you a birthday card and a present.
3 I remembered to buy a card but I forgot to get you a present.
4 I remembered to look for a present but I saw a pair of shoes instead.
5 When I got home I saw that Jane had arrived and was waiting for me.
6 I had forgotten that I had invited her for lunch/ inviting her for lunch.
7 So I did not remember to buy you a present.
8 Perhaps I will be able to make it up to you next week.
9 I shall be coming to town to do some shopping/for some shopping.
10 Would you like to have lunch with me?
11 I promise (that) I'll not forget to meet you/I promise not to forget to meet you!

EXERCISE B

1 g	2 h	3 e	4 f	5 d	6 a	7 b	8 j
9 i	10 l	11 n	12 m	13 c	14 k	15 o	

EXERCISE C

that	whose
which	whom
who, whom	

1 who	5 which
2 which/that	6 who
3 whose	7 (which/that)
4 (who/whom)	8 who

EXERCISE E

injure, injured/injurious	ruin, ruined
harm, harmful	hurt/hurtful
damage, damaged	spoiled/spoilt

1 injured	7 hurts
2 injuries	8 damage
3 harming	9 spoiled/spoilt/ruined
4 harm/damage	10 harm
5 hurt	11 ruin
6 spoiled/spoilt/ruined	12 spoil/ruin

EXERCISE F

1 B	2 D	3 B	4 C	5 A

EXERCISE G

1 knocked	5 at	9 in
2 scene	6 who/whom	10 as
3 until	7 It	11 injuries
4 to	8 was	12 in

EXERCISE I

2 I might have been asleep when you called because I didn't hear the phone.
3 I must have been in the bath when the phone rang.
4 I might have popped out to empty the rubbish.
5 You should have tried ringing later.
6 You might have caught me later on in the evening.
7 You must have known I was expecting your call.
8 John wasn't at home either. He might have been at the cinema.
9 He must have stayed out late because he sounded very tired this morning.
10 He should have gone out on Saturday instead.

EXERCISE J

1 A one-way street	6 A three-dimensional picture
2 A one-parent family	
3 A two-litre jug	7 A four-letter word
4 A two-seater car	8 A four-door car
5 A three-piece suit	9 A five-day week
	10 A five-minute interval

15
THE MAN IN THE PARK

FOCUS ONE   SB 113 – 114

- **PICTURE DISCUSSION**
- **READING**
- **VOCABULARY**
- **LANGUAGE STUDY**
- ☐ Talking about a long time ago

PICTURE DISCUSSION

Ask students, in groups of 2–3, to discuss answers to Nos. 1–4. Allow 3–4 minutes then invite different members of each group to describe one of the people, say what they are doing and tell the rest of the class what conclusion they arrived at for Nos. 3–4.

Extension activity

Ask students how they would react if someone begged some money from them in the street. Ask students to tell the rest of the class what they would do.

READING

EXERCISE A

Ask students to read through Nos. 1–5 in their books and guess what the passage will be about.

Now ask students in groups of 2–3 to take it in turns to read the passage aloud to each other without explaining any words they do not know.

Ask students individually to choose the best answer.

▶ Answers
1 D   2 C   3 A   4 C   5 D

EXERCISE B

In groups of 2–3 ask students to prepare a short history of what could have happened to Rogers if he really was the man in the park. Appoint a spokesperson to report back to the rest of the class on the group's theory.

VOCABULARY

▶ Answers

1 slave-driver	5 stumbled
2 shabby-(looking)	6 profile
3 shivering	7 resemblance
4 mumbled	8 begging

See if students can use these words in sentences of their own.

LANGUAGE STUDY

Talking about a long time ago

EXERCISE A

▶ Answers
   c) sounds strange, doesn't mean the speaker hasn't eaten recently.
   1 a), b) and d)
   2 c)

EXERCISE B

▶ Answers
   1 The last time I heard from Kevin was a long time ago.
   2 I haven't seen him for a long time.
   3 It has been ages since I had a holiday.
   4 The last time we had Chinese food was a year ago.
   5 It is six months since I saw a good film.
   6 You haven't written to me for years.
   7 It is five years since my wife spoke to me.
   8 My husband hasn't had a bath for five years.
   9 The last time Peter saw Kate was several years ago.
   10 It is ages since she wrote to him.

FOCUS TWO SB 115–116

- ■ USE OF ENGLISH
- ■ SPEAKING
- ■ LANGUAGE STUDY
- ☐ Reporting suggestions (*suggest + ing, suggest that . . . should*) ▷ GS 12.5
- ■ VOCABULARY
- ☐ *cost, value, expense, price,* or *worth*?
- ☐ Phrasal verbs (*fall, see, set*)

USE OF ENGLISH

Write the headline from the passage on the board and ask students in small groups to write down 10 words which they think might appear in the article.

Now ask them to skim read the article and see if any of the words they wrote down did appear. Make a list of any that did on the board and discuss the meaning of any others students do not understand.

In pairs, ask students to complete the blank-filling exercise.

► Answers

1 given	8 expense	15 did/realized
2 being	9 ago/before	16 power
3 as	10 introduced	17 up
4 future	11 for	18 asked/told
5 during/at	12 thought	19 to
6 known	13 had	20 value
7 seen	14 see	

LANGUAGE STUDY

Reporting suggestions

EXERCISE A

► Answers

1 She suggested meeting/that they should meet at one o'clock.
2 She suggested going/that they should go to the opera on Friday evening.
3 She suggested having dinner/that they should have dinner at the Coliseum restaurant afterwards.
4 She suggested spending/that they should spend the weekend in Paris.
5 She suggested making/that they should make a reservation at the Ritz.
6 She suggested that he should make the reservations immediately.

Point out that No. 6 can only be reported as *She suggested that he should . . .* because -*ing* can only be used when the speaker is included in the suggestion.

EXERCISE B

► Answers

1 Let's call the company 'Cartegna'.
2 Wouldn't it be a good idea if you found the customers and I looked after the money?
3 I think we should rent an office in London and another in Paris.
4 Why don't we go to Paris immediately to look for an office?
5 Wouldn't it be a good idea if you ran the London office and I ran the Paris one?
6 Why don't you buy a fast car?
7 Wouldn't it be a good idea if I used it and you paid for it?
8 What about going to a nightclub and charging it to your expense account?

VOCABULARY

***cost, value, expense, price* or *worth*?**

EXERCISE A

Ask students to try to explain the difference in meaning between the five words, using their dictionaries.

cost	= (verb) to be obtained for a certain price, (noun) the amount asked or paid for something
value	= (verb) to estimate what something is worth, (noun) what something is worth in terms of money or usefulness
expense	= (noun) financial cost, fee, money paid out for work done
price	= (noun) what you pay for goods, e.g. *The price of this soap is not marked.* Notice: *to price goods* (verb)
worth	= (adjective) value – used with expressions like: *What is this worth? It's not worth doing.*

Now ask them to complete Nos. 1–5 with one appropriate word.

► Answers

1 expense	3 cost	5 value
2 worth	4 price	

Phrasal verbs

EXERCISE B

▶ Answers

a) fell for	c) fell in	e) set-up
b) saw through	d) saw to	

1 b)　　2 e)　　3 d)　　4 c)　　5 a)

EXERCISE C

▶ Answers

1 through	3 off	5 in
2 out	4 out	6 about

FOCUS THREE　SB 117–118

■ USE OF ENGLISH
■ SPEAKING
■ LISTENING
■ LANGUAGE STUDY
□ *if* or *unless*? ▷ GS 4
□ *until* or *by*? ▷ GS 10.5, 10.18
■ VOCABULARY
□ Word combinations

USE OF ENGLISH

Give students 2–3 minutes to decide where the picture has been taken, who the people are and what they might be doing.

Now, in pairs, ask students to complete the dialogue in their books. Tell them to read through the skeleton dialogue first ignoring the missing parts, then go back and fill in the complete dialogue.

▶ Suggested answers

1 Yes, I would/I'd like to book a flight to Rio.
2 When do you intend to travel?
3 As soon as possible. No later than the end of this week.
4 Well, that will be difficult at this time of year, unless you are very lucky.
5 But it is absolutely essential (that) I get there at/by the end of this week!
6 All right, I'll do what I can. Would you like to sit down?
7 No. I'll be back in half an hour.
8 All right. I'll probably know (by) then. Could/Can/May I have your name?

Ask students to read or act this dialogue in pairs.

SPEAKING

In small groups, ask students to suggest a possible explanation of the connection between the dialogue and the mysterious disappearance of the Contessa.

▶ Suggested answer

The Contessa had left without paying her debts and she had deliberately tricked her boyfriend.

LISTENING

Tapescript

C = Clerk　W = Woman

C : . . . and I'm afraid that's the best we can do at such short notice.
W: Well, I had hoped to get a direct flight . . . but . . . very well . . . I'll take it. Could you repeat the information, please?
C : Yes . . . uh . . . have you got a pen? Or shall I write it down for you?
W: No, just repeat what you told me.
C : You'll have to go to Lisbon first and then . . .
W: Yes, yes, you've already told me that. Just give me the flight number and times again!
C : Uh . . . BA 438 . . . that's the 14th of March . . .
W: I know what month it is. What's important is that it's the day after tomorrow! Correct?
C : Yes, Friday. It leaves at sixteen forty and it takes two and a half hours so it arrives at . . .
W: The arrival time isn't important. Just tell me about the onward flight to Rio.
C : The same day . . . and the flight number is RG 709 . . . it departs from Lisbon at 23.50. Have you got all that?
W: Yes, yes . . . can you issue the ticket immediately?
C : No, I'm afraid not. That is, we can issue the British Airways ticket immediately but not the Varig one . . . not until tomorrow, but there's one thing I'd like to point out. The British Airways flight doesn't leave from London Heathrow but from . . .
W: You mean it isn't leaving from London? But I told you I wanted to l . . . .
C : No, no, please let me explain. There are two airports in London. Gatwick and Heathrow. Heathrow is the main airport but most British Airways flights to Spain and Portugal leave from Gatwick.
W: Ah yes, I remember . . . now remind me how I get to Gatwick?
C : By train from Victoria. You should leave from Victoria no later than a quarter to three . . . 2.45 in the afternoon . . . have you got that?
W: Yes, yes.

▶ Answers

1 B　　2 B　　3 B　　4 B　　5 A

EXERCISE B

Play the tape again and ask students to correct the two notes in their books.

▶ Answers

London	BA438	14/3	16.40
Lisbon	RG709	14/3	23.50

LANGUAGE STUDY

if or *unless*?

EXERCISE A

▶ Answers

1 unless	3 Unless	5 Unless
2 if	4 if	

EXERCISE B

▶ Answers

1 The car won't start unless there is some petrol in the tank.
2 Unless you help me, I'm lost!
3 Unless you give me that money, I'll shoot.
4 Unless you work harder, you'll never pass your exam.
5 Unless you turn off that radio, I'll break it!
6 Unless you hurry, you'll miss the train.
7 Unless I find a job, I'll starve.

until or *by*?

Point out that *until* = up to a certain time, and *by* = not later than.

▶ Answers

1 by	3 until	5 by
2 until	4 by	6 until

VOCABULARY

Word combinations

EXERCISE A

▶ Suggested answers

1 a businessman who is forty years old
2 a woman who writes with her left hand
3 a team consisting of eleven men
4 a man who looks poor and who is dressed in old clothes
5 a woman who wears beautiful clothes
6 a car which has three wheels

EXERCISE B

▶ Answers

1 a dark-haired woman
2 a tired-looking man
3 well-dressed people
4 a ten-minute walk
5 a ten-day trip
6 an eight-year-old child (point out that there is no 's' on *year*)
7 a candle-lit restaurant
8 a badly-built house

Now read out the explanations again and see if students can form the word combinations from memory.

EXERCISE C

Give students 3–4 minutes to fill in the spaces in Nos. 1–8 with the appropriate form of the words in capitals. See if they can explain what kind of word they have made.

▶ Answers

1 wintry (adjective)	5 hopefully (adverb)
2 foggy (adjective)	6 well- (adverb)
3 beggar (noun)	7 guiltily (adverb)
4 lucky (adjective)	8 dirty (adjective)

FOCUS FOUR SB 119

■ COMPOSITION (sequence)

COMPOSITION

EXERCISE A

▶ Answers
Correct order:

Paragraph 1	Paragraph 3
2, 1, 3	11, 9, 12, 10
Paragraph 2	Paragraph 4
5, 7, 6, 8, 4	16, 13, 18, 17, 14, 15

EXERCISE B

▶ Answers

1 Link words: examples in sentences 11, 15, 18
2 Time expressions: examples in sentences 8, 10, 16
3 The Past perfect: no examples
4 Using the -ing form: example in sentence 5

EXERCISE C

▶ Suggested answers

1 A year later he started working for a London insurance company.
2 After working for them for two years he was promoted. After that he moved to Edinburgh.
3 The following year he met Jane Simpson.
4 After they had been going out together for a year, they got married.
5 After living in Edinburgh for four years, they moved back to London.
6 A year later their first child was born.

EXERCISE D

Ask students to prepare a CV (curriculum vitae) for themselves, then write a biography of 120–180 words. For homework, ask them to write a similar biography (using an encyclopaedia if they wish) of someone famous, mentioning their major life events and using the expressions suggested in Exercise B.

FOCUS FIVE   SB 120

■ REVISION AND EXTENSION
☐ Further forms of the future ▷ GS 13.3
☐ Four types of infinitive
☐ Review of tenses
☐ Revision transformations

REVISION AND EXTENSION

Further forms of the future

EXERCISE A

Ask students to make a rough timetable for the term ahead putting down any dates which are important, e.g. half term, end of term, trip to the theatre etc.

In pairs tell students to ask each other questions about the timetable such as:

What'll you be doing on July 10th?
What'll you be doing at half-term/when the term finishes?
What do you think we'll have studied by the end of term?

Point out the use of *on* with *What'll you be doing on July 10th?* and the use of *by* with *By the end of term we'll have studied . . .* and tell students that *on* means 'at a precise time' and *by* means 'just before' or 'right up to a certain time'.

In groups of 3–4 ask students to read through the timetable notes from Jennifer's diary in their books and put Nos. 1–8 into the correct tense.

▶ Answers
1 she'll be revising
2 half term will have finished
3 she'll be moving
4 she'll be looking
5 she'll have found
6 she'll have found
7 she'll be living and working
8 she'll be travelling

Four types of infinitive

EXERCISE B

▶ Answers
1 c)   2 a)   3 d)   4 b)

EXERCISE C

Write the newspaper headline on the board and ask students to guess what the article might be about. In small groups ask students to skim read the article and see whether they guessed correctly. In the same groups, ask students to rewrite Nos. 1–8 using one of the infinitive forms in Exercise B.

▶ Answers
1 to have found   5 to have been carrying
2 to be studying   6 to be lying
3 to have sunk   7 to be
4 to have been   8 to be
  returning

Review of tenses

EXERCISE D

▶ Answers
have not written, have been, have not had, had, were, gave, had, put, have been living, have been, have done, have bought, have laid, made, have been painting, have not finished, have been putting

Revision transformations

EXERCISE E

Ask students to form small groups. Tell students in turn to read out an example from the exercise and give the others the beginning of the transformed sentence. The other students should write down the transformation after listening to the spoken example.

▶ Answers
1 I must remember to buy some cheese.
2 He might have gone to London.
3 The last time he wrote to his parents was two months ago.
4 It's ages since I saw a good film.
5 I haven't taken an exam for three years.
6 He suggested having a Chinese meal.
7 She suggested that he should ring his lawyer.
8 If it doesn't stop snowing, we won't get home.
9 He won't phone unless he changes his mind.
10 You should have given the letter to Peter.

WORKBOOK KEY   WB 63 – 6

UNIT 15   WB 63 — 67

EXERCISE A

1 C   2 A   3 A   4 D

EXERCISE B

1 homeless	6 strict
2 tramps	7 valued
3 demonstrations	8 retire
4 slim	9 relatives
5 fit	10 whispers

EXERCISE C

1 trial	7 lawyer, defence
2 accused	8 cross-examined, evidence
3 jury, court	9 verdict
4 judge	10 guilty
5 prosecution	11 sentenced
6 witnesses	12 fined

EXERCISE D

1 It's three weeks since I had a letter from Jenny.
2 The last time the builders did any work on the house was over a week ago.
3 I haven't been to the dentist for more than six months/for over six months.
4 I haven't seen her since January.
5 We haven't gone out for a meal together for ages.
6 It's over a week since she (last) phoned me.
7 It's so long since I last saw her I can hardly remember what she looks like.
8 The last time I went to France was in 1986.

EXERCISE E

(sample answers)

(Two main types of answer are possible, as shown in numbers 1 & 4.)

1 The last time I had a row with anyone in my family was when my sister broke my radio/I haven't had a row with anyone in my family for years.
2 The last time I went on holiday was a few weeks ago.
3 I haven't taken an exam for years.
4 I haven't been given a present for years/The last time I was given a present was a couple of months ago.
5 I haven't had anything to drink for days.
6 The last time I took some exercise was on Monday.
7 I haven't made anyone really angry for a long time.
8 I last went out for a meal at the weekend.

EXERCISE F

1 value	5 price
2 expense	6 worth
3 cost	7 cost
4 price	8 value

EXERCISE G

1 costly	5 valuable
2 priceless	6 priced
3 inexpensive	7 expensive
4 worthless	

EXERCISE H

(sample answers)

1 Why don't you use your credit card?
2 Wouldn't it be a good idea to phone his mother?
3 Let's go out and have a meal.
4 What about hiring a car for the weekend?
5 I think we ought to go to the theatre.

EXERCISE I

1 I suggested (that) she should use her credit card.
2 I suggested (that) he should phone Peter's mother.
3 I suggested going out for a meal.
4 I suggested (that) he should hire a car for the weekend.
5 I suggested going out to the theatre.

EXERCISE J

1 if	6 if
2 unless	7 Unless
3 unless	8 If
4 unless	9 unless
5 if	10 if

EXERCISE K

1 if . . .	4 unless . . .
2 unless . . .	5 if . . .
3 if . . .	

EXERCISE L

1 until	6 by
2 by	7 until
3 until, by	8 by
4 by, until	9 until, until
5 by	10 until

EXERCISE M

1 three-legged	6 two-faced
2 left-handed	7 best-dressed
3 self-centred	8 fair-haired
4 short-tempered	9 kind-hearted
5 old-fashioned	10 one-sided

PROGRESS TEST 3   WB 68 — 69

EXERCISE A

1 B	2 A	3 C	4 A	5 C
6 B	7 B	8 B	9 A	10 D
11 B	12 D	13 D		

EXERCISE B

1 of	11 so
2 also	12 of
3 memory	13 can
4 be	14 For
5 been	15 like
6 on	16 which
7 which/that	17 to
8 what	18 find
9 the	19 than
10 colours	20 to

EXERCISE C

1 I had expected (that) the exam would be much more difficult/much harder/much less easy; I had expected the exam to be much more difficult/much harder/much less easy.
2 Not only did she sprain her ankle, but she broke her wrist as well.
3 I'm going to have some new curtains made.
4 Marina felt upset because she hadn't been invited to the wedding.
5 Harry told his son that he shouldn't have stayed out so late/had been wrong to stay out so late.
6 Chinese food is said to be the best in the world.
7 Could you remind me to go to the dentist, please?
8 I haven't seen Robin for three weeks.
9 Jack suggested (to me) that I should apply for a job with the local paper.
10 The bank manager won't give me a loan unless I am sure I can repay it/the money.

EXERCISE D

1 keep up with	4 keep off
2 keeping (back) from	5 kept on
3 keep up	

EXERCISE E

1 attractive	4 innocence
2 indecisive	5 disconnect
3 shocked	

16 SERVANTS OF THE FUTURE

FOCUS ONE SB 121–122

- ■ PICTURE DISCUSSION
- ■ READING
- ■ VOCABULARY
  - □ *false* or *artificial*?
  - □ *clean* or *wash*?
- ■ LANGUAGE STUDY
  - □ *needs doing* ▷ GS 5.3
  - □ *myself, yourself* etc.

PICTURE DISCUSSION

Give students 1–2 minutes to look at the picture and write down as many words as they can to describe it. Write a complete list of vocabulary on the board. In pairs, ask students to write three questions to ask a partner about the picture. Allow time for students to interview each other about the picture.

In different pairs, ask students to take it in turns to ask each other the questions in their books.

Topics for further discussion

1 Will robots ever be able to think in the same way as human beings?
2 What kinds of jobs will be done by machines in the future?

Extension activity

Ask students to make a list of as many labour-saving devices as they can think of and suggest how these devices may change in the future. Tell students to divide the list into two parts: devices in the home and devices at work.

READING

Ask students to take it in turns to read a few lines of the passage aloud to the rest of the class. Tell the other students to make notes as they listen.

Ask some check comprehension questions about the passage and invite students to answer them from their notes, e.g.
What do some experts believe will happen within the next twenty years?
What has one London company developed?

Now ask students in small groups to choose the best answer to Nos. 1–3.

▶ Answers

   1 B   2 A   3 D

VOCABULARY

false or *artificial*?

EXERCISE A

Explain the difference in meaning between the two words, i.e.
false = (adjective) can mean not true, unfaithful, deceiving, based on mistaken ideas, not real.
Notice: *false teeth, eyelashes*
artificial = (adjective) can mean made by human work or art, not natural, made in imitation of, unnatural in an affected way. Notice: *artificial flowers, artificial respiration*.

Ask students to choose which word would be correct in Nos. 1–4.

▶ Answers

1 artificial	3 artificial
2 false	4 false

clean or *wash*?

EXERCISE B

Explain the difference between the two words, i.e.
clean = (verb and adjective) can mean remove dirt, stains etc. often with a chemical.
wash = (verb and noun) can mean make clean, usually with (soap and) water.

Read out Nos. 1–4 and ask students to supply the correct verb.

▶ Answers

1 clean	3 wash	5 clean
2 clean	4 wash	

Ask students which verb they would use with the following: the silver (*clean*), the shirts (*wash*), the house (*clean*), the coffee cups (*wash*), your shoes (*clean*).

LANGUAGE STUDY

needs doing

EXERCISE A

▶ Answers

b) and c) mean that someone else has to program the robots.

Sentence a) is false according to the passage because it means that the robots do the programming.

EXERCISE B

▶ Answers

1 The floor needs cleaning.
2 These clothes need ironing.
3 These things need washing.
4 Pets need looking after.
5 The car doesn't need repairing.
6 Does this structure need explaining?

myself, yourself etc.

EXERCISE C

Point out the form in the singular (*-self*) and plural (*-selves*) and tell students that these words can be used as reflexive pronouns, e.g. *to wash yourself*, or as emphasizing pronouns, e.g. *I painted this picture myself*.

Ask them to complete Nos. 1–6 with the correct word.

▶ Answers

1 herself	4 himself
2 yourself	5 myself
3 ourselves	6 themselves

FOCUS TWO   SB 123 – 124

- ■ LISTENING
- ■ READING
- ■ USE OF ENGLISH 1
- ■ USE OF ENGLISH 2
- ■ LANGUAGE STUDY
- □ *small enough . . .* or *too small . . .* ?

LISTENING

EXERCISE A

Tapescript

A: Service Department. May I help you?

B: Uh . . . yes . . . I've got a problem here with one of your robots.

A: I see. What exactly is the problem, sir?

B: Well . . . uh . . . the thing just doesn't do what I tell it to.

A: Which model is it, sir?

B: It's the ALP three five something.

A: Sorry, sir. Do you mean the three five seven or the three five nine?

B: Just a moment. I'll look. It's the 357.

A: I see. When did you buy it, sir?

B: This year. In . . . uh . . . let's see . . . was it March? Uh . . . no, it was April. I . . . uh . . . can't remember the exact date. Let me find the receipt.

A: No, wait, sir. That's enough about that for now. Just tell me what you mean when you say it doesn't do what you tell it to. Could you give me an example?

B: Well, uh . . . take yesterday, that was typical. I told it to watch the cat and feed the fish. And . . . uh . . . well . . . it did everything wrong!

A: Excuse me, sir, but I don't think I quite understand. What did you tell it to do?

B: Watch the cat and feed the fish.

A: Uh . . . watch the cat? What did you mean?

B: What I said. 'Watch the cat! Look after it. Take care of it. Don't let it out of the house.' You see, she was almost run over a few days ago and I didn't w . . .

A: But what happened, sir? What exactly did the robot do?

B: I don't know! I went out . . . but when I came back an hour later, you should have seen the mess!

A: Mess?

B: Yes, a terrible mess. There was soap all over her . . . and she was still wet. I can't im . . .

A: Over who, sir? Who was wet?

B: The cat, of course! I've just told you! And that wasn't all! The fish were gone. All three of them. Beautiful goldfish, they were. I told the robot to feed the fish, not free them!

A: Perhaps the robot didn't quite understand, sir.

B: Why not? I speak clearly enough, don't I? Can't the damned thing understand simple English? You say it will respond to simple spoken instructions but it doesn't!

B: Well, you see, at first it may have a few problems in . . . uh . . . understanding your voice. It has to get used to your voice and your way of speaking. So . . . uh . . . we may have to readjust it a little.

B: Readjust it?

A: Yes, reprogram it a little. Now, when can our service engineer call on you?

B: The sooner the better!

A: What about tomorrow afternoon?

B: Yes, after lunch. Let's say 2 p.m.
A: All right, sir. Now, may I have your name and address, please.
B: L. Pynge.
A: Would you spell that, please?
B: 'L' . . . that's my initial, 'L' for Lester . . . P–Y–N–G–E.
A: And your address?
B: 2456 Nelson Street . . . N–E–L–S–O–N.
A: Is that here, in Toronto, sir?
B: Yes.
A: And your telephone number?
B: 778856.
A: Thank you, Mr Pynge. Our service engineer will call on you at 2 p.m. tomorrow, June 19th.
B: Thank you.
A: Thank you, sir.

► Answers

CUSTOMER DETAILS

Name L. Pynge
Address 2456 Nelson Street
Telephone 778856
Robot Model No. ALP 357
Purchased April

Possible cause of malfunction
(✓ Where appropriate)

Mechanical failure ☑

Incorrect operation of controls ☐

Incorrect instructions to robot ☐

Service call required
state a.m. or p.m. June 19th p.m.
Today's date June 18th

EXERCISE B

Play the tape again and ask students to make notes as they listen to be able to discuss Nos. 1–3 with a partner.

► Possible answers
1 The robot washed the cat and freed the goldfish.
2 Maybe the cat has eaten them? Or perhaps the robot put them down the sink, or in a pond outside?
3 The robot heard *wash* for *watch*, and *free* for *feed*.

READING

Tell students, in groups of 2–3, to read the extract from the Amstrad user's guide and discuss answers to Nos. 1–3 in their books. Allow 4–5 minutes, then tell 2 groups to compare answers. Did they agree?

USE OF ENGLISH 1

Guided discussion and writing

Allow students, in pairs, 5–6 minutes to read through the information in their books and discuss (and make a note of) answers to Nos. 1–4.

Now invite different pairs to interview each other, asking and answering one question in turn.

Tell students to write out their answers using complete sentences, either in class or for homework.

USE OF ENGLISH 2

► Suggested answers
1 I am writing this letter in order to complain about the operating instructions for the Maestro M–1700.
2 I bought one of these machines a month ago and I have found learning how to use it very difficult.
3 The most difficult thing of all was understanding the instructions.
4 I often needed to read some sentences several times.
5 I believe you are hoping/hope to sell your machines in/to many different countries.
6 I am sure it will/would be too expensive to translate the instructions into many different languages.
7 This means/will mean that many of your foreign customers will have to use the English instructions.
8 How do you expect them to understand your instructions if well-educated English people like myself aren't able to understand them?

LANGUAGE STUDY

***small enough* . . . or *too small* . . . ?**

Point out that *small enough* means *not too big* and *too small* means *not big enough*. Read out the example then ask students to complete Nos. 1–6.

► Answers
1 The machine is light enough for a child to carry.
2 This machine is too heavy for me to carry.
3 You are speaking too fast for me to understand.
4 You should speak clearly enough for everyone to understand (you).
5 This problem should be easy enough for a child to solve.
6 And this problem is too difficult even for you to solve.

FOCUS THREE SB 125 – 126

- ■ USE OF ENGLISH
- ■ VOCABULARY
- □ Phrasal verbs (*put* and *do*)
- □ *do* or *make*? ▷ GS 15.2
- □ *to* or *with*?
- ■ LANGUAGE STUDY
- □ *-ing* clauses as the subject of a sentence ▷ GS 5.4

USE OF ENGLISH

► Answers

1 do	8 correct	15 holiday
2 tired/sick	9 All	16 act
3 in	10 rest	17 solve
4 putting	11 dinner	18 simplicity
5 give	12 out	19 used
6 need	13 care	20 impossible/
7 wonder	14 capable	unbearable

VOCABULARY

Phrasal verbs

EXERCISE A

► Answers
1 b) *put on* = dress in
2 c) *put . . . through* = connect people on the telephone

EXERCISE B

Ask students to interview each other in pairs using the suggestions in Nos. 1–4 and using the phrasal verbs in Exercise A in their replies.

► Suggested answers
1 homework, housework, writing letters etc.
2 clothing, shoes, hat etc.
3 noise, being late, deceit etc.
4 put (me) through

EXERCISE C

► Answers
1 b)   2 c)   3 a)

EXERCISE D

► Answers
1 without   2 away with   3 out of

do or *make*?

EXERCISE E

► Answers

1 make	4 make	7 make
2 do	5 do	8 make
3 do	6 do	

to or *with*?

EXERCISE F

► Answers
What have you done with the furniture? = a)
What have you done to the furniture? = b)

1 with	2 to	3 to	4 with

LANGUAGE STUDY

-ing clauses as the subject of a sentence

► Answers
1 Is learning English difficult?
2 Will learning English help me?
3 How will learning English help me?
4 Telling the truth is usually better than lying.
5 But sometimes telling the truth hurts people.
6 Is smoking bad for your health?
7 Teaching a robot how to prepare an omelette isn't as difficult as teaching it how to recognize a bad egg.
8 Sitting in the sun too long can be dangerous.

FOCUS FOUR SB 127

■ COMPOSITION (giving advice)

COMPOSITION

EXERCISE A

Conduct a brainstorming session and ask students to list any ways they know of giving advice. Write a complete list on the board and discuss any expressions students may not know. See if students can divide them into formal and informal expressions.

EXERCISE B

Ask students to read through the passage in small groups and make a note of any expressions they did not list.

EXERCISES C and D

▶ Answers

Advising someone to do something	Advising someone not to do something
– *do (go)*	– *whatever you do, don't . . .*
– *If I were you, I'd take . . .*	– *I wouldn't take . . .*
– *As far as . . . are concerned, the most essential is . . .*	– *It's best not to . . .*
– *it's a good idea to bring . . .*	
– *You ought to bring . . .*	
– *it's well worthwhile getting . . .*	
– *you'd better remember . . .*	

Divide the class into groups of 3–4. Ask them to prepare questions asking for advice about a trip to England. Now ask two groups to ask each other their questions and provide suitable advice. Another country could be suggested or perhaps a trip to somewhere very cold (the Arctic Circle) or very hot (the desert). Groups could be given different places.

▶ Suggested questions

If you were me, what would you . . . ?
Would you . . . ?
Is it best (not) to . . . ?
As far as . . . is/are concerned, what is the best . . . ?
Is it a good idea to . . . ?
Is it worthwhile . . . -ing?
Is there anything I need to remember?

EXERCISE E

Divide students into pairs or threes and ask them to prepare to read or act out the roles suggested. Tell Student A to make a list of questions asking for advice about learning English, (they can use a lot of the question forms from Exercise D) and Student B to make a list of as many ways as possible of improving his/her partner's English. Reverse roles and invite several pairs of students to perform their role play for the rest of the class.

EXERCISE F

Ask students to do topic 1 as a class composition. Allow about 45 minutes for this. Make a list of points to be included by asking students for their ideas then writing them all on the board. Now ask students to decide on the order in which the points will appear and then write the composition on their own.

Topic 2 could be set for homework.

FOCUS FIVE SB 128

■ REVISION AND EXTENSION
■ LISTENING TEST 8

REVISION AND EXTENSION

Set students a timed test (about 20 minutes) and see if they complete Nos. 1–20. When they have finished, ask them to mark a partner's work. Give out the correct answers after they have tried to correct each other's mistakes. Tell students to count the number of correct answers and give a mark out of 20.

▶ Answers

1 D	6 A	11 A	16 D
2 A	7 D	12 C	17 A
3 A	8 C	13 C	18 B
4 B	9 D	14 D	19 C
5 A	10 D	15 B	20 C

Check on any areas of revision students may need.

LISTENING TEST 8

Tapescript

J = Jenny   **S** = Steve

J: You've been to the Lake District, Steve. You know it, don't you?

S: Yes . . . long time ago though. Why, are you thinking of going, Jenny?

J: Yes, I was going to go up for a week or so at the end of the month, with Katie, but, um, we're not quite sure what to do about where to stay . . . and I was wondering if you could do us a big favour . . .

S: Yes, I should think so.

J: You know your tent . . . ? Could we borrow it?

S: Yes, of course you can.

J: We'll pay you for it.

S: No, don't be silly. It's no use to me because it would never fit the three of us, so you can have it as long as you like. You're sure you want to go camping? I mean, you've been before?

J: No, we haven't; but we just want to get away from all this noise and traffic and pollution and get some fresh air and have a change of scene . . . and we could go walking and spend the night more or less where we wanted, you know. And it should be quite cheap, too, because we haven't got very much to spend and we couldn't afford a hotel or anything like that.

S: Hmm. Have you got boots and rucksacks and things like that?

J: No, not yet, but we thought we'd ask you about the tent first, and then go and get what we need.

S: Tell me, are you going there because you want to go camping, or . . . ?

J: No, we don't particularly want to go camping, we just want to see the place . . .

S: You want to see it?

J: Yes. And not too expensive.

S: Well, the thing is, I mean, you're quite welcome to borrow the tent if you want to, you know, but if you're going to go camping and walking you're going to have to buy loads of other things like gas stoves, and lights and torches and something to cook on and boots and you name it . . . and by the time you finish you'll have spent much more on all of that than you would have done if you'd stayed in a hotel . . . so it's a sort of false economy, really.

J: But neither of us really like hotels anyway and, you know, it's nice to be able to get up when you want and cook for yourself and have cups of coffee whenever you feel like it . . .

S: Did I tell you about where we stayed?

J: Where . . . in the Lake District?

S: Yeah.

J: No, I don't think so.

S: It was one of these self-catering flats – just a couple of rooms really and a small sort of kitchen . . . but it'd be perfect.

J: Was it expensive?

S: No, not at all. It belonged to this woman who only used it once or twice a year, and the rest of the time she rented it out to people she knew, or friends of friends, so there are . . . there are really very few people who even know about it.

J: Do you think she'd let us have it?

S: I'm sure she would as long as it hasn't been booked . . . I'll get you her phone number and you can give her a ring.

J: That'd be great.

S: It'll be much better than a tent, really, because you'll be able to come and go when you want, and cook, and it's all fully-furnished so you won't have to buy all that equipment.

J: That sounds ideal, and it's nice to have a sort of base, you know.

S: Yes, and it means that you'll be OK even if it rains, and you'll be able to have hot baths and things which is much nicer than camping, which can be pretty awful if the weather's bad.

J: No, that's a really good idea. I'll have a word with Katie and then I'll give the woman a ring and see if we can get it.

▶ Answers

1 F	2 F	3 T	4 F	5 F
6 F	7 T	8 F	9 F	10 T

WORKBOOK KEY WB 70 – 73

UNIT 16

EXERCISE A

1 F	2 F	3 T	4 T
5 T	6 F	7 T	8 T

EXERCISE B

range: assortment
tasks: jobs
expert: specialist
unusual: extraordinary
repair: mend
slightly: a little
sophisticated: highly-developed
equivalent: corresponding
recognize: identify
respond: answer

1 repaired	6 slightly
2 tasks	7 experts
3 sophisticated	8 recognize
4 range	9 responding
5 equivalent	10 unusual

EXERCISE C

1 imitation	6 false
2 fake	7 wrong/dishonest
3 man-made	8 artificial
4 wrong	9 false
5 lying	10 artificial/man-made/imitation/ fake

EXERCISE D

1 You must speak clearly enough for everyone to understand you.
2 The suitcase is light enough for me to carry.
3 There is never enough time to do what you want.
4 The cake is big enough for everyone.
5 I haven't got enough money to go to the cinema.
6 I can't type quickly enough to get a good job.

EXERCISE E

1 This dress is too big for me to wear.
2 This car is cheap enough for us to buy.
3 The restaurant is good enough for us to take the manager to.
4 We have enough food to feed everybody.
5 The table is too small for us all to fit round.
6 The work is too complicated for me to understand.
7 It's too wet for us to go out.
8 It's hot enough for us to go for a swim.

EXERCISE F

1 When we bought the house it needed repairing.
2 My hair needs cutting.
3 The kitchen floor needs cleaning.
4 The windows need replacing.
5 His shoes needed repairing/replacing.
6 The car needed refuelling/filling up (with petrol).
7 The bath needs cleaning.
8 The cat needs feeding.
9 The garden needs weeding.
10 My watch needs winding/mending.

EXERCISE G

1 do without
2 Put on
3 done away with
4 put up with
5 do . . . out of
6 put . . . through
7 put off
8 put up with
9 put off
10 do without

EXERCISE H

(Sample answer)

Dear Mark,

Thank you for your letter. If I were you, I'd take these problems one by one. Firstly, I don't think it matters if your brothers like their own kind of music. You can get some headphones if you want to listen to pop music.

As for food, it's worth making an effort to eat your mother's food, but you could ask her if she could cook sausages, chips and peas now and again for you.

Finally, I wouldn't insist on wearing jeans for church – after all, you can wear jeans every other day of the week.

Dear Sue,

Thank you for your letter. I don't think you should worry. There's nothing selfish about enjoying a good holiday and wishing it would go on longer.

The fact that you don't miss your family shows how secure and independent you are. You should feel glad that you *can* enjoy yourself on holiday, and I'm sure that your parents are proud to have brought you up that way.

Dear Jim,

Thank you for your letter. Don't worry – the dangerous swamps in Florida will probably be a long way from where you live.

I think what you're really afraid of is all the new things you're going to meet in your daily life – new friends, teachers and so on. It's worth finding out as much as you can about your new house, school and town before you go. Then you won't find everything so strange when you go there.

17
DEATH-TRAP

FOCUS ONE   SB 129 – 130

- PICTURE DISCUSSION
- READING
- LANGUAGE STUDY
- ☐ More about the passive ▷ GS 8.2
- VOCABULARY

PICTURE DISCUSSION

In pairs, ask students to think of as many words as possible connected with fire. Put a complete list of vocabulary on the board. In the same pairs tell students to take turns interviewing each other about the picture using the questions in their books. Discuss any unknown vocabulary.

Topics for further discussion

1 Describe any precautions you can think of to prevent fire in the home or in the countryside.
2 What exactly causes death when there is a fire?
3 Describe any fire you have witnessed or heard about.

Extension activity

Take in some photocopies of a newspaper article about a fire (it could be in the students' mother tongue). Ask students in groups of 3–4 to prepare a short spoken news item in English to read out to the rest of the class. Ask one student from each group to read out the news item.

READING

Write the newspaper headline on the board and ask students to suggest two or three facts which might appear in the article they are going to read. Now divide the class into two groups. Ask group 1 (in pairs) to write 3–4 comprehension questions about the first three paragraphs of the article, ending with *. . . attempt to escape.*

Ask group 2 (also in pairs) to do the same for the last four paragraphs beginning with *Throughout the day . . . .*

Ask each group to skim read the paragraphs they have not already read then answer the questions prepared by the students in the other group.

Now ask students to choose the best answer to Nos. 1–5.

▶ Answers
1 D   2 B   3 B   4 C   5 D

LANGUAGE STUDY

More about the passive

EXERCISE A

▶ Answers
b) and c)

EXERCISE B

▶ Answers
1 The match was being watched on TV.
2 Many of the rescuers were burned by the intense heat.
3 The fire-extinguishers had been taken away.
4 An investigation has been set up.
5 Many people have been treated for burns and shock.
6 The identity of one of the victims is known by/to the police.
7 Stadiums are sometimes inspected by fire-officers.
8 Many existing stands will have to be rebuilt.
9 The stand was destroyed in a matter of minutes.
10 The fire was probably started by a dropped cigarette.

VOCABULARY

▶ Answers
1 C   3 A   5 A   7 B
2 B   4 C   6 A   8 C

FOCUS TWO SB 131–132

■ LISTENING
■ LANGUAGE STUDY
☐ *could* or *managed to*?
☐ *could*, *managed to* and *couldn't*
☐ *must have been done* ▷ GS 7.8
☐ *must be done* ▷ GS 7.8
■ VOCABULARY

LISTENING

Tapescript
M = Man   **W** = Woman

M: It's been a bad year for me as far as football goes. I mean, it *is* supposed to be good family entertainment, and it should be better than just staying at home. But this year has been terrible. First of all, I was in Brussels, and there was that riot and all those people were killed. And now there's been this fire, and more people killed. It's more like a war than a game.

It's a tragedy, an absolute tragedy and as far as I'm concerned, that's it. You won't find me going to a football match again with the children . . . or even by myself for that matter. I've had enough, I'm even going to give up watching it on TV.

W: I didn't go to the game, but the boys went by themselves . . . that's John who's 13 and Steven, he's 11. They've been to all the matches. Anyway, you can see the ground from our window, and I don't know why, but I looked out and could see all the smoke coming from the stadium, and I thought 'Oh my God, it's on fire.' Then the fire-engines started coming out and the ambulances, and then you could see the flames–they were hundreds of feet high. So I rushed downstairs as fast as I could and ran to the stadium. When I got there it was just terrible. The heat from the stand was so bad that you couldn't get anywhere near it so I went round to the main entrance. But it was impossible to get through the crowd, because there were already hundreds of people in the street shouting and screaming, and the road was completely blocked.

Well I just stood and waited, but I couldn't see the boys because then people started coming out of one of the gates, thousands and thousands of them, and there was no hope of finding anyone. Finally I asked a policeman how I could find out about the boys, and he told me to go to the police station. I was there for about three hours and they didn't have any news, so I went to the main hospital and they couldn't tell me anything either so I went home. I tell you, going home that night, not knowing where they were, was really terrible. I'd seen what it was like in the main police station, no-one there knew what was happening, and I'd seen the hospital too, and I feared the worst. But when I got back they were both there in front of the TV, and they were OK. You can't imagine how happy I felt, you just can't imagine.

▶ Answers
    1 D   2 D   3 A   4 C   5 D

LANGUAGE STUDY

***could* or *managed to*?**

EXERCISE A

▶ Answers
    b) means *I escaped.*
    a) is about a general ability, not an action.

could*, *managed to* and *couldn't

EXERCISE B

▶ Answers
    1 couldn't   4 couldn't   7 managed to
    2 managed to   5 managed to   8 could
    3 couldn't   6 could   9 could

must have been done

EXERCISE C

▶ Answers
    In b) and d) the speaker is making a guess.
    In a) and c) the speaker is talking about something actually seen or known.
    1 The gates must have been locked.
    2 The fire must have been started by a cigarette.
    3 The seats must have been made of plastic.
    4 Some of them must have been badly injured.
    5 The gates must have been locked before the match.

must be done

EXERCISE D

▶ Answers
    In b) the speaker is ordering or recommending something.
    1 The gates must be left open.
    2 Rubbish must not be thrown under the stands.
    3 Seats must not be made of plastic.
    4 Fire-extinguishers must not be removed.
    5 Rescuers must be provided with protective clothing.
    6 Stadiums must be inspected regularly.

EXERCISE E

▶ Answers
    1 He must have been arrested.
    2 It must have been stolen.
    3 It must be rebuilt.
    4 That letter must be posted today.
    5 The door must have been painted.
    6 This telephone must not be used without permission.
    7 It must be watered regularly.
    8 It must have been cleaned.

VOCABULARY

Put each word on the board and invite students to shout out what each word reminds them of, e.g. *enter* – a notice on a building or a door; *detect* – TV programmes about private investigators etc.

After discussing students' ideas ask them to complete the exercise in pairs.

▶ Answers

1	entrance	5	efficiency
2	detectives	6	admiration
3	inquiry	7	refreshments
4	destruction	8	casually

FOCUS THREE   SB 133–134

■ USE OF ENGLISH
☐ Paragraph completion

USE OF ENGLISH

EXERCISE A

▶ Answers

1	such	12	efficiently/
2	out		quickly/easily
3	for	13	high
4	begun	14	divided
5	extent	15	each
6	brought	16	supporters
7	to/with	17	use
8	taken	18	emergency
9	been	19	fact
10	case	20	which/that
11	better		

Paragraph completion

EXERCISE B

In groups of 3–4 ask students to read the passage carefully and see if they can explain in their own words what each paragraph is saying. Allow 10–15 minutes for this as the passage is quite challenging but similar to authentic material which students may come across in the exam.

Now ask students in the same groups to complete the three paragraphs as indicated in their books. Point out that the facts may not be in chronological order and students will have to read the whole passage to extract their information.

▶ Suggested answers

1 You should use different extinguishers for different types of fire. Carbon dioxide extinguishers, for example, can be used to put out fires caused by electrical equipment or flammable liquids and foam extinguishers for fires caused by burning liquids such as petrol. For most other fires you can use a water extinguisher.

2 Where and how you stand when fighting a fire is important. For any type of fire, you should never stand up straight. Stay down and this will help you to avoid the smoke and get closer to the fire. Make sure the wind is behind you. Make sure you are standing near an exit in case the fire gets out of control.

3 In certain circumstances, you must not stay and fight a fire. For example, if there is any danger of the fire spreading to anything which could explode, or if you think your escape route might be cut off by smoke or fire and you might be trapped, leave the building immediately. In other words, do not stay if there is any real danger of your being injured or suffocated.

FOCUS FOUR   SB 135

■ COMPOSITION (argument)

COMPOSITION

EXERCISE A

▶ Answers

1 Introduction
2 Tourism and a country's economy
3 Tourism and the environment
4 The influence of tourism on culture.
5 Conclusion

FOCUS FIVE   SB 136

■ REVISION AND EXTENSION
☐ Modals ▷ GS 7
☐ Revision transformations

REVISION AND EXTENSION

Modals

EXERCISE A

► Answers

1 D	6 A	11 C	16 C	21 B
2 A	7 B	12 B	17 B	22 A
3 B	8 A	13 D	18 B	23 C
4 D	9 A	14 B	19 A	24 A
5 D	10 D	15 B	20 A	25 C

Revision transformations

EXERCISE B

► Answers

1 He is too young to vote.
2 It is often very difficult to remember lists of words.
3 The stolen money has been found.
4 The window was almost certainly broken on purpose.
5 Will my pronunciation be improved by going to England?/Will my pronunciation improve if I go to England?
6 He isn't tall enough to be a policeman.
7 They say Charles is a very rich man.
8 He must be told the truth.
9 I won't put up with this behaviour for a minute longer.
10 The road must be finished before next summer.

WORKBOOK KEY WB 74 – 78

UNIT 17

EXERCISE A

1 B   2 A   3 D   4 C

EXERCISE B

1	reasOn	8	althouGh
2	vioLent	9	fAns
3	especiallY	10	ashaMed
4	staMp	11	sensEless
5	Proclaiming	12	worSe
6	furIous		
7	reCognising		

EXERCISE D

1 pitch/field	2 centre	3 rink	4 course
5 pitch	6 courts	7 track	8 pool

EXERCISE E

Earth: landslide, earthquake, avalanche
Wind: hurricane, sandstorm, typhoon, blizzard, tornado, whirlwind, gale
Fire: volcano, forest fire
Water: flood, tidal wave, drought

1 volcano   2 tornado   3 avalanche   4 tidal wave

EXERCISE F

a I could speak, I even managed to pass, I couldn't understand, I could say, I managed to have

b Have you managed to get hold of, couldn't get through, Did you manage to, couldn't hear, managed to explain, could see

EXERCISE G

a 7, b 5, c 9, d 4, e 6, f 2, g 3, h 8, i 10, j 1.
1 I'm afraid that your car can't be repaired.
2 Your cheque book might have been handed in at the bank.
3 The burglars must have been disturbed – they didn't take the video.
4 The letter won't arrive on time. It should have been posted earlier.
5 He might be arrested if he tries to leave the country.

EXERCISE H

1 sent   2 giving   3 get   4 held   5 called

EXERCISE I

1 turned into   2 cut off   3 do without
4 broke down   5 clear up/away

EXERCISE J

1 are being carried out, is being diverted, is being widened, is causing, are being advised

2 have swept, have been burned, have been destroyed, has been killed, have been injured, have been warned, have cancelled, have been arranged

3 had been set off, had taken, had stolen, had broken, had been, had been taken

4 was being transferred, was trying, was being held, was being questioned, was being searched, were staying, were helping

5 need, provide, are answered, go, are not given, are supported, is needed

6 lost, fell, was torn off, was taken, worked, sewed, was said

THE WOMAN WITHOUT A NAME

FOCUS ONE SB 137 – 138

■ PICTURE DISCUSSION
■ READING
■ SPEAKING
■ LANGUAGE STUDY
□ *in case* and *if* ▷ GS 6.6

PICTURE DISCUSSION

In pairs, students look at the two pictures and write down 5 sentences about things which they notice are different about the pictures, e.g.
The furnishings in the first picture look more comfortable and luxurious than those in the other picture.

The pairs then compare their sentences with those of another pair of students, and see if they had any which were the same.
Students should then in pairs discuss who they think might go to the two places, what type of food they could get and which kinds of eating places they themselves prefer and why. They can mention actual restaurants and tell their partner what they are like and how to get there.

READING

Ask one student to read aloud about 8 lines of the passage (other students' books closed) then ask students to say what they think is going to happen next in the story. Repeat the process asking another student to read the following 8 lines and so on.

Now in groups of 3–4 ask students to decide which answer in Nos. 1–5 is correct.

▶ Answers
   1 D   2 C   3 B   4 C   5 A

LANGUAGE STUDY

EXERCISE A

▶ Answers
   1 b)   2 a)   3 c)   4 d)

EXERCISE B

▶ Answers
   1 Put your raincoat on in case it rains.
   2 I am building a bomb shelter in case there is a war.
   3 In America a lot of people carry guns in case someone tries to rob them.
   4 Let me say goodbye now in case I don't see you again.
   5 Don't talk so loud in case the boss is listening.
   6 Get to the restaurant early in case it's crowded.
   7 Remind me again in case I forget.
   8 You'd better leave by the side door in case someone is watching.

FOCUS TWO SB 139 – 140

■ PICTURE DISCUSSION
■ SPEAKING
■ LISTENING
■ VOCABULARY
□ Phrasal verbs with *make*
□ *careful* or *careless*?
■ LANGUAGE STUDY
□ *if* or *whether*? ▷ GS 6.6
□ *a, an* or *some*? ▷ GS 3.3

PICTURE DISCUSSION

Ask students to write 10 words describing the two pictures (5 per picture). The words can be about the appearance of the woman, or her expression, or the place she seems to be in.

Now in pairs or threes students should ask and answer Nos. 1–3 using the words they have written if possible. The following expressions may help them:

Comparing and Speculating
She appears to be much (happier) in the (first) picture.
She seems/looks (richer) in the (second) picture.

SPEAKING

Allow 3–4 minutes for students, in groups of 2–3, to discuss answers to Nos. 1–5. Invite different members of each group to tell the rest of the class about their **own** answers.

LISTENING 📼

EXERCISE A

Tapescript

A man and a woman are sitting in an expensive restaurant in Beverly Hills, not far from Hollywood. They are looking at a photograph of two people, which the woman has brought with her.

A: You know who *she* is, I suppose.
B: Of course. And the man? Who's he?
A: Carl Earlham. Ever heard of him?
B: No, I'm afraid not.
A: He was one of her favourite photographers. He was her friend . . . he spent a lot of time with her just before she died, in '62.
B: Where is he now? What's he doing?
A: He's dead. He died last year. I knew him well. Very well. Do you understand?
B: I think so.
A: Well? Are you interested?
B: In what?
A: In using the information in the book you're writing about her, of course. You *are* doing some research into her death, aren't you?
B: Yes, but . . . I'm not sure. How did you know I was writing such a book?
A: Someone told me.
B: Who?
A: Just a friend. I have a lot of friends.
B: What's the name of your friend?
A: That doesn't matter! The only thing that matters is whether you want the information or not.
B: What information?
A: It's all in the letters.
B: Letters? What are you talking about?
A: She wrote Earlham several letters before she died. She told him all about things like her relationship with someone very . . .
B: Look. A lot of people say they've got letters like that. And just about everyone in Hollywood can tell stories about what happened just before she died.
A: What I've got isn't a story. I'm not making it up! It's the truth. In her own handwriting. I can prove she wrote the letters. And what's in them is dynamite. Pure dynamite.
B: Are you sure? It isn't exactly news any more, is it? It happened more than 25 years ago.
A: It's still dynamite.
B: How did you get hold of these letters?
A: I told you. I was Earlham's friend. We were . . . very close. He gave me the letters before he died. Well? Do you want to see the letters?
B: That depends.
A: On what?
B: On what you want in return.
A: Money, of course.
B: I thought so. How much?
A: $100,000.
B: That's a lot of money.
A: Yes, and it's worth it! Every penny. Look, I hope you understand what I'm offering you. Letters. *Her* letters. Some of which she wrote only a few days before she died.

B: Yes.
A: Yes? Yes, what?
B: Yes, I understand.
A: Well, you'd better decide whether you want them or not. And you'd better decide quickly! Because if you don't want them, I know a lot of other people who will! And believe me! $100,000 is nothing to pay. Not for these letters. Marilyn's letters! Marilyn Munroe's letters!

▶ Answers

1 True	4 False	7 True
2 True	5 True	8 False
3 False	6 True	

EXERCISE B

▶ Possible answers
1 She is trying to sell him some letters.
2 Either he is going to buy the letters or she is going to try and sell the letters to someone else.

VOCABULARY

Phrasal verbs with *make*

Ask students to look at the illustrations and explain what they can see using a verb with *make*. Point out the two meanings of *make up*, i.e. 'become friends again' and '(use) cosmetics'.

EXERCISE A

Ask students to explain the meanings of *make out* and *make for*. In pairs, ask them to complete Nos. 1–6 with the appropriate word.

▶ Answers

1 up	3 for	5 -up
2 out	4 out	6 up

EXERCISE B

1 make out	4 make up
2 make out	5 make up
3 make-up	6 make for

'make-up' in 3 is a noun from a phrasal verb

***careful* or *careless*?**

EXERCISE C

Explain that *-ful* at the end of certain words (as a suffix) can mean 'with' and that *-less* means 'without'.

Ask students to complete Nos. 1–10 with a suitable word.

▶ Answers

1 careless	5 endless	8 useful
2 helpful	6 painless	9 harmless
3 useless	7 restless	10 painful
4 restful		

LANGUAGE STUDY

if or *whether?*

Explain that both *if* and *whether* can mean 'on the condition that' but *whether* is often used with *or not* at the end of the clause it introduces, or before an infinitive, e.g.
*I don't know **whether to buy** the car **or not**.*

EXERCISE A

► Answers

1 if/whether   4 whether
2 whether   5 whether
3 if/whether   6 if

a, an or *some*

EXERCISE B

► Answers

1 some	5 an	8 some
2 some	6 some	9 a
3 a	7 some	10 some
4 some		

FOCUS THREE   SB 141–142

- ■ USE OF ENGLISH
- ■ LISTENING
- ■ VOCABULARY
- ■ LANGUAGE STUDY
  □ *had better (not)*

USE OF ENGLISH

Ask students to work on this exercise in pairs.
Tell them to make a list of as many words as possible which they think might fill the gaps, then choose the most likely word but be prepared to justify why they think their other answers might have been correct.

► Answers

1 whether	7 worth
2 sip/drink	8 depended
3 prove	9 would
4 getting/becoming	10 waited
5 fear/suspicion/	11 condition
anxiety	12 cash
6 what/everything	13 have

14 bites	18 tell
15 touch/contact	19 had
16 made	20 waving/holding/
17 After/When	dropping

LISTENING   📼

Tapescript

A: Well, have you made up your mind?
B: Yes, I have.
A: Well?
B: You'll have the $10,000 in advance.
A: In cash. I don't want cheques or anything like that.
B: That can be arranged.
A: There's one more condition. Are you listening?
B: Go on.
A: You can't keep the letters. Not until you've paid the rest of the $100,000.
B: But that's impossible. How can the handwriting expert examine the letters unless we keep them?
A: I'll bring them to your hotel the day after tomorrow. Make sure your expert is there . . . in your room . . . you'll have an hour to examine them. And I'll be in the room with both of you all the time!
B: That isn't long enough to prove they're really her letters.
A: Yes, it is! Your expert can bring copies of Monroe's handwriting with him. If he can't decide in an hour, he isn't an expert.
B: I . . . I don't know . . . how c . . .
A: That's my offer. Take it or leave it! Decide now. Well?
B: All right.
A: Good.
B: But I have a condition, too.
A: What?
B: I need at least two hours to make sure I can find a handwriting expert who's willing to do the tests the day after tomorrow.
A: Oh no!
B: Oh, yes! That's *my* condition. Now *you* can take it or leave it! And you'd better make up your mind *now*.
A: All right. I'll phone back in exactly two hours!

► Suggested answers

1 The journalist means he will pay her in cash.
2 She will bring the letters to his hotel room for examination by a handwriting expert but she will remain in the room.
3 To confirm that he has found a handwriting expert willing to do the tests the day after tomorrow.

VOCABULARY

Mime the words which appear in the students' books and see if students can tell you how to express these words in English, i.e. *bite, sip, chew, gulp, lick, swallow.*

EXERCISE A

► Answers

1 lick	3 chew	5 sip
2 bite	4 gulp	6 swallow

Read out the words in a jumbled order and ask different students to mime what the word means.

EXERCISE B

▶ Answers

1 chew	4 licked
2 swallowed	5 bite
3 sip	6 gulp . . . chewing

The spy probably died. 'Chew' and 'chewing' (infinitive and gerund).

LANGUAGE STUDY

had better (not)

EXERCISE A

▶ Answers

    1 b) and c)   2 a)

EXERCISE B

▶ Answers

1 see/consult	3 drink
2 take	4 be/arrive

The verbs are all in the infinitive without *to*.

EXERCISE C

▶ Suggested answers

1 You had ('d) better put something warm on.
2 You'd (had) better drink your coffee quickly/ finish your coffee.
3 You had ('d) better not go down there. It might be dangerous!
4 You'd (had) better not drink that water. It might be polluted.

FOCUS FOUR   SB 143

- ■ COMPOSITION (describing a process)
- □ The passive ▷ GS 8.2

COMPOSITION

EXERCISE A

▶ Answers

The correct order is 9, 2, 6, 8, 5, 1, 7, 4, 10, 3

The passive

EXERCISE B

▶ Answers

1 After being heated the mixture is left to cool.
2 Then the yeast is mixed with some warm water and added to the beer.
3 After being poured into a container the beer is left to ferment.
4 Before being put into sterilized bottles the beer is tested.
5 Some sugar is added to the bottles.
6 The beer is put in a cool place and left for several weeks before drinking.

EXERCISE C

Conduct a class brainstorming session to decide on the different processes necessary to send a letter. Write all the points mentioned on the board. Divide the class into 5 or 6 groups and ask each group to arrange the points in the correct order for a composition.

Now ask each student to write a composition individually. Allow 20–30 minutes. Collect in the finished compositions to be marked at home and ask students to choose one of the alternatives in No. 2 to write a timed composition exercise for homework. Tell students to spend no longer than 40 minutes on their composition.

FOCUS FIVE   SB 144

- ■ REVISION AND EXTENSION
- ■ LISTENING TEST 9

REVISION AND EXTENSION

▶ Answers

1 D	6 B	11 A	16 A
2 A	7 A	12 A	17 C
3 C	8 D	13 C	18 B
4 D	9 A	14 B	19 B
5 D	10 D	15 B	20 B

LISTENING TEST 9

Tapescript

A: Could you tell us a little bit about stencilling, because I know that's one of the techniques that you use.
B: Well, with stencilling you can just decorate a small part of a room if you want, unlike some of the other techniques we were talking about. Essentially, stencilling involves cutting out a shape on a

piece of paper, for example, the shape of a rose; and then you put the paper on the wall and paint over the shapes you've cut out, so that when you take the paper away, you are left with the shape you want on the wall.

A: What kind of designs work best?

B: Well, that depends on the house you're working in, but on the whole, simple, clear designs are the most effective. Stencils with patterns of leaves or flowers work very well, I find. You can, of course, use more than one colour – for example, if you were doing the stencil of the rose that I mentioned, you would have one stencil of the leaves – only the leaves – and paint that onto the wall, and another stencil of the flower, which you would paint on afterwards.

A: Um, what kind of paint do you use?

B: I use special stencilling paints which you can buy in most good art shops these days, and they come in a nice wide range of colours, but if you can't get hold of them, then just ordinary cans of spray paint will do. Obviously you have to be careful with spray paint not to cover all the furniture with it. But it can give quite good results and, of course, it's much faster than using a paintbrush, so I sometimes use it myself if I've got large areas to cover. The one thing that I don't like about it is that you can't really control the colours as well as you can with a paintbrush.

A: Um, what are the advantages of stencilling over other techniques?

B: The nearest other technique is using wallpaper really, and the problem there is that you're limited to what you can find in the shops. With a stencil you can choose almost any pattern you like and any colour. One of the nice things is that with a stencil, you can make a pattern to match the other furniture or decoration in a room. I was working in a hotel in Charlbury the other day and I noticed a really nice pattern in the carpet; so I made a stencil of the pattern and used it in one of the rooms and it looked very good.

A: We've talked about stencilling walls, but is there anything else you can use stencils on?

B: Oh, yes, absolutely. You can use stencils on furniture – er, wooden mainly, tables and chairs, and of course on fabrics like cotton and silk. Stencilling fabrics can be very satisfying and very exciting. In the home you can make your own cushions or curtains or tablecloths, for example. If you like you can even use stencils to make patterns and designs on clothes – I've seen some lovely jackets and dresses made using stencils. You do need to use special fabric paint though, which is different from what you use for the walls, because your fabrics need to be washable. In fact, fabrics tend to be best for beginners, because you can practise on a small piece of cloth. A lot of people are – quite understandably – a bit afraid of stencilling a piece of furniture or a wall in case something goes wrong, so fabrics are a good place to start.

▶ Answers

1 B   2 A   3 B   4 C

WORKBOOK KEY WB 79 – 82

UNIT 18

EXERCISE B

1 subtle
2 revenge
3 insult
4 impulsive

5 pushy
6 insincere
7 sympathetic

a outgoing: reserved
b thinker: doer
c bright: dull
d lively: quiet

e serious: light
f colourful: pastel
g seldom: often

EXERCISE C

1 Tell me again now in case I forget.
2 We can stay at the hotel if they have a room.
3 We can go to the museum if we have time.
4 I'll take some extra money in case we need it tomorrow.
5 I'm going to hide the silver objects in case someone steals them.
6 I'll phone you if I find time.
7 We'll book in advance in case the restaurant is full.
8 She's going to university if she passes the final school exam.

EXERCISE D

1 careful	2 helpful	3 careless	4 harmful
5 endless	6 restless	7 useful	8 hopeful
9 painless	10 harmless		

EXERCISE E

(sample answers)

1 You'd better not have anything else to eat.
2 You'd better pay attention/You'd better not fall asleep.
3 You'd better not tell my parents.
4 You'd better have a rest.
5 You'd better work/study hard/You'd better revise.
6 You'd better not forget your passport/You'd better remember your passport.
7 You'd better slow down.
8 You'd better find a service station.
9 You'd better have/get a haircut.
10 You'd better hurry up.

EXERCISE F

1 sing	2 whisper	3 scream	4 say
5 shout	6 speak	7 gossip	8 tell

1 shout	2 sing	3 gossiping	4 whisper
5 screamed	6 speak	7 told	8 said

EXERCISE G

1 march	2 hop	3 run	4 step
5 climb	6 stroll	7 skip	8 leap

1 run	2 marched	3 hopping	4 skip
5 stepped	6 climb	7 stroll	8 lept

EXERCISE H

some advice	an office
some homework	an exercise
some furniture	a sofa
some work	some baggage
an assistant	some news
some help	a newspaper
some information	a job
a handbag	

19 LEAVING HOME

FOCUS ONE   SB 145 – 146

- ■ PICTURE DISCUSSION
- ■ READING
- ■ VOCABULARY
- ☐ Phrasal verbs (*stand*)
- ■ LANGUAGE STUDY
- ☐ Cause and result in conditional sentences
  ▷ GS 4.3

PICTURE DISCUSSION

Tell students, in pairs, to ask and answer Nos. 1–5. Put a list of suggestions for Nos. 3 and 4 on the board.

Now ask students (in the same pairs) to write a TV script for one of the pictures. Tell them to make it 2–3 minutes long (or suggest a number of lines, e.g. 15–20) and they should be prepared to read/act it out for the other students.

Topics for further discussion

1 What kind of things do people say in your country when they are leaving each other, perhaps for a long time?
2 Are real life happenings anything like events which we see in TV plays or films?
3 Why are TV 'soap operas' like *Dallas* and *Dynasty* so popular?

READING

Read out the last three lines of the passage aloud and ask students to tell you what they think will come before these lines in the passage.

Now allow students 3–4 minutes to skim read the passage and see if their ideas were correct or not.

EXERCISE A

In groups of 3–4 ask students to discuss Nos. 1–6 then join with another group to compare their answers and suggestions.

▶ Suggested answers
  1 'What would you say if I told you I was thinking of going to live in London?'
  2 (as passage)

3 The writer had been offered a job in the head office in London of the bank he was working for and he had accepted it.
4 Hurt/angry/upset/sad/disappointed.
5 He was probably tired of the small village he had lived in all his life and wanted to see something of the world.
6 He probably took the job and went to live in London.

VOCABULARY

Phrasal verbs

EXERCISE A

▶ Answers
  a) stand by   c) stand up to
  b) stand for   d) stand for
  1 c)   2 b)   3 a)   4 d)

EXERCISE B

▶ Answers
  1 for   2 by   3 for   4 up to

LANGUAGE STUDY

Cause and result in conditional sentences

EXERCISE A

▶ Answers
  a) 1st part – result, 2nd part – cause
  b) 1st part – cause, 2nd part – result
  c) 1st part – result, 2nd part – cause
  d) 1st part – result, 2nd part – cause
  The difference is:
  a) and c) express cause with *because*
  b) and d) express cause with *if*

EXERCISE B

▶ Answers
  1 If Mary's father had let her meet boys she wouldn't have been shy with them.
  2 If Tom hadn't seemed so pleasant, she wouldn't have been attracted to him.
  3 If she hadn't been rich, Tom wouldn't have wanted to marry her.

4 If her father hadn't thought Tom was a prince, he wouldn't have liked him.

5 If Mary hadn't had so little experience of men, she wouldn't have believed his story.

6 If she hadn't thought he really loved her, she wouldn't have married him.

7 If he hadn't been so terrible to her, she wouldn't have shot him.

8 If her father hadn't been so foolish, all this wouldn't have happened.

FOCUS TWO   SB 147–148

- ■ USE OF ENGLISH
- ■ VOCABULARY
- □ *between* or *among*? ▷ GS 10.1, 10.3
- ■ LANGUAGE STUDY
- □ *It's time . . .*

USE OF ENGLISH

EXERCISE A

▶ Answers

1	hoping/wanting/ longing	10	apart
		11	in
2	looking/searching	12	tired
3	especially/ particularly	13	time
		14	reason
4	out	15	rest
5	test	16	member
6	latest	17	arrange
7	with/to	18	with
8	for	19	fill
9	country/field	20	off/away

VOCABULARY

EXERCISE A

▶ Answers

1	scientific	6	chemist
2	romantic	7	loneliness
3	artistic	8	happily
4	specialist	9	similarities
5	pianist	10	activities

between or *among*?

EXERCISE B

▶ Answers

1	between	4	between	7	among
2	among	5	between	8	between
3	Among	6	Among		

between = 2 people, things or points
among = more than 2 people, things or points

LANGUAGE STUDY

It's time . . .

EXERCISE A

▶ Answers

b) means that the speaker has let time go by without doing anything about the problem.

d) means 'You've been lying in bed too long.'

EXERCISE B

▶ Answers

1 It's time you found a job.
2 It's time I got out of bed.
3 It's time we had a talk about this problem.
4 It's time you got married.
5 It's time I had a holiday.
6 It's time we got down to work.
7 It's time you bought some new clothes.
8 It's time the government did something about this problem.

EXERCISE C

▶ Answers

1 It's time you learned to tie your shoelaces.
2 It's time you took/had a bath.
3 It's time I paid those bills.
4 It's time I had the brakes (on the car) repaired.

FOCUS THREE   SB 149–150

- ■ USE OF ENGLISH
- □ Paragraph completion
- ■ LISTENING 1
- ■ VOCABULARY
- □ Prefixes
- ■ LISTENING 2

USE OF ENGLISH

Paragraph completion

In groups of 5–6 ask students to read carefully the details about Alice, then read through the three potential partners one by one and decide verbally which would suit her best, giving reasons for their answers.

Now ask students individually to complete the paragraphs as suggested in their books.

▶ Sample answers

1 I think the best partner for Alice would be Donald because he likes films, classical music and good food. She would probably get on well with him because he does not smoke much and is in no hurry to start a family. He would get on well with her because he is looking for an independent partner who will also be a good friend.

2 In some ways, Alice and Sebastian would be suited to each other because he doesn't smoke and he is looking for an 'intelligent woman'. However, they have little else in common. For example he does not like spending money on the cinema and meals. He prefers open air activities and he wants to have children as soon as possible.

3 I don't think Bernie and Alice would get on very well because they have absolutely nothing in common at all. He likes basic, boring food. He watches cowboy films and football, which are not very intellectual interests! He probably chain-smokes and does not like women to talk too much, so this relationship would be a disaster.

LISTENING 1

EXERCISE A

Tapescript

A: I've been living in London now for three years, and I still don't think I've got used to it. Life is . . . well . . . very impersonal here . . . people in the South of England are rather unfriendly compared with people in the North. I come from a rather small town in Lancashire called Ormskirk . . . it's close to both Liverpool and Manchester. So . . . uh . . . perhaps I'm just not the sort of person to live in a place like London. For one thing, I find it's very difficult to talk to people here about anything. They're all so . . . indifferent. Perhaps it's because they get so tired just travelling to and from work.

In Ormskirk I had plenty of friends. Here in London I have very few friends . . . in fact, I don't think I have any. Acquaintances. That's what they are. Acquaintances. I know a lot of people but I haven't any friends. Perhaps it's my fault. Or perhaps it's just the place.

B: I was born in a small village in the West of Ireland near Cork and personally, I couldn't wait to get out of it. I came here when I was eighteen. I actually stole the money to come here, although I *have* paid it back since.

People say village life is so much better than life in a city like London . . . half the people I know here in London say they would prefer to live in a village somewhere, but I think they have a very unrealistic idea of what life in a village is really like. In most villages, people gossip about each other all the time. They've nothing else to talk about. They've nothing else to do! It's impossible to keep anything private for long. Your life is everybody else's property.

Now, I don't like to say anything very nice about the English, but I must admit they're more tolerant than the people back home. People in small villages who've lived there all their lives are very intolerant, you know. They think everybody should be the same as they are. Here in England . . . well, here in London, at least, people really don't care what you do, what you wear or how you behave as long as you don't actually disturb them. Now, I don't know if that's tolerance or indifference. And I don't really care. But I think I've made a lot of friends here . . . well, many of them are Irish, like myself . . . but I have some English friends. It isn't difficult to make friends in a place like this . . . as long as you're prepared to make contact . . . to talk to people. It's no good just sitting in your room and waiting for people to come to you. You've got to go out to them. And if you don't, it's not their fault you haven't any friends. It's yours!

▶ Answers

1 B   2 D   3 C   4 D

EXERCISE C

In pairs, ask students to interview each other using the questions in their books and make notes about each other to report back to the rest of the class.

VOCABULARY

Prefixes

EXERCISE A

▶ Answers

Negative prefixes for words in column B:
im-, un-, dis-, un-, in-, ir-

EXERCISE B

▶ Answers

1 incapable	6 irregular
2 inaccurate	7 disloyal
3 impossible	8 disorderly
4 impolite	9 unlucky
5 irresistible	10 unhappy

11 insensitive
12 unreasonable
13 unwilling
14 displeased

15 unpleasant
16 inconvenient
17 incorrect
18 uncertain

LISTENING 2 📼

Ask students to read through the table before listening to the passage. As you play the tape tell them to fill in as many details as possible.

Tapescript

R = Reporter **D** = Director

R: How many members have you actually got?
D: In round numbers, 42,000.
R: What's the average age of a typical member?
D: We don't think in terms of a typical average age. However, we do divide our members into three age-groups . . . and the biggest of these is the group between 21 and 25 . . . sixty per cent of our members fall into that group . . . the next largest group is between 26 and 29 . . . twenty-eight per cent of our members belong to this group . . . and the smallest group is the youngest . . . between 17 and 20, and only twelve per cent of our members fall into this category.
R: All your members have to pay an entry or initial fee, is that right?
D: Yes. It costs £50 to join.
R: And what happens then?
D: We give them a personality test and our computer works out a list of potential partners. The new member can choose up to three people from each list and we arrange a meeting.
R: Does that cost anything?
D: Well, there is a charge of £10 for each list, but no charge for the meetings we arrange.
R: Do you know how many of your members are actually satisfied with the service you provide?
D: Yes. By far the majority are satisfied. Only an insignificant percentage are not.
R: Well, can you give me exact figures? Or better, what percentage of your members say they are satisfied?
D: Almost eighty per cent.
R: Almost?
D: Yes. To be exact, seventy-nine and a half per cent.
R: Yes. But doesn't that leave twenty per cent who are dissatisfied? And can you really say that twenty per cent is an insignificant percentage?
D: No.
R: No? So you adm . . .
D: Just a moment, please. I answered 'no' to your first question. Not the second.
R: Which . . . which question was that?
D: No, it doesn't leave twenty per cent who are dissatisfied. It leaves in fact only five per cent. I wish it were lower than that. But I still don't think five per cent is significant.
R: Well, what about the other fifteen per cent? I mean, what happened to them?
D: I was coming to that. Fifteen per cent of our members said they didn't know if they were satisfied or dissatisfied with the service we provided . . . they said they needed more time to decide.

▶ Answers

1	Total number of members	42,000
2	Percentage between 17 and 20	12%
3	Percentage between 21 and 25	60%
4	Percentage above 25	28%
5	Initial membership fee	£50
6	Cost for each 'list of potential partners'	£10
7	Percentage of members who say they are satisfied with the service provided	79½%
8	Percentage who say they are dissatisfied	5%
9	Percentage of 'Don't know's'	15%

FOCUS FOUR   SB 151

■ COMPOSITION (letter and narrative)

COMPOSITION

Point out to students that in the exam they may be asked to write a composition which is a combination of two types – for example, to write a letter telling a story as well as asking for something. This Focus contains an example of this type of composition.

EXERCISE A

▶ Suggested answers

   1 Introduction – setting the scene
   2 Detailed explanation
   3 Reason for writing

EXERCISE B

▶ Answers

1 c)	3 a)	5 d)	7 b)	9 b)
2 b)	4 a)	6 c)	8 d)	10 a)

EXERCISE C

In pairs, ask students to write a joint composition for No. 1. Allow 30–40 minutes for this. Set No. 2 to be written individually for homework. Remind students to follow the suggestions carefully when they write their compositions.

FOCUS FIVE   SB 152

■ REVISION AND EXTENSION
☐ *if, unless, when* or *in case*? ▷ GS 6.6
☐ Conditional 3
☐ Conditionals 1, 2 and 3 ▷ GS 4
☐ Mixed tense forms

REVISION AND EXTENSION

if, unless, when or *in case*?

EXERCISE A

▶ Answers

1 when	4 if	7 when
2 unless	5 unless	8 Unless
3 in case	6 If	

Conditional 3

EXERCISE B

In pairs ask students to read the conversation to each other and fill in the correct form of the verb in brackets.

▶ Answers

had been able, would have passed,
had known, could have borrowed,
would have been, had not wanted,
had not stopped, might have run,
had done, would have failed,
would you do/would you have done, were driving/
had been driving, happened/had happened,
would do/would have done,
should have done, had been,
would have done,would not have changed,
had made

EXERCISE C

▶ Answers

1 If he hadn't written a best-selling novel, he wouldn't have earned a lot of money.
2 If Anna hadn't worked in a language school, she wouldn't have met Kostas.
3 If he hadn't accepted the job, he wouldn't have earned a lot of money.
4 If you hadn't been careless, you wouldn't have had an accident.
5 If the goalkeeper hadn't saved the penalty, we wouldn't have won the match.

Conditionals 1, 2 and 3

EXERCISE D

▶ Suggested answers (there are many other possibilities)

1 + Present tense, e.g. I will be very pleased if you *come* to Anne's wedding.
2 + Past tense, e.g. I would never hurt an animal unless it *bit* me.
3 + Perfect conditional, e.g. If I had been born in England, I *wouldn't have needed* to learn English.
4 + Present conditional, e.g. Unless I was very angry, I *would never hit* anybody.
5 + Future tense, e.g. If I pass the exam, we'*ll have* a party.
6 + Perfect conditional, e.g. If I had started playing a musical instrument when I was four, I *would have been* a good player by now.
7 + Present conditional, e.g. If I were five years younger, I *would apply* for that job.
8 + Present tense, e.g. You can't get a good job unless you *are prepared* to go out looking for one.

Mixed tense forms

EXERCISE E

▶ Answers

1 went/ were going	3 to get	6 would get
	4 had been	7 had been
2 had not come	5 started	8 went

WORKBOOK KEY WB 83 – 86

UNIT 19

EXERCISE A

1 B   2 C   3 D   4 C   5 A

EXERCISE B

1 If I hadn't had a baby, I wouldn't have given up my job.
2 If my husband hadn't lost his job, we wouldn't have come back to England.
3 If my husband hadn't found another job, we wouldn't have stayed in England.
4 If I hadn't had another baby, I wouldn't have given up my job.
5 If we hadn't saved some money, we wouldn't have been able to buy a house.

6 If we hadn't bought a large four-bedroom house, we
  wouldn't have found it difficult to make ends meet.
7 If we hadn't worked hard for many years, we
  wouldn't have finished paying for the house.
8 If we hadn't won the football pools, our problems
  wouldn't have disappeared.

EXERCISE C

1 a chemist
2 a pianist
3 a teacher
4 a nurse
5 a lawyer/solicitor
6 a musician
7 an astronaut
8 a cook/chef
9 an architect
10 a pilot

EXERCISE E

1 It's time you did your homework.
2 It's time he found a job.
3 It's time they settled down and had a family.
4 It's time we went home.
5 It's time I had a break.
6 It's time they changed their policy.
7 It's time you took on new staff.
8 It's time we bought a new TV.

EXERCISE F

1 don't get
2 'll/will/shall go
3 have
4 'll/will/shall go
5 had not gone
6 would have spent
7 had
8 would you do
9 had
10 would travel
11 hadn't given
12 would/could never have caught
13 see
14 tell

EXERCISE G

1 gets by
2 gets round to (going)
3 standing by
4 get out of
5 stand for
6 stand up to
7 get over
8 stand for
9 stand in for
10 get up to

20
THE LOST CIVILIZATION

FOCUS ONE   SB 153 – 154

- ■ PICTURE DISCUSSION
- ■ READING
- ■ VOCABULARY
- ■ LANGUAGE STUDY
- □ Revision transformations 1

PICTURE DISCUSSION

Ask students to study the picture without looking at the questions in their books and suggest what it could be/mean and where it could/might come from.

In groups of 3–4 ask students to discuss the explanation and questions in their books, taking it in turn to ask each other the questions.

READING

Divide the class into 3 groups. Ask each group to read and take notes on one of the 3 paragraphs to be able to explain to the rest of the class, using only their notes, what their paragraph was about. Invite one student from each group to explain in chronological order what the paragraph said.

Now ask students in pairs to discuss which answer seems correct in Nos. 1–4.

▶ Answers
    1 D   2 A   3 D   4 B

VOCABULARY

false or **artificial**?

1 desert	4 plain	7 develop
2 crowded	5 general	8 ordinary
3 inhabit	6 wood	

LANGUAGE STUDY

Revision transformations

▶ Answers
1 What an extraordinary story this is!
2 Stephens was looking forward to seeing the ruins.
3 He was astonished by what he saw.
4 He said he had never seen anything so beautiful.
5 He wondered where all the people had gone.
6 Despite his illness/the fact that he was ill, he visited other ruins.
7 The other cities were difficult to reach.
8 Stephens and Catherwood were almost killed by two robbers.
9 Stephens told Catherwood not to be afraid.
10 They succeeded in returning to New York nine months later.
11 It took Stephens three months to write his book.
12 People found it very interesting.
13 If Catherwood's pictures had not been so good, it would not have been so successful.
14 It was such an interesting book that people could not put it down.
15 It has been a long time since I read it.

FOCUS TWO   SB 155 – 156

- ■ LISTENING 1
- ■ USE OF ENGLISH
- ■ LISTENING 2
- ■ VOCABULARY
- □ Review of phrasal verbs 1

LISTENING 1   ▣

Give students about 2 minutes to study the diagram and the places mentioned below it in their books. Ask them to predict which place will be which, and why.

Now ask them to read through what they are going to hear. Play the tape twice with a short pause in between plays and ask students to number the places in the correct positions on their diagrams.

Tapescript

G = Guide

G: Ladies and gentlemen, Chichen Itza is one of the most famous Mayan cities. But I should warn you that the stories behind the beautiful buildings we are about to visit can be frightening . . . even . . . uh . . . rather horrifying.

And here we are now in front of the Temple of Kukulcan . . . the god of the Mayas. The building at the top with the flat roof is the temple itself and, as you can see, it's quite a climb to the top. In fact, if you count the steps as we climb them you will find that there are exactly 364 steps . . . and if you count the roof, it comes to 365, the same number as the days in the year. The Mayas were very interested in astronomy, you see. Their religion was based on it, and every year they would sacrifice children to the gods in this very temple . . . where you can see the carving of their god, Kukulcan, the snake with feathers.

And now here we are at the top of the pyramid, and the building you can see behind us and to your right is the Observatory; can you see it over there, sir? With the round building on the top? Scientists believe that the Mayas made a number of important discoveries and observations of the stars in the Observatory. They knew a great deal about the planets. For instance, they knew that the earth was round as well as how long the years were on Mars and Venus.

This wonderful building is known as 'The Temple of the Warriors'; it was probably built around 1100 AD, later than the other buildings. It is also known as 'The Thousand Columns', because of all the columns you can see around you. This is where the soldiers of the Mayas would pray before going into battle. It is believed, by the way, that the Mayas went to war mainly in order to capture prisoners from other tribes. These prisoners were sacrificed to the gods. Perhaps they spent their last days here, among the thousand columns, before the . . . uh . . . day of the sacrifice came.

And now we're standing by the 'Well of Sacrifice' . . . where more sacrifices used to take place. The Mayas used to throw the bodies of their victims into the black water of the well in order to make Chac, their rain god, happy. The water was thought to be bottomless. Perhaps you can imagine, ladies and gentlemen, the terrible screams of the victims just before they were sacrificed . . . right here, where we are standing now.

And this is known as the 'Ball Court' . . . it was the scene of a very strange game. The purpose of the game was to throw a hard rubber ball through one of the rings you can see in the middle of the court. It seems that the captain and sometimes the players of the losing team were beheaded after the end of a game. Perhaps we would win the next World Cup if we started doing the same thing to the captain and players of our national football teams.

► Answers

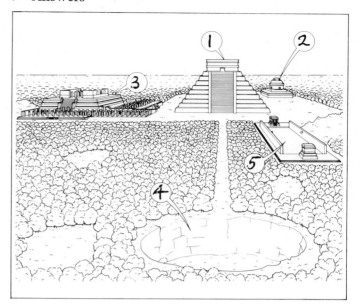

USE OF ENGLISH

► Suggested answers

1 out	11 until/till
2 dirty/polluted	12 enough
3 decided/started/had	13 soon
4 about/going	14 bottom
5 spirit/soul/ghost	15 Among
6 known	16 by
7 take	17 proof/evidence
8 were/was	18 have
9 ignoring/despite	19 within
10 on	20 in

LISTENING 2

Give students about 2 minutes to read through the instructions and questions in their books. Play the tape twice and compare answers after the second playing.

Tapescript

The Ball Court at Chichen Itza is the most splendid of its kind anywhere in the world. The two parallel walls that form its sides are 82.6 metres in length and have a height of 8.2 metres. They are exactly 30 metres apart.

These ball courts are found all over the area once inhabited by the Mayas. If you look carefully at the two parallel walls you will notice two iron rings in the centre and at the top of each wall. The game was played with a rubber ball, and the object was to throw the ball through the ring.

It is not known exactly how many players were used by each team, but it is believed that the number varied between nine and twelve. It seems to have been a very popular sport, although at times it does not really seem to have been a 'sport' in our sense of the word, at all. There is evidence that sometimes the members of the losing team were killed as soon as the game ended. Their heads were then placed on top of one of the walls and left there for weeks and even months.

However, the game was not always this serious. Sometimes all that was lost was money, or rather coffee beans which were often used at that time in place of money. It is said that sometimes the winning team was given not only this reward but the clothes of the losing team and of the spectators, as well.

▶ Answers

1 5
2 82.6 metres long
3 8.2 metres high
4 The walls are exactly 30 metres apart.
5 A game was played with a rubber ball and you had to throw the ball through an iron ring. There were 9–12 players.
6 Sometimes the members of the losing team were killed when the game ended and their heads were put on top of the wall and left there.
7 Coffee beans were often exchanged as money and could be won as a prize for this game.

VOCABULARY

EXERCISE A

Give students 3–4 minutes to complete the exercise on their own then ask them to explain what part of speech they made with the words in capitals.

▶ Answers

1 length (noun)	8 distance (noun)
2 height (noun)	9 proof (noun)
3 depth (noun)	10 strength (noun)
4 weight (noun)	11 weakness (noun)
5 width (noun)	12 warning (noun)
6 measurements (noun)	13 sharpness (noun)
7 calculations (noun)	14 frighten (verb)
	15 threatening (verb)

Review of phrasal verbs 1

EXERCISE B

▶ Answers

1 broke	5 through	10 keep/go
2 about	6 carry	11 up
3 switched/ turned/put	7 on	12 come
4 out	8 cut	13 to
	9 down	14 give

FOCUS THREE   SB 157–158

■ READING
■ LANGUAGE STUDY
☐ Revision transformations 2
■ VOCABULARY
☐ Review of phrasal verbs 2

READING

Tell students to read through the passage silently on their own and choose the best answer to Nos. 1–3. Allow 5–6 minutes, then ask students to compare answers with a partner.

▶ Answers

1 C   2 D   3 C

LANGUAGE STUDY

Revision transformations 2

▶ Answers

1 I didn't think Uxmal was as impressive as Chichen Itza.
2 I thought Uxmal was less impressive than Chichen Itza.
3 Roger wished he hadn't eaten that salad.
4 It can be dangerous to eat raw vegetables in hot countries.
5 He was too ill to go on the excursion.
6 Would you rather talk about something else?
7 You had better not eat raw fruit either.
8 Do you prefer fruit to vegetables?
9 I've never heard a sillier (such a silly) question.
10 This is the most beautiful place I have ever seen.
11 Neither have I.
12 I didn't like the town we visited yesterday.
13 The place we saw last week was almost as beautiful.
14 The people around here are said to believe in rain gods.
15 I can't help laughing at such a foolish idea.
16 I'm tired of revising.

VOCABULARY

Review of phrasal verbs 2

▶ Answers

1 go	8 put	15 out
2 take/write	9 down	16 do/manage
3 down	10 turned	17 down
4 take	11 away	18 see
5 down	12 get	19 like
6 get	13 up	20 call
7 up	14 get	

FOCUS FOUR   SB 159

■ COMPOSITION (narrative)
☐ An account of an event

COMPOSITION

EXERCISE A

▶ Answers

1 d)   2 a)   3 c)   4 b)

EXERCISE B

▶ Answers

1d) A few weeks ago I took the opportunity of going to the Computer Exhibition in Earls Court. It is one of the biggest exhibitions of electronic equipment in the country, so I thought it might be interesting.

2a) It was very well organized and laid out. Each of the different manufacturers had their own stand, with displays of their latest models. Representatives were there to answer questions about them and to give demonstrations.

3c) I was particularly interested in small business computers, and was able to talk to the sales people and try the machines out. However, there were also all kinds of new machines and gadgets that I found fascinating. For example, there were machines that can send copies of colour photographs by satellite, computers that can speak and understand English, and even home robots for domestic use.

4b) To sum up, the exhibition was well worth a visit, and I would recommend it to anyone interested in computers. For people who are seriously thinking about buying one, the exhibition should not be missed, as it gives the opportunity of comparing so many different models.

EXERCISE C

Allow students 40–50 minutes to prepare and write the composition in their books following the suggestions and advice given. Ask them to choose one of the visits for their composition in class, then choose another to write for homework.

FOCUS FIVE   SB 160

REVISION AND EXTENSION

Divide students into teams and tell them that the first team to finish the exercise correctly wins!

▶ Answers

1 C	6 A	11 B	16 D	21 B
2 C	7 D	12 A	17 B	22 A
3 D	8 A	13 A	18 D	23 D
4 C	9 B	14 D	19 C	24 C
5 D	10 D	15 A	20 B	25 D

EXERCISE B

▶ Answers

1 Take some cash in case the bank is shut.
2 He must have been seen leaving the building.
3 I wasn't allowed to stay in the country.
4 If she had concentrated more/harder, she wouldn't have made a lot of mistakes.
5 I haven't been to the dentist for ages.
6 The computer was not very expensive.
7 Not only could he speak French well, he could also write it.
8 He has been playing football for Manchester United for six months.
9 He asked me if I would open the window/to open the window.
10 He wouldn't have run away from home if he hadn't been unhappy.

WORKBOOK KEY WB 87 – 92

UNIT 20   WB 87 — 90

EXERCISE A

1 B   2 D   3 A   4 C

EXERCISE B

1 dissolved	2 carvings	3 eroded	4 ancient
5 ruins	6 spectacular	7 reduced	8 debts

EXERCISE C

1 funds	4 income	7 owe	10 borrow
2 lend	5 repay	8 debt	
3 interest	6 loan	9 earn	

EXERCISE D

1 It was such a successful musical (that) all the tickets were sold.
2 Graham told me to drop in and see him the next day.
3 Although he was ill, he carried on working.
4 It's quite a long time since I saw my aunt and uncle.
5 If Henry hadn't been wearing a seat belt, he would have been hurt.
6 I'll remind you about your appointment.
7 It took them just over three days to cross the Atlantic.
8 She is too young to play in the championship.
9 The car must have been stolen during the night.
10 If he hadn't failed his exams he would have become an accountant.

EXERCISE E

1 between	6 artificial	11 wash/clean
2 among	7 do	12 wash
3 between	8 make	13 remind
4 false	9 done	14 remember
5 false	10 cleaning	15 remember

EXERCISE F

1 brouGht	5 caLled
2 brOke	6 cUt
3 loOked	7 piCk
4 maDe	8 maKe

EXERCISE G

(Sample answer)

My first choice for an award would be the Water Well Group because the Salmon Foundation aims to help people and promote international understanding. People in the Third World would be helped, and because WWG is a voluntary organization, they could not go ahead without a great deal of financial help.

I would also consider giving the award to the Maya Site Group because they want to control the effects of pollution in Mexico, and their techniques may also help other countries in the world. The West has led the way in increasing pollution, so it ought to lead the way in reducing its effects.

I would not recommend giving the award to the Yoshiaki Corporation because the aim of their project is simply to make money for the company. The Corporation is already wealthy, and the Foundation wants all people, including the poor, to benefit from new ideas. Only the Yoshiaki Company would benefit from this.

PROGRESS TEST 4   WB 90 — 92

EXERCISE A

1 B	2 B	3 A	4 D	5 B
6 C	7 D	8 A	9 B	10 C

EXERCISE B

1 on/during	6 no	11 on	16 too
2 waking/being	7 us	12 made	17 even
3 was	8 for	13 of	18 was
4 out	9 had	14 to	19 have
5 must	10 used	15 up	20 had

EXERCISE C

1 The grass needs cutting as it's getting very long.
2 I think your cakes are good enough to sell.
3 Milan is too far from London to drive to in a day.
4 When they got back, the house had been broken into.
5 This year a lot of tourists have been put off by the high cost of living.
6 The escaped prisoner must have had a key to the prison gates.
7 It's best to have your insurance documents with you in case you have an accident.
8 You'd better not be late.
9 If I had realised (that) you were at home I would have phoned you.

EXERCISE D

1 do without	4 put up
2 putting off	5 put on
3 put . . . through	

EXERCISE E

1 engine	4 fireman
2 brigade	5 extinguishers/hoses
3 fireplace/hearth/grate	

REVISION TESTS

Each set of ten questions is based on a unit in the book, so if students find any set difficult, go back to that unit and revise it. There are two types of test: *multiple choice* and *sentence transformation*.

Multiple choice

Units 1, 3, 5, 7, 9, 12, 14, 16, 18. Pages 142–150.

Sentence transformation

Units 2, 4, 6, 8, 10, 11, 13, 15, 17, 19. Pages 151–155.

The Key to the Revision Tests appears in numerical order on pages 156–158.

You may make photocopies of these tests for classroom use (but please note that copyright law does not normally permit mutiple copying of published material).

UNIT 1

Choose the best answer.

1 It was a secret – you weren't supposed to .... anyone anything.

A tell   B say   C speak   D talk

2 Some people marry for .... and some for money.

A a love   B to love   C the love

D love

3 Look over there. Isn't that the woman .... son you played tennis with the other day?

A who   B which   C of which

D whose

4 I .... many people at the party, just a few old friends.

A met   B have met   C didn't meet

D haven't met

5 You've really got to stop .... the door unlocked, or one day someone will just walk in and steal things.

A having left   B to leave   C to have left

D leaving

6 She was upset because her watch, ... she had been given as a 21st birthday present, was lost in the fire.

A which   B whose   C which one

D what

7 I can't stand her, and I find that even .... her voice gets on my nerves.

A the sounds   B a sound of

C the sound of   D a sound from

8 It's hard to .... the difference between this forgery and the real painting.

A say   B speak   C tell   D talk

9 One of the main disadvantages .... the old machine was that it used up so much electricity.

A to   B of   C for   B from

10 The car stopped suddenly .... a child who ran across the road.

A avoiding   B to avoiding

C for to avoid   D to avoid

UNIT 3

Choose the best answer.

1 In her first year in business, my aunt came
.... more problems that she had expected.

A down on   B out of   C in to
D up against

2 The other day I came .... an advert for a job
you might be interested in.

A through   B over   C across
D around

3 I wouldn't go and see that film if I were you. It's
incredibly ....

A bored   B bores   C bore   D boring

4 Mrs Mason felt very .... when her two
children were rude to the shopkeeper.

A embarrassment   B embarrassing
C embarrassed   D embarrass

5 Martha Fox has been transferred from the Sales
Department to the .... Department.

A Personal   B Personality
C Persons   D Personnel

6 The new car factory will be the largest .... in
the area.

A employee   B employed
C employment   D employer

7 I would be grateful if you could give me some
.... about what to say in the interview.

A advice   B advising   C advises
D advisers

8 I haven't had a reply to that invitation I sent you
last week. .... to my party?

A Are you coming   B Do you come
C Should you come   D Shall you come

9 I'm coming to Athens next week, and I'll give you a
ring when I ....

A arrive   B am arriving
C will have arrived   D will arrive

10 I'm afraid I can't see you this afternoon, because I
.... tennis with Graham.

A will play   B shall play
C am playing   D go to play

UNIT 5

Choose the best answer.

1 Does anyone mind .... the TV on?

  A to my turning   B if I turned
  C if I turn   D me to turn

2 Would it be all right .... you the composition next week?

  A for to give   B my giving   C if I gave
  D if I give

3 I expect you'd rather be at home right now, ... ?

  A hadn't you   B didn't you
  C wouldn't you   D weren't you

4 I'm sorry, but this is a library, so could I ask you .... ?

  A not talking   B don't talk
  C not to talk   D no talking

5 I hope you won't be .... by what I'm about to say, but I think I ought to talk to you frankly.

  A offensive   B offending   C offended
  D offence

6 He got very angry and .... that no one had warned him that he would have to move to a smaller office.

  A suggested   B insisted
  C requested   D admitted

7 Seat belts can prevent passengers .... their heads.

  A to hit   B against hitting
  C from hitting   D not to hit

8 It's an excellent murder story, and in the end it turns .... that everyone had a part in the murder.

  A out   B up   C in   D away

9 It's a couple of years since I .... in Paris.

  A was   B had been   C haven't been
  D am

10 Before she started university, Stella .... in the States for six months working as a nanny.

  A has lived   B lived   C lives
  D has been living

UNIT 7

Choose the best answer.

1 At the factory, every Friday is ....-day, and the men go out to the pub after work.

   A cash   B wages   C money   D pay

2 I'm still using the same computer that I bought when I left school, and I .... any trouble with it in all that time.

   A have never had   B haven't
   C didn't have   D haven't been having

3 I saw you with Laura the other day; how long .... her?

   A did you know   B have you been knowing
   C do you know   D have you known

4 Could I .... £5 until tomorrow? The bank was closed and I've absolutely no money on me.

   A lend   B borrow   C loan   D hire

5 The lights aren't working. I think there must be a .... somewhere in the wiring.

   A error   B mistake   C fault
   D wrong

6 If I had the opportunity, I think I .... one of those round-the-world air tickets.

   A bought   B buy   C will buy
   D would buy

7 Drop in for a coffee tomorrow, if you .... too busy.

   A aren't   B won't be   C wouldn't be
   D don't be

8 The garage said the car would be ready on Wednesday, but by the following Friday, they .... hadn't finished mending it.

   A even   B still   C yet   D already

9 I think you ought to write your aunt a letter and apologize .... so late at night.

   A to ring   B for ring   C for ringing
   D to be ringing

10 A holiday in Spain is unlikely to cost very much .... you stay in the top class luxury hotels.

   A when   B if   C unless
   D otherwise

UNIT 9

Choose the best answer.

1 I managed to beat him at squash .... I think he's probably a bit better than me.

A even B although C despite
D because

2 She was given the job .... her lack of formal qualifications.

A despite B although C even though
D in spite

3 .... arriving nearly half an hour late, Michael finished the exam paper and answered all the questions.

A Although B Despite C Even though
D In spite

4 The government wants to .... football hooligans from travelling abroad.

A protect B miss C prevent
D avoid

5 You'll have to get down low and hide behind the wall to .... being seen by the police.

A protect B prevent C avoid
D leave

6 I knew from the start he was dishonest so I wasn't taken .... by him, but some of my friends lost money.

A in B down C at D to

7 You .... say things like that to people or you'll lose all your friends.

A don't have to B needn't
C haven't got to D mustn't

8 You can come with me to the shops but you .... if you don't want to.

A mustn't B needn't C can't
D haven't

9 You .... have any vaccinations or injections if you're travelling around Europe.

A mustn't B don't need C don't have to
D needn't to

10 I'm really looking forward .... you both again next week.

A for seeing B on seeing C to see
D to seeing

UNIT 12

Choose the best answer.

1 Not only .... with speeding, but she was accused of drinking and driving as well.

   A charged she   B they charged her
   C was she charged   D did she charge

2 Not only .... properly, but that cooker is dangerous because of all those loose wires at the back.

   A does it not work   B it doesn't work
   C it works not   D doesn't work it

3 Could you give me a hand with .... the table?

   A lying   B laying   C to lay   D to lie

4 I could never really take her word for anything again after I found out that she had .... to me.

   A laid   B lay   C lain   D lied

5 My luggage is at the station. You couldn't go and .... it for me, could you?

   A take   B bring   C carry   D fetch

6 Since we're going to spend the weekend with them, I think we ought to .... them some flowers or chocolates.

   A carry   B take   C bring   D donate

7 Your coat is made of wool, so I really think you ought to .... it dry-cleaned.

   A let   B leave   C make   D have

8 His car needed a lot of attention because he hadn't .... it serviced for such a long time.

   A let   B left   C made   D had

9 He kept .... trying to annoy me and in the end I just hit him.

   A in   B on   C at   D with

10 Some time ago we were .... that our rent would be increased.

   A let to know   B said   C known
   D told

UNIT 14

Choose the best answer.

1 When it's very important for me to .... something, I write it on my hand.

  A remind   B recall   C remember
  D realize

2 I've got her business card, but strangely I don't .... meeting her at all.

  A remind   B recall   C memorize
  D forget

3 Before they left at the end of their holiday, they went shopping to buy a few ....

  A souvenirs   B memories
  C recollections   D reminders

4 I met a girl yesterday who .... me strongly of someone I used to know years ago.

  A reminded   B recalled
  C recollected   D remembered

5 It's your own fault that you're so tired. You .... have stayed up so late last night.

  A needn't   B shouldn't   C mustn't
  D couldn't

6 Why on earth did you run across the road? You .... have been killed!

  A can   B might   C must   D would

7 She was supposed to be here over an hour ago; I think she .... have forgotten about coming for supper.

  A must   B should   C can   D would

8 As people grow older, they tend to become more and more .... and can't remember where they have put things.

  A forgotten   B forgetting   C forgets
  D forgetful

9 A lot of children .... parents were not very good at school often do well themselves.

  A who   B their   C which   D whose

10 Jimmie is a long – .... lorry driver; he travels from London to Istanbul every ten days.

  A way   B travel   C road   D distance

UNIT 16

Choose the best answer.

1 Computer scientists are doing a lot of research into .... intelligence.

A unreal   B false   C fake
D artificial

2 The spy had hidden the documents in a ....
bottom in his suitcase.

A unreal   B false   C fake
D artificial

3 Big gardens seem like quite a nice idea, but they need .... after.

A to look   B being looked
C looking   D to be looking

4 Hello Henry, Kate, Peter. Help .... to some food and I'll be with you in a moment.

A you   B yours   C yourself
D yourselves

5 I had to take the wardrobe to pieces because it was .... to go up the staircase.

A so big   B very big   C big enough
D too big

6 You must do this homework again; it's full of mistakes, and it's really not ....

A enough good   B much too good
C good enough   D good too

7 I find her husband unbearable, and I can't imagine how she can put .... his awful behaviour.

A on to   B up with   C down on
D away from

8 I .... this homework all by myself, and nobody helped me.

A did   B answered   C worked
D made

9 What have you done .... the TV? It doesn't work.

A with   B to   C by   D for

10 It's difficult for older people .... new words.

A remembering   B memorizing
C to remember   B to remind

UNIT 18

Choose the best answer.

1 I think you'd better take a credit card with you
   .... you run out of cash.

   A unless   B otherwise   C if
   D in case

2 Simon is so rude, aggressive and ungrateful that
   trying to please him is completely ....

   A worthless   B endless   C careless
   D pointless

3 I'll come and see you later on .... I have the
   time.

   A unless   B otherwise   C if
   D in case

4 She wears bright clothes, has lots of jewellery and
   her face is always very heavily made ....

   A out   B up   C on   D away

5 She decided she ought to do the work at once
   .... he phoned her later in the evening and
   asked for it.

   A unless   B otherwise   C if
   D in case

6 I have got .... good news for you about your
   exams.

   A a   B the   C a few   D some

7 Gina's getting married, isn't that wonderful? It's
   .... best news I've heard all year.

   A a   B the   C a few   D some

8 I told her that she should think about moving out
   .... she was really feeling unhappy.

   A if   B whether   C in spite
   D providing

9 These new aspirins are round and much smaller, so
   they're easier to ....

   A chew   B gulp   C sip   D swallow

10 You .... better get a move on if you don't
   want to miss your plane.

   A should   B would   C did   D had

UNIT 2

Finish the second sentence without changing the meaning.

1 Jason felt lonely because he didn't have many friends in the new town.
   Jason felt lonely because he had ....
   ....

2 There was little I could do to help her when she was ill.
   There wasn't ....
   ....

3 It will take us three hours to fly to Barcelona.
   The ....
   ....

4 I may be late, so don't wait for me.
   It's ....
   ....

5 It is essential that these catalogues are sent off by Friday.
   These catalogues ....
   ....

6 I'm sure Peter's at home because the phone is engaged.
   Peter must ....
   ....

7 I would like that letter sent off at once, please.
   Will ....
   ....

8 Do these shoes look nice with the green skirt?
   Do these shoes and the green skirt go ....
   ....

9 Mary and her boyfriend have stopped going out together.
   Mary and her boyfriend are ....
   ....

10 My case was examined by the customs officer.
   The customs officer went ....
   ....

UNIT 4

Finish the second sentence without changing the meaning.

1 John and Mary were both unable to do the work.
   Neither ....
   ....

2 Neither I nor Peter could find the purse.
   Peter ....
   ....

3 Both Jason and I learned the violin.
   Jason learned ....
   ....

4 My brother explained that I was out when he called.
   'You ....
   ....

5 'Look at my hand, John,' said Mary.
   Mary told ....
   ....

6 'When are you going to leave the country?' Mary asked Peter.
   Mary asked ....
   ....

7 'Have you seen the missing child?' the policewoman asked me.
   The policewoman ....
   ....

8 'More wine?' the smiling waiter asked us.
   The smiling waiter ....
   ....

9 We haven't got any coffee left.
   We have run ....
   ....

10 Stop arguing or I'll turn you out.
   I'll turn you out ....
   ....

UNIT 6

Finish the second sentence without changing the meaning.

1 I couldn't borrow you car next week, could I?
   You couldn't ....
   ....

2 Manchester United won the match against Aston Villa.
   In the match Aston Villa were ....
   ....

3 It's a pity that I haven't got my exam results.
   I wish ....
   ....

4 I'm sorry that I am not going with you to the ball.
   I wish ....
   ....

5 They succeeded in getting the dates of their tickets changed.
   They managed ....
   ....

6 Most of the action in the film happens in London.
   Most of the action in the film takes ....
   ....

7 If I earn more money, I spend more
   The ....
   ....

8 I'm upset because she didn't come to see us.
   I wish ....
   ....

9 Don't keep on telling people I failed my driving test – it upsets me.
   I wish ....
   ....

10 I'm upset because I am so overworked.
   I wish..
   ....

UNIT 8

Finish the second sentence without changing the meaning.

1 Someone broke into our house while we were out.
   When we got back, we found that the house ....
   ....

2 It's such a well-made film that I never get tired of seeing it.
   That film is ....
   ....

3 There were so many people on the train that I had to stand.
   There were such ....
   ....

4 You're such a fast swimmer that I think you could win the competition.
   You swim ....
   ....

5 The storm damaged the houses badly.
   The houses ....
   ....

6 I smoked when I was young, but I don't any more.
   I used ....
   ....

7 After you've been in the army for a while, getting up early won't be difficult for you.
   After you've been in the army for a while, you'll .....
   ....

8 Having to speak English all day is new to me.
   I am ....
   ....

9 She lost her temper and hung up.
   She lost her temper and put ....
   ....

10 Margaret is between 63 and 67 years old.
   Margaret is in her ....
   ....

UNIT 10

Finish the second sentence without changing the meaning.

1 Some people find it difficult to criticize their friends.
   It ....
   ....

2 They say French is easier to learn than German.
   They say it ....
   ....

3 In your opinion, was the second book in the series as good as the first?
   Did you ....
   ....

4 I speak English better than I write it.
   I am better ....
   ....

5 My son's behaviour worries me a lot.
   I am very ....
   ....

6 I'm on good terms with everyone in my family.
   I get ....
   ....

7 I wondered when you were going to tell me.
   I wondered when you were going to get ....
   ....

8 I like coffee much more than tea.
   I much ....
   ....

9 I'd prefer not to work late this evening.
   I'd rather ....
   ....

10 I think sunbathing is nicer than sightseeing.
   I prefer ....
   ....

UNIT 11

Finish the second sentence without changing the meaning.

1 They announced their engagement yesterday.
   Yesterday they said they were going ....
   ....

2 The Prime Minister said she did not intend to resign.
   The Prime Minister said she had ....
   ....

3 There's no point trying to please him.
   It's ....
   ....

4 It was over a week before he found the time to reply to her letter.
   He didn't get ....
   ....

5 She felt so tired that she couldn't drive any further.
   She was too ....
   ....

6 Unfortunately he forgot to send off the card.
   Unfortunately he didn't ....
   ....

7 I've had enough of clearing up after you.
   I'm ....
   ....

8 The lessons were much more interesting than I had expected.
   I hadn't expected ....
   ....

9 I didn't think the party would be so expensive.
   The party ....
   ....

10 I am allowed to use the kitchen if I want.
   They let ....
   ....

UNIT 13

Finish the second sentence without changing the meaning.

1 I went to a show in London; it was marvellous.
The ....

....

2 I broke a window in the kitchen, but it's been repaired.
They've repaired ....

....

3 She told us something, and it was very interesting.
What ....

....

4 You need some things, and you can get them at that shop.
You can get what ....

....

5 There's something I don't like about him, and that's the way he talks about people behind their backs.
What ....

....

6 A lot of people were attracted to the Prime Minister's proposals.
A lot of people found ....

....

7 Mr Fujihara wants that painting, and the price doesn't matter to him.
Mr Fujihara wants that painting, and he doesn't ......

....

8 Where can I see if this skirt fits me?
Where can I try ....

....

9 He's got a new car with an electric sunroof.
He's got a new car, and ....

....

10 It is believed that the young man who was arrested yesterday lives in East London.
The young ....

....

UNIT 15

Finish the second sentence without changing the meaning.

1 My boyfriend hasn't written to me for ages.
It's ....

....

2 The last time I went to London was nearly three years ago.
I haven't ....

....

3 We haven't invited them round to dinner for several months now.
The ....

....

4 'Let's have a barbecue on Friday,' Katie said to me.
Katie suggested ....

....

5 'I think you ought to try and get another job,' my brother said to me.
My brother suggested ....

....

6 Anne suggested to Jim that he should buy a new car.
Anne said to Jim, 'Why ....

....

7 The value of Henry's oil painting has gone up a great deal since last year.
Henry's oil painting is ....

....

8 I can't leave work before 6.30 tonight.
I'll have to ....

....

9 Visiting Moscow will not be possible without a visa.
Unless ....

....

10 They say the British Museum is one of the most popular tourist attractions in London.
The British Museum ....

....

UNIT 17

Finish the second sentence without changing the meaning.

1 I'm glad to say that they have painted all the windows.
I'm glad to say that all ....
....

2 The police are holding a man in London on a murder charge.
A man ....
....

3 In the next 30 years, they will have to rebuild most of the bridges in this country.
In the next 30 years, most of ....
....

4 He ran to the station and succeeded in getting onto the train.
He ran to the station and managed ....
....

5 Because of where I was sitting, it wasn't possible for me to see the stage properly.
Because of where I was sitting, I ....
....

6 It is essential that office telephones are not used for personal calls.
Office telephones must ....
....

7 Their dog hasn't been home for a week. I'm sure someone has stolen it.
Their dog hasn't been home for a week. It ....
....

8 Someone must have left the back door open.
The ....
....

9 I admire what he has done a great deal.
I have a great deal ....
....

10 It wasn't necessary for you to write your speech again, because it was fine the first time.
You needn't ....
....

UNIT 19

Finish the second sentence without changing the meaning.

1 I'll support you even if things go wrong for you.
I'll stand ....
....

2 We only found out about this house because Claire showed us the advertisement for it.
If Claire ....
....

3 Jennifer didn't go to the village school because her parents had to move to London.
If ....
....

4 I didn't send Mary a birthday card because I didn't know it was her birthday.
I would ....
....

5 If the bill hadn't been so unreasonable, I would have paid it at once.
I didn't ....
....

6 You're nearly twenty-one, so you ought to be earning your own living by now.
You're nearly twenty-one, so it's ....
....

7 It's getting a bit late, so I think we'd better go.
It's getting a bit late, so it's time to ....
....

8 Jane says she'll only ring us if she misses the train.
Jane says she won't ....
....

9 It's a shame you didn't come to the party.
I wish ....
....

10 Take a book with you, because there's a chance that the plane might be delayed.
Take a book with you in ....
....

REVISION TESTS KEY

UNIT 1

1 A	2 D	3 D	4 C	5 D
6 A	7 C	8 C	9 B	10 D

UNIT 2

1 Jason felt lonely because he had few friends in the new town.
2 There wasn't much I could do to help her when she was ill.
3 The flight to Barcelona will take (us) three hours.
4 It's possible (that) I will be late, so don't wait for me.
5 These catalogues must be sent off by Friday.
6 Peter must be at home because the phone is engaged.
7 Will you send that letter off at once, please?
8 Do these shoes and the green shirt go (well/nicely) together?
9 Mary and her boyfriend are no longer going out together/not going out together any more.
10 The customs officer went through my case.

UNIT 3

1 D	2 C	3 D	4 C	5 D
6 D	7 A	8 A	9 A	10 C

UNIT 4

1 Neither John nor Mary could do the work.
2 Peter and I were (both) unable to find the purse; Peter could not find the purse and nor could I; Peter and I could not find the purse.
3 Jason learned the violin and so did I/and I learned it too.
4 'You were out when I called,' explained my brother.
5 Mary told John to look at her hand.

6 Mary asked Peter when he was going to leave the country.
7 The policewoman asked me if/whether I had seen the missing child.
8 The smiling waiter asked us if/whether we would like (some) more wine.
9 We have run out of coffee.
10 I'll turn you out unless you stop arguing/if you don't stop arguing.

UNIT 5

1 C	2 C	3 C	4 C	5 C
6 B	7 C	8 A	9 A	10 B

UNIT 6

1 You couldn't lend me your car next week, could you?
2 In the match Aston Villa were defeated/beaten by Manchester United.
3 I wish I had my exam results.
4 I wish I was/were going with you to the ball.
5 They managed to get the dates of their tickets changed.
6 Most of the action in the film takes place in London.
7 The more I earn, the more I spend.
8 I wish she had come to see us.
9 I wish you wouldn't keep (on) telling people (that) I failed my driving test; I wish you'd stop telling people (that) I failed my driving test.
10 I wish I weren't/wasn't so overworked.

UNIT 7

1 D	2 A	3 D	4 B	5 C
6 D	7 A	8 B	9 C	10 C

UNIT 8

1 When we got back, we found (that) the house had been broken into.
2 The film is so well made (that) I never get tired of seeing it.
3 There were such a lot of people on the train (that) I had to stand.
4 You swim so fast (that) I think you could win the competition.
5 The houses were badly damaged by the storm.
6 I used to smoke when I was young but I don't any more.
7 After you've been in the army for a while, you'll not find it difficult to get up early/have no difficulty in getting up early.
8 I am not used/accustomed to having to speak English all day.
9 She lost her temper and put down the phone/the phone down.
10 Margaret is in her mid sixties.

UNIT 9

1 B	2 A	3 B	4 C	5 C
6 A	7 D	8 B	9 C	10 D

UNIT 10

1 It is difficult for some people to criticise/criticize their friends.
2 They say it is easier to learn French than German.
3 Did you think (that) the second book in the series was as good as the first?
4 I am better at speaking English than ((I am) at) writing it.
5 I am very worried by my son's behaviour.
6 I get on well with everyone in my family.
7 I wondered when you were going to get round to telling me.
8 I much prefer coffee to tea.
9 I'd rather not work late this evening.
10 I prefer sunbathing to sightseeing.

UNIT 11

1 Yesterday they said they were going to get engaged/married.
2 The Prime Minister said she had no intention of resigning.
3 It's pointless trying to please him/pointless to try and please him.
4 He didn't get time to reply to/round to replying to her letter for over a week.
5 She was too tired to drive any further/farther.
6 Unfortunately he didn't remember to send off the card.
7 I'm tired of clearing up after you.
8 I hadn't expected the lessons to be (nearly) so interesting.
9 The party was more expensive than I thought/expected it would be; the party was more expensive than I (had) expected it to be.
10 They let me use the kitchen if I want.

UNIT 12

1 C	2 A	3 B	4 D	5 D
6 B	7 D	8 D	9 B	10 D

UNIT 13

1 The show I went to in London was marvellous.
2 They've repaired the window (that) I broke in the kitchen.
3 What she told us was very interesting.
4 You can get what you need at that shop.
5 What I don't like about him is the way he talks about people behind their backs.
6 A lot of people found the Prime Minister's proposals attractive.
7 Mr Fujihara wants that painting, and he doesn't care/mind about the price/what the price is.
8 Where can I try on this skirt?
9 He's got a new car and it's got an electric sunroof/it has an electric sunroof.
10 The young man who was arrested yesterday is thought/believed to live in East London.

UNIT 14

1 C	2 B	3 A	4 A	5 B
6 B	7 A	8 D	9 D	10 D

UNIT 15

1 It's ages since my boyfriend (last) wrote to me.
2 I haven't been to London for nearly three years.
3 The last time we invited them round to dinner was several months ago.
4 Katie suggested to me that we should have a barbecue on Friday.
5 My brother suggested (that) I should try and/to get another job.
6 Anne said to Jim, 'Why don't you buy a new car?'
7 Henry's oil painting is worth a great deal/lot more than it was last year.
8 I'll have to stay at work until 6.30 tonight.
9 Unless you have a visa, you can't visit Moscow.
10 The British Museum is said to be one of the most popular tourist attractions in London.

UNIT 16

1 D	2 B	3 C	4 D	5 D
6 C	7 B	8 A	9 B	10 C

UNIT 17

1 I'm glad to say that all the windows have been painted.
2 A man is being held by police in London on a murder charge.
3 In the next thirty years, most of the bridges in this country will have to be rebuilt.
4 He ran to the station and managed to get onto the train/to board the train.
5 Because of where I was sitting I wasn't able to see the stage properly/I was unable to see the stage properly.
6 Office telephones must not be used for personal calls.

7 Their dog hasn't been home for a week. It must have been stolen.
8 The back door must have been left open.
9 I have a great deal of admiration for what he has done.
10 You needn't have written your speech again because it was fine the first time.

UNIT 18

1 D	2 D	3 C	4 B	5 D
6 D	7 B	8 A	9 D	10 D

UNIT 19

1 I'll stand by you even if things go wrong for you.
2 If Claire hadn't shown us the advertisement (for it), we wouldn't have found this house; if Claire hadn't shown us the advertisement for this house, we wouldn't have found it.
3 If her parents hadn't moved to London, Jennifer would have gone to the village school.
4 I would have sent Mary a birthday card if I had known (that) it was her birthday.
5 I didn't pay the bill at once because it was so unreasonable.
6 You're nearly twenty-one, so it's time you earned your own living.
7 It's getting a bit late, so it's time for us to go.
8 Jane says she won't ring unless she misses the train.
9 I wish you had come to the party.
10 Take a book with you in case the plane is delayed.

NEW PACKAGE

A complete new package for the First Certificate

COURSEBOOKS

Success at First Certificate
Robert O'Neill, Michael Duckworth & Kathy Gude

Success at First Certificate consolidates and extends students' knowledge of the language and their ability to use it for communication, at the same time providing practice for all five papers of the First Certificate examination.

The book has twenty units, each based on an interesting theme, which thoroughly cover the areas of vocabulary, structure and language which the First Certificate student needs. There are regular revision and extension sections: many of these are presented in the format of the examination.

A Grammar Summary at the back of the book is cross-referenced to points in the course itself and so provides a useful reference aid for students and teachers, particularly for students working alone.

There is an accompanying cassette which contains the recordings for the listening material in the Student's Book, and a separate Listening Tests cassette. The Teacher's Book gives detailed teaching notes, answer keys, transcripts of the recorded material, and photocopyable Revision Tests. There is also a Workbook with new authentic reading material, revision and extension exercises, and four Progress Tests.

Success at First Certificate Practice Tests 1 and 2

Each book contains five complete and up-to-date practice tests for the First Certificate examination. The tests will familiarize students with the examination format and provide valuable practice and diagnosis of problem areas for students. The *with key* edition includes answer keys, suggested marking schemes and transcripts of the recordings.

SUPPLEMENTARY BOOKS

Paper 3
Successful Use of English for First Certificate
Mary Spratt

This book provides learners with detailed preparation and practice for all types of question found in Paper 3. The nine units contain reading and vocabulary based on typical exam themes, exam preparation, and grammar revision which is presented in the format of the exam. There are also three complete Practice Papers.

Paper 4
Successful Listening for First Certificate
Shelagh Rixon

Using the techniques of learner training, the book is organized around the different question types students might meet in the listening test, such as filling in grids, identifying pictures and answering multiple choice questions. Students are shown how to use the question paper to predict what they will hear, to listen for helpful words and phrases, and to analyse what information questions are asking for. There are practice tests at the end of each unit and two complete tests at the end of the book.

Paper 5
The Interview
Devised by Rob Nolasco

The Interview is a forty-minute video designed to familiarize students with Paper 5 (the oral interview) and to provide them with strategies for success. An accompanying Video Guide contains suggestions for class viewing activities, teacher's notes, and transcripts. The video (which features genuine First Certificate candidates and examiner) consists of three parts:

ONE **The content of the interview** - presents the options available, the different stages of the interview, what the examiner looks for and how the student is assessed.

TWO **How to succeed** - looks at ways in which students can improve their performance in the exam.

THREE **A complete interview**

The student interviews seen on the video use the oral test material from *Success at First Certificate Practice Tests 1* - and, while the video can be used independently of the Practice Tests, together they provide a unique combination of teaching and practice for Paper 5.

The Interview is available in VHS, Betamax and Umatic formats for PAL. SECAM and NTSC television standards.

All papers
Successful Vocabulary for First Certificate
Norman Whitney

This book illustrates and practises the different ways in which vocabulary and vocabulary skills are tested in the examination. Each of the thirty units focusses on different parts of the exam and suggests ways students can improve their vocabulary and vocabulary skills. A Word Banks appendix provides valuable reference material and opportunity for further practice.

If you would like more information about any of these titles, please contact: ELT Marketing, Oxford University Press, Walton Street, Oxford OX2 6DP